A STORY TELLER'S STORY

A STORY TELLER'S STORY

Sherwood Anderson

GROVE PRESS INC.
NEW YORK

TO ALFRED STIEGLITZ,

who has been more than father to so many
puzzled, wistful children of the arts in this
big, noisy, growing and groping America, this
book is gratefully dedicated.

Portions of this book have been published in the *American Mercury, Century* and *Phantasmus* and to these magazines the author makes due acknowledgment.

A STORY TELLER'S STORY

A STORY-TELLER'S STORY

In all the towns and over the wide countrysides of my own mid-American boyhood there was no such thing as poverty, as I myself saw it and knew it later in our great American industrial towns and cities.

My own family was poor, but of what did our poverty consist? My father, a ruined dandy from the South, had been reduced to keeping a small harness-repair shop and, when that failed, he became ostensibly a house-and-barn painter. However, he did not call himself a house-painter. The idea was not flashy enough for him. He called himself a "sign-writer." The day of universal advertising had not yet come and there was but little sign-writing to do in our town, but still he stuck out bravely for the higher life. At any time he would let go by the board the privilege of painting Alf Mann the butcher's house (it would have kept him busily at work for a month) in order to have a go at lettering signs on fences along country roads for Alf Granger the baker.

There was your true pilgrimage abroad, out into the land. Father engaged a horse and a spring wagon and took the three older of his sons with him. My older brother and the one next younger than myself were, from the first, adept at sign-writing, while both father and myself were helpless with a brush in our

3

hands. And so I drove the horse and father supervised the whole affair. He had a natural boyish love for the supervision of affairs and the picking out of a particular fence on a particular road became to him as important a matter as the selection of a site for a city, or the fortification that was to defend it.

And then the farmer who owned the fence had to be consulted and if he refused his consent the joy of the situation became intensified. We drove off up the road and turned into a wood and the farmer went back to his work of cultivating corn. We watched and waited, our boyish hearts beating madly. It was a summer day and in the small wood in which we were concealed we all sat on a fallen log in silence. Birds flew overhead and a squirrel chattered. What a delicate tinge of romance spread over our commonplace enough business!

Father was made for romance. For him there was no such thing as a fact. It had fallen out that he, never having had the glorious opportunity to fret his little hour upon a greater stage, was intent on fretting his hour as best he could in a money-saving prosperous corn-shipping, cabbage-raising Ohio village.

He magnified the danger of our situation. "He might have a shotgun," he said, pointing to where in the distance the farmer was again at work. As we waited in the wood he sometimes told us a story of the Civil War and how he with a companion had crept for days and nights through an enemy country at the risk of their lives. "We were carrying messages," he said, raising his eyebrows and throwing out his hands. By the gesture there was something implied. "Well, it was an affair of life or death.

4

Why speak of the matter? My country needed me and I, and my intrepid companion, had been selected because we were the bravest men in the army," the raised eyebrows were saying.

And so with their paint pots and brushes in their hands my two brothers presently crept out of the wood and ran crouching through cornfields and got into the dusty road. Quickly and with mad haste they dabbed the name of Alf Granger on the fence with the declaration that he baked the best bread in the State of Ohio, and when they returned to us we all got back into the spring wagon and drove back along the road past the sign. Father commanded me to stop the horse. "Look," he said, frowning savagely at my two brothers, "your *N* is wrong. You are being careless again with your *Bs*. Good gracious, will I never teach you two how to handle a brush?"

If our family was poor, of what did our poverty consist? If our clothes were torn the torn places only let in the sun and wind. In the winter we had no overcoats, but that only meant we ran rather than loitered. Those who are to follow the arts should have a training in what is called poverty. Given a comfortable middle-class start in life, the artist is almost sure to end up by becoming a bellyacher, constantly complaining because the public does not rush forward at once to proclaim him.

The boy who has no warm overcoat throws back his head and runs through the streets, past houses where smoke goes up into a clear cold sky, across vacant lots, through fields. The sky clouds and snows come and the bare hands are cold and chapped. They are raw and red but at night, before the boy sleeps.

5

his mother will come with melted fat and rub it over the raw places.

The warm fat is soothing. The touch of a mother's fingers is soothing. Well, you see, with us, we were all of us—mother father and the children—in some way outlaws in our native place and that thought was soothing to a boy. It is a soothing thought in all my memories of my boyhood. Only recently one connected with my family said to me: "You must remember, now that you are an author, you have a respectable place in the world to maintain"; and for a moment my heart swelled with pride in the thought.

And then I went out of the presence of the cautious one to associate with many other respectables and into my mind flashed thoughts of the sweetness I have seen shining in the eyes of others—of waiters, horsemen, thieves, gamblers, women, driven by poverty to the outer rim of society. Where were the respectables among those who had been kindest and sweetest to me?

Whatever may be said in this matter, and I admit my feet have slipped many times toward solid respectability we of our family were not too respectable then.

For one thing father never paid his rent and so we were always living in haunted houses. Never was such a family to take the haunts out of a house. Old women riding white horses, dead men screaming, groans, cries—all were quieted when we came to live in a haunted house. And how often because of this talent—inherent in my family—we lived for months scot-free in a fairly comfortable house, while at the same time conferring a benefit on the property owner.

6

It is a system—I recommend it to poets with large families.

There were not enough bedclothes so three boys slept in one bed and there was a window that, in summer, looked out upon fields, but in winter had been painted by the hand of the frost king so that moonlight came softly and dimly into the room. It was no doubt the fact that there were three of us in one bed that drove away all fear of the "haunts."

Mother was tall and slender and had once been beautiful. She had been a bound girl in a farmer's family when she married father, the improvident young dandy. There was Italian blood in her veins and her origin was something of a mystery. Perhaps we never cared to solve it—wanted it to remain a mystery. It is so wonderfully comforting to think of one's mother as a dark, beautiful and somewhat mysterious woman. I later saw her mother—my own grandmother—but that is another story.

She the dark evil old woman with the broad hips and the great breasts of a peasant and with the glowing hate shining out of her one eye would be worth a book in herself. It was said she had shuffled off four husbands and when I knew her, although she was old, she looked not unwilling to tackle another. Some day perhaps I shall tell the tale of the old woman and the tramp who tried to rob the farm house when she was staying alone; and of how she, after beating him into submission with her old fists, got drunk with him over a barrel of hard cider in a shed and of how the two went singing off together down the road—but not now.

Our own mother had eyes that were like pools lying

7

in deep shadows at the edge of a wood but when she grew angry and fell into one of her deep silences lights danced in the pools. When she spoke her words were filled with strange wisdom (how sharply yet I remember certain comments of hers—on life—on your neighbors!), but often she commanded all of us by the strength of her silences.

She came into the bedroom where three boys lay on one bed, carrying in one hand a small kerosene lamp and in the other a dish in which was warm melted fat.

There were three boys in one bed, two of them almost of the same size. The third was then a small silent fellow. Later his life was to be very strange. He was one who could not fit himself into the social scheme and, until he was a grown man, he stayed about, living sometimes with one, sometimes with another of his brothers—always reading books, dreaming, quarreling with no one.

He, the youngest of the three, looked out at life always as from a great distance. He was of the stuff of which poets are made. What instinctive wisdom in him. All loved him but no one could help him in the difficult business of living his life and when on summer evenings, as the three lay in the bed the two older boys fought or made great plans for their lives, he lay beside them in silence—but sometimes he spoke and his words came always as from a far place. We were perhaps discussing the wonders of life. "Well," he said, "it is so and so. There will be no more babies, but the new babies do not come as you say. I know how they come. They come the same way you grow corn. Father plants seed in the earth and mother is the earth in which the seed grows."

8

I am thinking of my younger brother after he had grown a little older—I am thinking of him grown into a man and become habitually silent like mother—I am thinking of him as he was just before he mysteriously disappeared out of our lives and never came back.

Now, however, he is in bed with the other brother and myself. An older brother, he who crept through the cornfields to paint the name of Alf Granger on the fence, had already gone from our lives. He had a talent for drawing, and a drunken half-insane cutter of stones for graveyards has taken him away from our town to another town where he is already sitting at a desk drawing designs for gravestones. A dove descends out of the sky and holds a leaf in its bill. There is an angel clinging to a rock in the midst of a storm at sea.

Rock of ages, cleft for me,
Let me hide myself in Thee.

The three boys are in the bed in the room and there are not enough bedclothes. Father's overcoat, now too old to be worn, is thrown over the foot of the bed and the three boys have been permitted to undress downstairs, in the kitchen of the house, by the kitchen stove.

The oldest of the boys remaining at home (that is myself) must undress first and must arrange his clothes neatly on a kitchen chair. Mother does not scold about such a trifling matter. She stands silently looking and the boy does as he has been told. There is something of my grandmother in a certain look that can come into her eyes. "Well, you'd better,"

9

it says. How unsuccessfully I have tried all my life to cultivate just that look, for myself!

And now the boy has undressed and must run in his white flannel nightgown barefooted through the cold house, past frosted windows, up a flight of stairs and, with a flying leap into the bed. The flannel nightgown has been worn almost threadbare by the older brother—now gone out into the world—before it has come down to him who wears it now.

He is the oldest of the brothers at home and must take the first plunge into the icy bed, but soon the others come running. They are lying like little puppies in the bed but as they grow warmer the two older boys begin to fight. There is a contest. The point is not to be compelled to lie on the outside where the covers may come off in the night. Blows are struck and tense young bodies are intertwined. "It's your turn to-night! No it's yours! You're a liar! Take that! Well then, take that! I'll show you!"

The youngest brother of the three brothers has already taken one of the two outside positions. It is his fate. He is not strong enough to fight with either of the other two and perhaps he does not care for fighting. He lies silently in the cold in the darkness while the fight between the other two goes on and on. They are of almost equal strength and the fight might possibly last for an hour.

But there is now the sound of the mother's footsteps on the stairs and that is the end of the struggle. Now—at this moment—the boy who has the coveted position may keep it. That is an understood thing.

The mother puts the kerosene lamp on a little

table by the bed and beside it the dish of warm, comforting melted fat. One by one six hands are thrust out to her.

There is a caress in her long toil-hardened fingers. In the night and in the dim light of the lamp her dark eyes are like luminous pools.

The fat in the little cracked china dish is warm and soothing to burning itching hands. For an hour she has had the dish sitting at the back of the kitchen stove in the little frame house far out at the edge of the town.

The strange, silent mother! She is making love to her sons, but there are no words for her love. There are no kisses, no caresses.

The rubbing of the warm fat into the cracked hands of her sons is a caress. The light that now shines in her eyes is a caress.

. . . .

The silent woman has left deep traces of herself in one of her sons. He is the one now lying stilly in the bed with his two noisy brothers. What has happened in the life of the mother? In herself, in her own physical life, even the two quarreling, fighting sons feel that nothing can matter too much. If her husband, the father of the boys, is a no-account and cannot bring money home—the money that would feed and clothe her children in comfort—one feels it does not matter too much. If she herself, the proud quiet one, must humiliate herself, washing—for the sake of the few dimes it may bring in—the soiled clothes of her neighbors, one knows it does not matter too much.

And yet there is no Christian forbearance in her.

She speaks sometimes as she sits on the edge of the bed in the lamplight rubbing the warm fat into the cracked frost-bitten hands of her children and there is often a kind of smoldering fire in her words.

.   .   .   .

One of the boys in the bed has had a fight with the son of a neighbor. He, the third son of the family, has taken a hatchet out of the neighbor boy's hands. We had been cramming ourselves with the contents of a book, "The Last of the Mohicans," and the neighbor boy, whose father is the town shoemaker, had the hatchet given him as a Christmas present. He would not lend it, would not let it go out of his hands and so my brother, the determined one, has snatched it away.

The struggle took place in a little grove of trees half a mile from the house. "Le Renard Subtil," cries my brother jerking the hatchet out of the neighbor boy's hand. The neighbor boy did not want to be the villain—"Le Renard Subtil."

And so he went crying off toward his home, on the farther side of the field. He lived in a yellow house just beyond our own and near the end of the street at the edge of the town.

My brother now had possession of the hatchet and paid no more attention to him but I went to stand by a fence to watch him go.

It is because I am a white man and understand the whites better than he. I am Hawkeye the scout, "La Longue Carabine," and as I stand by the fence *la longue carabine* is lying across the crook of my arm. It is represented by a stick. "I could pick him off

12

from here, shall I do it?" I ask, speaking to my brother with whom I fight viciously every night after we have got into bed but who, during the day, is my sworn comrade in arms.

Uncas—"Le Cerf Agile"—pays no attention to my words and I rest the stick over the fence, half determined to pick off the neighbor boy but at the last withholding my fire. "He is a little pig, never to let a fellow take his hatchet. Uncas was right to snatch it out of his hand."

As I withhold my fire and the boy goes unscathed and crying across the snow-covered field I feel very magnanimous—since at any moment I could have dropped him like a deer in flight. And then I see him go crying into his mother's house. Uncas has, in fact, cuffed him a couple of times in the face. But was it not justified? "Dare a dirty Huron—a squaw man— dare such a one question the authority of a Delaware? Ugh!"

And now "Le Renard Subtil" has gone into his mother's house and has blabbed on us, and I tell Uncas the news but, with the impenetrable stoicism of a true savage, he pays no attention. He is as one sitting by the council fire. Are words to be wasted on a dog of a Huron?

And now "Le Cerf Agile" has an idea. Drawing a line in the snow, he stands some fifty feet from the largest of the trees in the grove and hurls the hatchet through the air.

What a determined fellow! I am of the paleface race myself and shall always depend for my execution upon *la longue carabine* but Uncas is of another breed. Is there not painted on his breast a crawling tortoise?

13

In ink I have traced it there myself from a drawing he has made.

During the short winter afternoon the hatchet will be thrown not once but a hundred, perhaps two hundred, times. It whirls through the air. The thing is to throw the hatchet so that, at the end of its flight, the blade goes, just so, firmly into the soft bark of the tree. And it must enter the bark of the tree at just a particular spot.

The matter is of infinite importance. Has not Uncas, "The Last of the Mohicans," broad shoulders? He will later be a strong man. Now is the time to acquire infinite skill.

He has measured carefully the spot on the body of the tree where the blade of the hatchet must enter with a soft chug, deep into the yielding bark. There is a tall warrior, a hated Huron, standing by the tree and young Uncas has measured carefully so that he knows just where the top of the warrior's head should come. An idea has come to him. He will just scalp the unsuspecting warrior with the blade of the tomahawk; and has not he, Uncas, crept for many weary miles through the forest, going without food, eating snow for his drink? A skulking Huron has dared creep into the hunting grounds of the Delawares and has learned the winter abiding place of our tribe. Dare we let him go back to his squaw-loving people, bearing such knowledge? Uncas will show him!

He, Uncas, is absorbed in the problem before him and has not deigned to look off across the fields to where the neighbor boy has gone crying to his mother. "Le Renard Subtil" will be heard from again but for the present is forgotten. The foot must be advanced just so. The arm must be drawn back just so. When one hurls the hatchet the body must be swung forward just so. An absolute silence must be maintained. The skulking Huron who has dared come into our hunting grounds is unaware of the presence of the young Uncas. Is he, Uncas, not one whose feet leave no traces in the morning dew?

Deep within the breasts of my brother and myself there is a resentment that we were born out of our time. By what a narrow margin in the scroll of time have we missed the great adventure! Two, three, at the most a dozen generations earlier and we might so well have been born in the virgin forest itself. On the very ground where we now stand Indians have indeed stalked one another in the forest, and how often Uncas and myself have discussed the matter. As for our father, we dismiss him half contemptuously. He is born to be a dandy of the cities and has turned out to be a village house-painter, in the dwelling places of the paleface. The devil!—with luck he might have turned out to be an actor, or a writer or some such scum of earth but never could he have been a warrior. Why had not our mother, who might have been such a splendid Indian princess, the daughter of a great chief, why had she also not been born a few generations earlier? She had just the silent stoicism needed for the wife of a great warrior. A deep injustice had been done us, and something of the feeling of that injustice was in the stern face of Uncas as he crept each time to the line he had marked out in the snow and sent the hatchet hurtling through the air.

The two boys, filled with scorn of their parentage,

15

on the father's side, are in a little grove of trees at the edge of an Ohio town. In later days the father—also born out of his place and time—will come to mean more to them but now he has little except their contempt. Now Uncas is determined—absorbed—and I, who have so little of his persistence, am impressed by his silent determination. It makes me a little uncomfortable for, since he has snatched the hatchet out of the neighbor boy's hand, saying, "Go on home, crybaby," no word has passed his lips. There is but a small grunting sound when the hatchet is hurled and a scowl on his face when it misses the mark.

And "Le Renard Subtil" has gone home and blabbed to his mother, who in turn has thrown a shawl over her head and has gone to our house, no doubt to blab, in her turn, to our mother. "La Longue Carabine," being a paleface, is a little intent on disturbing the aim of "Le Cerf Agile." "We'll catch hell," he says, looking at the hatchet thrower who has not so far unbent from the natural dignity of the Indian as to reply. He grunts and taking his place solemnly at the line poises his body. There is the quick abrupt swing forward of the body. What a shame Uncas did not later become a professional baseball player. He might have made his mark in the world. The hatchet sings through the air. Well, it has struck sideways. The Huron is injured but not fatally, and Uncas goes and sets him upright again. He has marked the place where the Huron warrior's head should be by pressing a ball of snow into the wrinkled bark of the tree and has indicated the dog's body by a dead branch.

And so Hawkeye the scout—"La Longue Carabine"

16

—has gone creeping off among the trees to see if there are any more Hurons lurking about and has come upon a great buck, pawing the snow and feeding on dry grass at the edge of a small creek. Up goes *la longue carabine* and the buck pitches forward, dead, on the ice. Hawkeye runs forward and swiftly passes his hunting knife across the neck of the buck. It will not do to build a fire now that there are Hurons lurking in the hunting ground of the Delawares so Uncas and he must feed upon raw meat. Well, the hunter's life for the hunter! What must be must be! Hawkeye cuts several great steaks from the carcass of the buck and makes his way slowly and cautiously back to Uncas. As he approaches he three times imitates the call of a catbird and an answering call comes from the lips of "Le Cerf Agile."

"Aha! the night is coming on," Uncas now says, having at last laid the Huron low. "Now that the dirty lover of squaws is dead we may build a fire and feast. Cook the venison ere the night falls. When darkness has come we must show no fire. Do not make much smoke—big fires for the paleface, but little fires for us Indians."

Uncas stands for a moment, gnawing the bone of the buck, and then of a sudden becomes still and alert. "Aha! I thought so," he says, and goes back again to where he has drawn the mark in the snow. "Go," he says; "see how many come."

And now Hawkeye must creep through the thick forests, climb mountains, leap canyons. Word has come that "Le Renard Subtil" but feigned when he went off crying, across the field—fools that we were! While we have been in the forest he has crept into the very teepee of our people and has stolen the princess, the mother of Uncas. And now "Le Renard Subtil," with subtle daring, drags the stoical princess right across the path of her warrior son. In one moment from a great height Hawkeye draws the faithful Deer Killer to his shoulder and fires, and at the same moment the tomahawk of Uncas sinks itself in the skull of the Huron dog.

" 'Le Renard Subtil' had drunk firewater and was reckless," says Uncas, as the two boys go homeward in the dusk.

. . . .

The older of the two boys now homeward bound is somewhat afraid but Uncas is filled with pride. As they go homeward in the gathering darkness and come to the house, where lives "Le Renard Subtil," to which he has gone crying but a few hours before, an idea comes to him. Uncas creeps in the darkness, halfway between the house and the picket fence in front and, balancing the hatchet in his hand, hurls it proudly. Well for the neighbor's family that no one came to the door at that moment for Uncas' long afternoon of practicing has got results. The hatchet flies through the air and sinks itself fairly and deeply into the door panel as Uncas and Hawkeye run away home.

. . . .

And now they are in the bed and the mother is rubbing the warm grease into their chapped hands. Her own hands are rough, but how gentle they are! She is thinking of her sons, of the one already gone out into the world and most of all at the moment of Uncas.

There is something direct brutal and fine in the nature of Uncas. It is not quite an accident that in our games he is always the Indian while I am the despised white, the paleface. It is permitted me to heal my misfortune a little by being, not a store-keeper or a fur trader but that man nearest the Indian's nature of all the palefaces who ever lived on our continent, "La Longue Carabine"; but I cannot be an Indian and least of all an Indian of the tribe of the Delawares. I am not persistent patient and determined enough. As for Uncas, one may coax and wheedle him along any road and I am always clinging to that slight sense of leadership that my additional fifteen months of living gives me, by coaxing and wheedling, but one may not drive Uncas. To attempt driving him is but to arouse a stubbornness and ob-stinacy that is limitless. Having told a lie to mother or father, he will stick to the lie to the death while I—well, perhaps there is in me something of the doglike, the squaw man, the paleface, the very spirit of "Le Renard Subtil"—if the bitter truth must be told. In all my after years I shall have to struggle against a tendency toward slickness and plausibility in myself. I am the tale-teller, the man who sits by the fire waiting for listeners, the man whose life must be led into the world of his fancies, I am the one des-tined to follow the little, crooked words of men's speech through the uncharted paths of the forests of fancy. What my father should have been I am to become. Through long years of the baffling uncer-tainty, that only such men as myself can ever know,

19

I am to creep with trembling steps forward in a strange land, following the little words, striving to learn all the ways of the ever-changing words, the smooth-lying little words, the hard, jagged, cutting words, the round, melodious, healing words. All the words I am in the end to come to know a little and to attempt to use for my purpose have, at the same time, the power in them both to heal and to destroy. How often am I to be made sick by words, how often am I to be healed by words, before I can come at all near to man's estate!

And so as I lie in the bed putting out my chapped hands to the healing touch of mother's hands I do not look at her. Already I am often too conscious of my own inner thoughts to look directly at people and now, although I am not the one who has cuffed the neighbor boy and jerked the hatchet out of his hands, I am nevertheless busily at work borrowing the troubles of Uncas. I cannot let what is to be be, but must push forward striving to change all by the power of words. I dare not thrust my words forward in the presence of mother, but they are busily getting themselves said inside myself.

There is a consciousness of Uncas also within me. Another curse that is to lie heavily on me all through my life has its grip on me. I am not one to be satisfied to act for myself, think for myself, feel for myself but I must also attempt to think and feel for Uncas.

At the moment slick plausible excuses for what has happened during the afternoon are rising to my lips, struggling for expression. I am not satisfied with being myself and letting things take their course, but must be inside the very body of Uncas, striving to fill his stout young body with the questioning soul of myself.

As I write this I am remembering that my father, like myself, could never be singly himself but must always be a playing some rôle, everlastingly strutting on the stage of life in some part not his own. Was there a rôle of his own to be played? That I do not know and I fancy he never knew, but I remember that he once took it into his head to enact the rôle of the stern and unyielding parent to Uncas and what came of it.

The tragic little comedy took place in the woodshed back of one of the innumerable houses to which we were always moving when some absurd landlord took it into his head that he should have some rent for the house we occupied, and Uncas had just beaten with his fists a neighbor boy who had tried to run away with a baseball bat belonging to us. Uncas had retrieved the bat and had brought it proudly home, and father, who happened along the street at that moment, had got the notion fixed in his mind that the bat belonged, not to us, but to the neighbor boy. Uncas tried to explain, but father, having taken up the rôle of the just man, must needs play it out to the bitter end. He demanded that Uncas return the bat into the hands of the boy from whom he had just ravaged it and Uncas, growing white and silent, ran home and hid himself in the woodshed where father quickly found him out.

"I won't," declared Uncas; "the bat's ours"; and then father—fool that he was for ever allowing himself to get into such an undignified position—began

21

to beat him with a switch he had cut from a tree at the front of the house. As the beating did no good and Uncas only took it unmoved, father, as always happened with him, lost his head.

And so there was the boy, white with the sense of the injustice being done, and no doubt father also began to feel that he had put his foot into a trap. He grew furious and, picking up a large stick of wood from a woodpile in the shed, threatened to hit Uncas with it.

What a moment! I had run to the back of the shed and had thrown myself on the ground where I could look through a crack and as long as I live I shall never forget the next few moments—with the man and the boy, both white, looking at each other; and, that night, in the bed later, when mother was rubbing my chapped hands and when I knew there was something to be settled between her and Uncas, that picture danced like a crazy ghost in my fancy.

I trembled at the thought of what might happen, at the thought of what had happened that day in the shed.

Father had stood—I shall never know how long—with the heavy stick upraised, looking into the eyes of his son, and the son had stared, with a fixed determined stare, back into the eyes of his father.

At the moment I had thought that—boy as I was—I understood how such a strange unaccountable thing as a murder could happen. Thoughts did not form themselves definitely in my mind but after that moment I knew that it is always the weak, frightened by their own weakness, who kill the strong, and perhaps I also knew myself for one of the weak ones of the world. At the moment, as father stood with the stick upraised, glaring at Uncas, my own sympathies (if my own fancy has not tricked me again) were with father. My heart ached for him.

He was saved by mother. She came to the door of the shed and stood looking at him and his eyes wavered, and then he threw the stick back upon the pile from which he had taken it and went silently away. I remembered that he tramped off to Main Street and that, later in the evening when he came back to the house, he was drunk and went drunken to bed. The trick of drunkenness had saved him from the ordeal of looking into the eyes of Uncas or of mother, as so often words have later saved me from meeting fairly some absurd position into which I have got myself.

.   .   .   .

And so there was I now, in the bed and up to one of father's tricks: upstart that I was, dog of a Huron myself, I was trembling for mother and for Uncas—two people very well able to take care of themselves.

Mother dropped my hand and took the outstretched hand of my brother.

"What happened?" she asked.

And Uncas told her, fairly and squarely. "He was a cry-baby and a big calf and I walloped him one. I wanted the hatchet and so I took it—that's what I did. I banged him one on the nose and jerked it out of his hand."

Mother laughed—a queer unmirthful little laugh. It was the kind of laugh that hurts. There was irony

23

in it and that got to Uncas at once. "It doesn't take much of a fellow to snatch a hatchet out of the hands of a cry-baby," she said.

That was all. She kept on rubbing his hands and now it was my eyes, and not the eyes of Uncas, that could look directly into our mother's eyes.

Perhaps it was in that moment, and not in the moment when I lay on the ground peeking through the crack into the shed, that the first dim traces of understanding of all such fellows as father and myself came to me. I looked at mother with adoration in my own eyes, and when she had taken the kerosene lamp and had gone away, and when we boys were all again curled quietly like sleeping puppies in the bed, I cried a little, as I am sure father must have cried sometimes when there was no one about. Perhaps his getting drunk, as he did on all possible occasions, was a way of crying too.

And I cried also, I suppose, because in Uncas and mother there was a kind of directness and simplicity that father and all fellows, who like myself are of the same breed with him, can never quite achieve.

24

be had in our town and I presume Aldrich also had no work. I remember him as a quiet-looking middle-aged man with a red face. He also was a house-painter, during the summer months, and he and father had by some chance got hold of a secondhand magic-lantern outfit.

They were to show at country schoolhouses in the farming districts of northern Ohio. There was to be a sheet hung across the end of the room, near the place where the teacher's desk would sit, and on this would be thrown certain pictures Aldrich had got hold of.

Those of you who have lived in the farming sections of mid-America, in the days before the movies, will understand that show. There would be a picture of Niagara Falls—taken in the winter—Niagara Falls frozen into a series of ice bridges and with small black figures of men running over the bridges.

These, you are to understand, however, would not be moving men. They would be frozen still and still—petrified men with legs upraised to take a step, and holding them there—to the end of time—forever.

Then there would be a picture of President McKinley and one of Abe Lincoln and Grover Cleveland—one of an emigrant wagon going across the Western plains to California, with Indians on ponies circling in the middle distance—a picture of the driving of the last railroad spike, when the railroad builders coming from the West had met the railroad builders coming from the East—somewhere out on the plains. The spike would be a golden one, as everyone in the audience would know, but in the picture it would be black. Several men with silk hats

NOTE II

A FAMILY of five boys and two girls—a mother who is to die, outworn and done for at thirty—

A father, whose blood and whose temperament I am to carry to the end of my days. How futile he was—in his physical life as a man in America in his time—what dreams he must have had!

There was a dream he had of something magnificent—a lone rider on a horse, dressed in shining armor and riding in a city before a vast multitude of people—the beating of drums . . . "The man—he comes! Hurra!" People who live their lives by facts can never understand such a fellow. "He comes! All hail!" What has he done? Well, never mind—something grand, you may be sure of that. The dream that never can become a fact in life can become a fact in fancy. "There he goes . . . 'Teddy the magnificent'!" One both laughs and cries over the memory of him.

The showman was there, in him—it flowered within him—and it is in me too. When Carl Sandburg, the poet, long after said to me—speaking of his lecturing and reading his poetry aloud, to make a living—"I give 'em a good show," I understood what he meant and I understood the pride in his voice when he said it. And then, later still, when I was writing my own novel, "Poor White"; and when my boyhood friend, John Emerson, gave me a job—doing publicity for movie people, in order that I might have some income to write at my leisure—and for a time I saw a good deal of that strange perverted band, I could understand them also. They were people like my own father, robbed of their inheritance. In an odd way they were my own people too.

John Emerson, a boyhood friend from my own village, had given me the movie job, knowing I would be no good at it. He was a successful man, a money-maker, and was always planning out schemes for giving me money and leisure. I went often to the movie studios and watched the men and the women at work. Children, playing with dreams—dreams of an heroic kind of desperado cowboy, doing good deeds at the business end of a gun—dreams of an ever-virtuous womanhood walking amid vice—American dreams—Anglo-Saxon dreams. How they wanted to be the things they were always playing, and how impossible it all was!

My father lived in a land and in a time when what one later begins to understand a little as the artist in man could not by any possibility be understood by his fellows. Dreams then were to be expressed in building railroads and factories, in boring gas wells, stringing telegraph poles. There was room for no other dream and since father could not do any of these things he was an outlaw in his community. The community tolerated him. His own sons toler-ated him.

As for the movie people I saw, they worked in a strange land of fragments of dreams. The parts they were to play were given them in fragments. Everything was fragmentary and unfinished. A kind

26

of insanity reigned. A "set" having been made, at a certain cost in dollars and cents, half a dozen little bits of the dream they were to enact were gone through —sometimes a dozen times—and the very piece the actors were supposed to play they often did not know. A strange greenish light fell down over them, and when they were not playing, they sat stupidly hour after hour arrayed in their motley, often pawing one another over listlessly with their hands and seeking outside the studios—in drink, in dope, in futile love-making, in trying to carry on an absurd pretense to being ladies and gentlemen of parts—seeking in all these things to compensate themselves for being robbed of their inheritance as artists—the right to pour the emotional energies into their work.

The result of all this perversion of workman and of emotional energy in the movie world see to me to reduce human beings to a state that me all suggested to my mind angleworms squirming boy's bait-can; and why any human being, und conditions in which they must work and w materials with which they must work, should be a movie actor or a writer for the movies i my comprehension.

But to return to my father. At least, little of the dull listlessness of the anglewo He created his own, "dope," inside himse the time.

Once he actually set up as a showm man of our town, named Aldrich, who ov down horse and a spring wagon he strut his own little hour upon the boar It was winter and there was no wo

27

on their heads stood about while a workman drove the spike. The hammer was upraised. It stayed there. In the background was an engine, and several Indians wrapped in blankets and looking sad, as though to say: "This cooks our bacon."

Most of the pictures would be in dead blacks and whites, but there would be, at the very end, in colors, the old flag floating—that last of all. It was as good for a hand then as it was later when George Cohan got rich and became famous with it, and father and Aldrich evidently knew it would "go."

The admission charge would be ten cents.

As I have said, Aldrich was a red-faced mild middle-aged appearing man. What things will not such quiet-looking fellows sometimes do? No one in the world would ever be understood at all if your mild quiet-looking man did not have, buried away in him somewhere, the possibility of being almost any known sort of a fool.

In the arrangement that had been made father was to be the actor—a comedian. He was to sing certain songs.

First, a few pictures from the magic lantern; then a song by father, with a little dance. Then more pictures and another song; and at last the colored pictures, ending with the flag flying. The inference might be that the flag, at any rate, had survived the ordeal.

And a dream of a harvest of dimes too. As for expense—well, let us say, a dollar for the use of the country schoolhouse and enough firewood to heat it for the evening. A boy would build the fire for the chance to be admitted free; and the horse and the two men would be fed at the bounty of some farmer. Father would have promised that—he would have been very sure of being able to accomplish that—would have depended upon his personal charm. I can fancy him explaining to Aldrich, or rather not explaining. He would smile and throw out his hands in a peculiar way. "You leave that to me, just you leave that to me."

And his hopes would not be unjustified either. What a boon for a quiet, dull, farming family in the winter, to have such a one light down upon it! He and his companion would have to stay in the one school district for two or three days. Arrangements would have to be made about getting the schoolhouse, and he and Aldrich would have to drive around the neighborhood and distribute the play bills:

AT THE SCHOOLHOUSE
FRIDAY EVENING
MAJOR IRWIN ANDERSON
THE ACTOR
IN SONG AND DANCE
MARVELOUS MAGIC-LANTERN SHOW
A VISIT TO ALL THE WONDERS
OF THE WORLD
10 CENTS

And then the evenings in the farmhouses! Aldrich would sit like an Indian in his corner by the farmhouse stove; and he must have been saying to himself constantly: "Now, how did I get into this? How did I get into this?"

The farmer's wife the hired man and perhaps a

30

grown daughter would be there and there would be a maiden of uncertain age—the farm woman's sister, who had never married and so just stayed about and worked for her board—and, in a corner, two or three towheaded boys who would presently have to go off to bed.

All the others silent, but father talking and talking. An actor in the house! It was wonderful, like having Charlie Chaplin to dinner with you nowadays!

Father was in his element now. This was pie for him. No hungry sons about, no sick wife, no grocery bills or rent to be paid. This the golden age—timeless; there was no past, no future—the quiet, unsophisticated people in the room were putty to his hands.

Surely there was something magnificent in my father's utter disregard for the facts of life. In the picture I have of him—that is to say in my fancy—in the picture I have of him during his pilgrimages of that winter I always see his partner in the affair, Aldrich, fast asleep in a chair.

But the farmer and his wife, and the wife's sister —they are not asleep. The unmarried woman in the house is, let us say, thirty-eight. She is tall and gaunt and has several teeth missing and her name is Tilly. It would be bound to be Tilly.

And when father has been in the house two hours he is calling her "Tilly," and the farmer he is addressing familiarly as "Ed."

After the evening meal the farmer has had to go to his stable to look at his stock, to bed the stock down for the night, and father has gone with him. Father runs about the stable holding the lantern. He boasts about the horses and cattle in his father's

31

stables when he was a boy. Whether that early home of his ever existed anywhere but in his fancy is doubtful.

What a fellow, wanting to be loved, was my father!

And now he is in the farmhouse sitting room and it is late evening and the towheaded children have gone regretfully to bed. There is something in the air of the room, a kind of suspense, a feeling that something is about to happen. Father has so carefully worked that up. He would do it by silences, by sudden breakings out into suppressed laughter, and then by quickly looking sad. I have seen him do the thing, oh, many times. "My dear people—you wait! There is something inside me that is wonderful, and if you will only be patient you will presently see or hear it come forth," he seemed to be saying.

He is by the fire with his legs spread out and his hands are in his trousers pockets. He stares at the floor. He is smoking a cigar. In some ways he always managed to keep himself supplied with the little comforts of life.

And he has so placed his chair that he can look at Tilly, who has retired into her corner, without anyone else in the room seeing the look. Now she is sitting in deep shadows, far away from the kerosene lamp with which the room is lighted and as she sits there, half lost in the darkness, there is suddenly something—a haunting kind of beauty hangs over her.

She is a little excited by something father has managed in some indescribable way to do to the very air of the room. Tilly also was once young and must at some time have had her grand moment in life. Her moment was not very prolonged. Once, when she was a young woman, she went to a country dance and a man, who dealt in horses, took a fancy to her and carried her home after the dance in his buggy. He was a tall man with a heavy mustache and she—it was a moonlight night in October—she grew sad and wistful. The horse dealer half intended—well, he had been buying horses for a trucking company at Toledo, Ohio, had secured all he wanted and was leaving the neighborhood on the next day—the thing he felt during that evening later quite went out of his mind.

As for father he is, at the moment perhaps thinking of mother, when she was young and lovely and was a bound girl in just such another farmhouse, and surely he wanted something lovely for mother then as he does for Tilly now. I have no doubt at all that father always wanted lovely things for people —to happen to people—and that he had also an absurd and never-dying faith in himself—that he was, in some inscrutable way, appointed to be the bearer of lovely things to obscure people.

However, there is something else in his mind also. Is he not the fellow who, by his personal charm, is to earn for himself, Aldrich and the horse, board, a bed, a welcome—without pay—until the show is pulled off at the schoolhouse? That is his business now and this is his hour.

In fancy I can hear the tale he would now begin telling. There was that one about his escape from the guards when he was a Union soldier in the Civil War and was being marched off to a Southern prison camp. He would no doubt use that. It was a bull's-eye story and always hit the mark! Oh, how often and under what varying circumstances has not my father escaped from prisons! Benvenuto Cellini or the Count of Monte Cristo had nothing on him.

Yes, the story he would now tell would be that once when it rained and the Union prisoners, father among them—some forty men in all—were being marched off along a road in the deep mud—

That was indeed a night of adventure! It was a tale he loved telling, and what realistic touches he could put into it: the rain that wet the prisoners to the skin—the cold—the chattering teeth—the groans of weary men—the closeness of the dark forest on either hand—the steady weary chug-chug of the feet of the prisoners in the mud—the line of guards at either side of the road, with the guns over their shoulders—the curses of the Rebel guards when they stumbled in the darkness.

What a night of weary anguish on the part of the prisoners! When they stopped to rest the guards went into a house and left the prisoners to stand outside in the rain, or lie on the bare ground, guarded by part of the company. If any died of exposure—well, there would be that many less men to feed when they were got into the Southern prison camp.

And now, after many days and nights, marching thus, the souls of the prisoners were sick with weariness. A dreary desolated look would come upon father's face as he spoke of it.

They marched steadily along in the deep mud and the rain. How cold the rain was! Now and then, in the darkness, a dog barked, far away somewhere. There was a break in the solid line of timber along the road and the men marched across the crest of a low hill. There are lights to be seen now, in distant farmhouses, far away across a valley—a few lights like stars shining.

The story-teller has got his audience leaning forward in their chairs. Outside the farmhouse in which they sit a wind begins to blow and a broken branch from a near-by tree is blown against the side of the house. The farmer, a heavy, stolid-looking man, starts a little and his wife shivers as with cold and Tilly is absorbed—she does not want to miss a word of the tale.

And now father is describing the darkness of the valley below the hill and the lights seen, far off. Will any of the little company of prisoners ever see their own homes again, their wives, their children, their sweethearts? The lights of the farmhouses in the valley are like stars in the sky of a world turned upside down.

The Rebel commander of the guard has issued a warning and a command: "It's pretty dark here, and if any of the Yanks make a stir to move out of the centre of the road fire straight into the mass of them. Kill them like dogs."

A feeling creeps over father. He is, you see, a southern man himself, a man of the Georgia hills and plains. There is no law that shall prevent his having been born in Georgia, although to-morrow night it may be North Carolina or Kentucky. But to-night his birthplace shall be Georgia. He is a man who lives by his fancy and to-night it shall suit his fancy and the drift of his tale to be a Georgian.

And so he, a prisoner of the Rebels, is being marched over the low hill, with the lights from distant farmhouses shining like stars in the darkness below, and suddenly a feeling comes to him, a feeling such as one sometimes has when one is alone in one's own house at night. You have had the feeling. You are alone in the house and there are no lights and it is cold and dark. Everything you touch—feel with your hands in the darkness—is strange and at the same time familiar. You know how it is.

The farmer is nodding his head and his wife has her hands gripped, lying in her lap. Even Aldrich is awake now. The devil! Father has given this particular tale a new turn since he told it last. "This is something like." Aldrich leans forward to listen.

And there is the woman Tilly, in the half darkness. See, she is quite lovely now, quite as she was on that evening when she rode with the horse dealer in the buggy! Something has happened to soften the long, harsh lines of her face and she might be a princess sitting there now in the half-light.

Father would have thought of that. It would be something worth while now to be a tale-teller to a princess. He stops talking to consider for a moment the possibilities of the notion, and then with a sigh gives it up.

It is a sweet notion but it won't do. Tale-teller to a princess, eh! Evenings in a castle and the prince has come in from hunting in a forest. The tale-teller is dressed in flashy clothes and with a crowd of courtiers, ladies in waiting—whatever hangers-on a princess has —is sitting by an open fire. There are great, magnificent dogs lying about too.

Father is considering whether or not it is worth trying sometime—the telling of a tale of himself in

36

just that rôle. An idea crosses his mind. The
princess has a lover who creeps one night into the
castle and the prince has become aware of his presence, is told of his presence by a trusty varlet. Taking his sword in hand the prince creeps through the
dark hallways to kill his rival, but father has warned
the lovers and they have fled. It afterward comes
to the ears of the prince that father has protected the
lovers and he—that is to say, father—is compelled to
flee for his life. He comes to America and lives the
life of an exile, far from the splendor to which he
has been accustomed.

Father is thinking whether it would be worth trying—the telling of such a fable of his former existence, some evening at some farmhouse where he and
Aldrich are staying; and for a moment a sort of
George Barr McCutcheon light comes into his eyes,
but with a sigh he gives it up.

It wouldn't go over—not in a farmhouse in northern
Ohio, he concludes.

He returns to the tale, that so evidently is going
over; but, before he resumes, casts another glance at
Tilly. "Oh, Tilly, thou dear lovely one," he sighs
inwardly.

The farmhouse is in the North and he has set himself forth as a southerner enlisted in the northern
army. An explanation is in order, and he makes it,
with a flourish.

Born a southerner, the son of a proud southern
family, he was sent to school, to a college in the North.
In college he had a roommate, a dear fellow from the
state of Illinois. The "roommate's father was owner
and editor of the *Chicago Tribune*," he explains.

37

And during one summer, a few years before the breaking out of the war, he went on a visit to the home of his Illinois friend, and while he was there he, with his friend, went to hear the famous Lincoln-Douglas debates. It was odd, but the facts were that the young fellow from Illinois became enamored of the brilliant Douglas while he—well, to tell the truth, his own heart was wrung by the simplicity and nobility of the rail-splitter, Lincoln. "Never shall I forget the nobility of that countenance," he says in speaking of it. He appears about to cry and does in fact take a handkerchief from his pocket and wipe his eyes. "Oh, the noble, the indescribable effect upon my boyhood heart of the stirring words of that man. There he stood like a mighty oak of the forest breasting the storms. 'A nation cannot exist half slave and half free. A house divided against itself cannot stand,' he said, and his words thrilled me to the very marrow of my being."

And then father would have described his homecoming after that terrific experience. War was coming on and all the South was aflame.

One day at table in his southern home, with his brothers, his father and mother and his beautiful and innocent young sister sitting with him, he dared to say something in defense of Lincoln.

What a storm was then raised! The father getting up from his place at table pointed a trembling finger at his son. All eyes, except only those of his younger sister, were turned on him in wrath and disapproval. "Mention that hated name again in this house and I will shoot you like a dog, though you are my son," his father said, and the son got up from the table and went away, filled with the sense of filial duty that would not let a born southerner answer his own father, but nevertheless determined to stick to the faith aroused in him by the words of the noble Lincoln.

And so he had ridden away from his southern home in the night and had finally joined the Union forces.

What a night—riding away from his father's house in the darkness, leaving his mother behind, leaving all tradition behind, condemning himself to be an outlaw in the hearts of those he had always loved—for the sake of duty!

One can imagine Aldrich blinking a little and rubbing his hands together. "Teddy is laying it on rather thick," he no doubt says to himself; but he must nevertheless have been filled with admiration.

However, let us, who are together revisiting the scene of my father's triumph on that evening in the farmhouse long ago, be not too much in fear for the heart of the woman Tilly. At any rate her physical self, if not her heart, was safe.

Although there can be little doubt that the presence of the virgin Tilly, sitting in the half darkness, and the kindliness of the shadows that had temporarily enhanced her failing beauty, may have had a good deal to do with father's talent on that evening, I am sure nothing else ever came of it. Father, in his own way, was devoted to mother.

And he had his own way of treasuring her. Did he not treasure always the lovelier moments of her?

He had found her in a farmhouse when he was by way of being something of a young swell himself and she was a bound girl; and she was then beautiful

—beautiful without the aid of shadows cast by a kerosene lamp.

In reality she was the aristocrat of the two, as the beautiful one is always the aristocrat; and oh, how little beauty in woman is understood! The popular magazine covers and the moving-picture actresses have raised the very devil with our American conception of womanly beauty.

But father had delicacy, of a sort, of that you may be quite sure; and do you not suppose that Tilly, in the Ohio farmhouse, sensed something of his attitude toward what fragment of beauty was left in her, and that she loved him for that attitude—as I am sure my own mother also did?

> My fruit shall not be my fruit until it
> drops from my arms, into the arms of the
> others, over the top of the wall.

And now the weary prisoners with their escort have come down off the hillside to a valley and are approaching a large old southern mansion, standing back from the road they have been traveling, and the officers in charge of the prisoners—there were two of them—command the guards to turn in at a gate that leads to the house.

There is an open space before the house where the prisoners are gathered and the ground—covered with firm turf during most of the year—has, under the continuous rains, become soft and yielding. Where each prisoner stands a puddle gathers about his feet.

The house is dark, but for a single light at the back, and one of the officers begins shouting. A large pack of hunting dogs have come from a shed, hidden away in the darkness somewhere, and are gathered growling and barking in a half circle about the prisoners.

One of the dogs rushes through the mass of prisoners and with a glad cry leaps upon father, and all the others follow so that guards are compelled to drive the dogs off, kicking them and using the butts of their guns. Lights are lit inside the house. The people are astir.

You will understand what a moment this was for father. By one of those strange streaks of fate—which he is very careful to explain to his audience happen much more frequently in life than one imagines—he had been led, as a prisoner on his way to a southern prison pen, right to the door of his own father's house.

What a moment indeed! Being a prisoner he has of course no idea how long he will be kept there. Thank God, he has grown a thick, bushy beard since he left home.

As to his fate—if the prisoners are kept in the yard until daylight comes—well, he knows his own mother.

His own father, old man though he is, has gone off to the war and all his brothers have gone; and his mother has come from a proud old southern family, one of the oldest and proudest. Had she known he was there among the prisoners she would have seen him hanged without a protest and would herself have lent a hand at pulling the rope.

. . . .

Ah, what had not my father given for his country! Where will his equal be found, even among the whole world's heroes? In the eyes of his own mother and father, in his brother's eyes, in the eyes of all the branches and ramifications of his southern family, in the eyes of all—except only one unsophisticated and innocent girl—he had brought everlasting disgrace on one of the proudest names of the South.

Indeed it was just because he, the son, had gone off to fight with the northern army that his father, a proud old man of sixty, had insisted on being taken into the southern army. "I have a strong old frame and I insist," he had said. "I must make good the loss to my Southland for my own son, who has proven himself a dog and a renegade."

And so the old man had marched off with a gun on his shoulder, insisting on being taken as a common soldier and put where he could face constant and terrible danger, and the seeds of an undying hatred against the son had been planted deep in the hearts of the whole family.

The dullest mind surely will comprehend now what a position father was in when, in answer to the shouts of the officer, lights began to appear all through the house. Was it not a situation to wring tears from the heart of a man of stone! As for a woman's heart—one can scarcely speak of the matter.

And in the house, before father's eyes, there was one—a pure and innocent southern girl of rare beauty—a pearl of womanhood in fact—rarest example of the famed spotless womanhood of the Southland—his younger sister—the only woman child of the family.

You see, as father would so carefully have explained that evening in the farmhouse, he did not care so much for his own life. That had already been given to his country, he would have said proudly.

But, as you will understand quickly enough, had his presence among the prisoners been discovered, his proud mother—eager to wipe out the only stain on the family escutcheon—would at once have insisted that he be hanged to the doorpost of the very house in which he was born, her own hand pulling at the rope that was to jerk him up, into the arms of death—to make white again the family escutcheon, you understand.

Could a proud southern woman do less?

And in the event of such an outcome to the adventures of the night, see how that younger sister—the love of his life at that time—see how she would have suffered.

There she was, the pure and innocent girl, the one who understood nothing, to be sure, of the import of his decision to stick to the old flag and fight for the land of Washington and Lincoln, and who, in her innocent way, just loved him. On that day at his father's table, when he—so deeply affected by the Lincoln-Douglas debates—had dared say a word for the cause of the North, it had been her eyes and her eyes alone that had looked at him with love, when all the other eyes of his family had looked at him with hatred and loathing.

And she would just be bursting into womanhood now. The aroma of awakening womanhood would be lying over her as perfume over the opening rosebud.

Think of it! There she, the pure and innocent one, would have to stand and see him hanged. A blight would be brought down upon her young life and her head would, ever after that night, be bowed in lonely and silent sorrow. That brave pure and just girl made old before her time. Ah; well might it be that in one night the mass of golden locks, that now covered her head like a cloud just kissed by the evening sun—that very golden hair might be turned as white as snow!

I can, in fancy, hear my father saying the words I have set down here and coming very near to crying himself as he said them. At the moment he would have believed without question the story he himself was telling.

. . . .

And now the front door to the old southern mansion is thrown open and there, in the doorway facing the prisoners in the rain, stands a gigantic young negro—my father's own body servant before he left home. (Father stops the flow of his talk long enough to explain how he and the negro boy, as lads together, had fought, wrestled, hunted, fished and lived together like two brothers. I will not go into that, however. Any professional southerner will tell you all about it, if you care to hear. It would have been the most trite part of father's evening's effort.)

Anyway, there the gigantic young negro stands in the doorway and he is holding in his hand a candle. Back of him stands my grandmother and back of her the young and innocent sister.

The figure of father's mother is erect. She is old but she is yet tall and strong. One of the officers explains to her that he and his men have been on an all-night march, taking the crowd of Yankee prisoners to a prison camp, and asks for the hospitality of the house. Being a southerner himself he knows that southern hospitality can never fail, even at midnight. "A bite to eat and a cup of hot coffee in the name of our Southland," he asks.

It is granted, of course. The proud woman beckons him and his brother officer into the house and herself steps out into the cold, drizzling rain.

She has ordered the young negro to stand on the porch, holding the candle aloof, and now, marching across the wet lawn, approaches the prisoners. The southern guards have stepped aside, bowing low before southern womanhood, and she goes near the prisoners and looks at them, as well as one may in the uncertain light. "I have a curiosity to see some of the unmannerly dogs of Yanks," she says, leaning forward and staring at them. She is very near her own son now but he has turned his face away and is looking at the ground. Something however causes him to raise his head just as she, to express more fully her contempt, spits at the men.

A little speck of her white spittle lands upon father's thick, tawny beard.

And now his mother has gone back into the house and it is again dark on the lawn in front. The Rebel guards are relieved—two at a time—to go to the kitchen door, where they are given hot coffee and sandwiches. And once his young sister, she of the tender heart, tries to creep to where the prisoners stand in the darkness. She is accompanied by an old negro woman and has planned to give food aid and comfort to the weary men but is prevented. Her mother has missed her inside the house and coming to the door

45

calls to her. "I know your tender heart," she says, "but it shall not be. The teeth of no Yankee dog shall ever bite into food raised on the land of your father. It shall not happen, at least while your mother is alive to prevent."

NOTE III

So there was father, sitting comfortably in the warm farmhouse living room—he and Aldrich having been well fed at the table of a prosperous farmer—and having before him what he most loved, an attentive and absorbed audience. By this time the farmer's wife would be deeply moved by the fate of that son of the South that father had represented himself as being; and as for Tilly—while, in the fanciful picture he is making, he stands in the cold and wet outside the door of that southern mansion, Heaven knows what is going on in poor Tilly's heart. It is however bleeding with sympathy, one may be sure of that.

So there is father and, in the meantime, what of his own actual flesh-and-blood family, the family he had left behind in an Ohio village when he set forth on his career as an actor?

It is not suffering too much. One need not waste too much sympathy on his family. Although he was never what we called in our Ohio country, "a good provider," he had his points and as one of his sons I at least would be loath to trade him for a more provident shrewd and thoughtful father.

It must however have been a fairly hard winter, for mother at least and in connection with that winter and others that followed I have often since had an amusing thought. In later years, when my own name

47

had a little got up in the world as a teller of tales I was often accused of having got my impulse, as a story-teller, from the Russians. The statement is a plausible one. It is, in a way, based upon reason.

When I had grown to be a man, and when my stories began to be published in the pages of the more reckless magazines, such as *The Little Review*, the old *Masses* and later in *The Seven Arts* and *The Dial*, and when I was so often accused of being under the Russian influence, I began to read the Russians, to find out if the statement, so often made concerning me and my work, could be true.

This I found, that in Russian novels the characters are always eating cabbage soup and I have no doubt Russian writers eat it too.

This was a revelation to me. Many of the Russian tales are concerned with the lives of peasants and a Boston critic once said I had brought the American peasant into literature; and it is likely that Russian writers, like all the other writers who have ever lived and have not pandered to the popular demand for sentimental romances were fortunate if they could live as well as a peasant. "What the critics say is no doubt true," I told myself; for, like so many of the Russian writers, I was raised largely on cabbage soup.

Let me explain.

The little Ohio farming community, where I lived as a lad had in it, at that time, no factories, and the merchants artisans lawyers and other townspeople were all either owners of land which they rented out to tenant farmers, or they sold goods or their services to farmers. The soil on the farms about the town was a light sandy loam that would raise small fruits, corn, wheat, oats or potatoes, but that did particularly well when planted to cabbages.

As a result the raising of cabbages became a sort of specialty with us in our country; and there are now, I believe, in my native place, some three or four prosperous factories, devoted to the making of what before the war was called "sauerkraut." Later, to help win the war, it was called: "Liberty Cabbage."

The specialization in the raising of cabbage began in our Ohio country in my day, and in a good year some of the fields produced as high as twenty tons of cabbage an acre.

The cabbage fields grew larger and larger and, as we grew older, my brothers and I went every spring and fell to work in the fields. We crawled across the fields, setting out cabbage plants in the spring, and in the fall went out to cut cabbages. The huge round hard heads of cabbage were cut from their stalks and pitched to a man who loaded them upon a hay wagon; and on fall days I have often seen twenty or thirty wagons, each bearing its two or three tons of cabbages and waiting its turn to get to the cars on the railroad siding. The waiting wagons filled our streets as tobacco-laden wagons fill the streets of a Kentucky town in the fall, and in the stores and houses everyone for a time talked of nothing but cabbages. "What would the crop bring on the markets at Cleveland or Pittsburgh?" Pittsburgh, for some reason I have never understood, had a passion for cabbages; and why Pittsburgh hasn't produced more so-called realistic writers, in the Russian manner, I cannot understand.

49

However, one may well leave that to the modern psychologists.

During the fall of that year, after father had set out on his adventures as an actor, mother did something she had often done before. By a stroke of strategy she succeeded in getting a winter's supply of cabbages for her family, without the expenditure of any monies.

The fall advanced, father had gone, and the annual village cut-up time, called among us "Hallowe'en," came on.

It was the custom among the lads of our town, particularly among those who lived on the farms near town, to make cabbages part of their celebration of the occasion. Such lads, living as they did in the country, had the use of horses and buggies, and on Hallowe'en they hitched up and drove off to town.

On the way they stopped at the cabbage fields and, finding in some of the fields many cabbages yet uncut, pulled them out by the roots and piled them in the backs of their buggies.

The country lads, giggling with anticipated pleasure, drove into one of the quieter residence streets of our town and, leaving the horse standing in the road, one of them got out of the buggy and took one of the cabbages in his hand. The cabbage had been pulled out of the ground with the great stalklike root still clinging to it and the lad now grasped this firmly. He crept toward one of the houses, preferably one that was dark—an indication that the people of the house, having spent a hard day at labor, had already gone to bed. Approaching the house cautiously, he swung the cabbage above his head, holding it by the long stalk, and then he let it go. The thing was to just hurl the cabbage full against the closed door of the house. It struck with a thunderous sound and the supposition was that the people of the house would be startled and fairly lifted out of their beds by the hollow booming noise, produced when the head of cabbage landed against the door and, as a matter of fact, when a stout country boy had hurled the cabbage the sound produced was something quite tremendous.

The cabbage having been thrown the country boy ran quickly into the road, leaped into his buggy and, striking his horse with the whip, drove triumphantly away. He was not likely to return unless pursued. and there it was that mother's strategy came into play.

On the great night she made us all sit quietly in the house. As soon as the evening meal was finished the lights were put out and we waited while mother stood just at the door, the knob in her hand. No doubt it must have seemed strange to the boys of our town that one so gentle and quiet as mother could be so infuriated by the hurling of a cabbage at the door of our house.

But there was the simple fact of the situation to tempt and darkness had no sooner settled down upon our quiet street that one of the lads appeared. It was worth while throwing cabbages at such a house. One was pursued, one was scolded, threats were hurled: "Don't you dare come back to this house! I'll have the town marshal after you, that's what I'll do! If I get my hands on one of you I'll give you a drubbing!" There was something of the actor in mother also.

What a night for the lads! Here was something

worth while and all evening the game went on and on. The buggies were not driven to our house, but were stopped at the head of the street, and town boys went on pilgrimages to cabbage fields to get ammunition and join in the siege. Mother stormed scolded and ran out into the darkness waving a broom while we children stayed indoors, enjoying the battle—and when the evening's sport was at an end, we all fell to and gathered in the spoils. As she returned from each sally from the fort mother had brought into the house the last cabbage thrown—if she could find it; and now, late in the evening when our provident tormentors were all gone, we children went forth with a lantern and got in the rest of our crop. Often as many as two or three hundred cabbages came our way and these were all carefully gathered in. They had been pulled from the ground, with all the heavy outer leaves still clinging to them, so that they were comparatively uninjured and, as there was also still attached to them the heavy stalklike root, they were in fine shape to be kept. A long trench was dug in our back yard and the cabbages buried, lying closely side by side, as I am told the dead are usually buried after a siege.

Perhaps indeed we were somewhat more careful with them than soldiers are with their dead after a battle. Were not the cabbages to be, for us, the givers of life? They were put into the trench carefully and tenderly with the heads downward and the stalks sticking up, mother supervising, and about each head straw was carefully packed—winding sheets. One could get straw from a strawstack in a near-by field at night, any amount of it, and one did not pay or even bother to ask.

When winter came quickly, as it did after Hallowe'en, mother got small white beans from the grocery and salt pork from the butcher, and a thick soup, of which we never tired, was concocted. The cabbages were something at our backs. They made us feel safe.

And there was also a sense of something achieved. In the land in which we lived one did not need to have a large income. There was food all about, plenty of it, and we who lived so precariously in the land of plenty had, by our " mother's wit," achieved this store of food without working for it. A common sense of pride in our cleverness held us together.

One went out into our back yard on a winter's night when there was snow on the ground and looked abroad. Already we lads read books, and snow-covered fields stretching away under the winter moon suggested strange, stirring thoughts—travelers beset by wolves on the Russian Steppes—emigrant trains lost in whirling snowstorms on the Western sagebrush deserts of our own country, men in all sorts of strange terrible places wandering, desperate and starving, under the winter moon—and what of us? The place where the cabbages were buried made a long white mound, directly across our back yard, and when one looked at it there was a sense of fullness and plenty in the land. One remembered that down under the snow, buried away in the straw, were those long rows of cabbages. Deer, buffaloes, wild horses and equally wild long-horned cattle, far out on the Western plains, did not worry about food because the ground was covered with snow. With their hoofs they pawed the snow away, and found buried beneath the snow the sweet little clusters of bunch grass, that again sent the warmth of life singing through their bodies.

It was a chance for the fancy to play, to kick up its heels and have a good time. One could imagine the house in which one lived as a fort, set far out on the Western frontier. The cabbages had been put into the ground with the stalks straight up. They stuck up straight and stiff, like sentinels standing and, after looking, one went into the fort and slept quietly and peacefully. There the soldiers were—they were standing firm and unyielding. Were there enemies prowling out there in the white darkness, the little wild dogs of want? One could laugh at such thoughts. Were not the sentinels standing—quietly and firmly waiting? One could go into the fort and sleep in peace, hugging that thought.

To us at home, father was always, somewhat strangely, a part and at the same time not a part of our lives. He flew in and out as a bird flies in and out of a bush, and I am quite sure that, all through the years of our childhood, it never occurred to him to ask, when he set off on one of his winter adventures, whether or not there was anything to eat in our house. The fall came with its snows, and the little creeping fear of actual starvation for her brood, that must often have been in mother's mind, followed by the spring, the warm rains, the promise of plenty and his return. If he brought no money, he did bring something—a ham, some combs of honey, a jug of cider, or even perhaps a quarter of beef. There he was again and there was food on the table. He made a gesture.

"There!" he seemed to be saying; "you see! Who says I'm not a provider?"

There were tales to be told and he was the teller of tales. "It is sufficient. Can man live by bread alone? There is food on the table now. Eat! Stuff yourselves! Spring has come and there are signs to be painted. The night has passed and it is another day. I am a man of faith. I tell you a sparrow shall not fall to the ground without my notice. I will make a tale of it—tell why and how it fell. The most marvelous tale in the world might be made from the fall of a sparrow. Is not the workman worthy of his hire? What about the lilies of the field, eh? They toil not and neither do they spin—do they?"

And yet, was Solomon, in all his glory, arrayed like one of these?

.   .   .   .

I remember a day in the early spring when we were compelled to move out of one house and into another. The rent for the house in which we had lived all during the winter had been long unpaid and mother had no money. Father had just returned from one of his long adventures, but early in the day of the moving he disappeared again and, as we could not afford a moving wagon, mother and we boys carted our poor belongings to the new place on our backs.

As for father, he had managed to borrow a horse and a spring wagon from a neighbor and had set off again into the country. The house to which we were moving was far out at the edge of the town and next to it was a field in which there was a great straw stack—a convenience, as what we called our "bed ticks," on which we slept, had to be emptied of the straw that had become fine and dustlike from long use, and then refilled with the new straw.

When all was done and we were quite settled in the new place, father drove into the yard. He had noticed, he explained, a special kind of straw at a farmhouse some five miles away, at a place he had visited during his wanderings of the winter just past, and he had thought he would give us all a treat by getting that particular kind of straw for our beds.

And so he had driven off at daybreak, and, while we packed our furniture to the new place, had dined with the farmer and his family and had now returned. Although our beds had been made for the night the bed ticks must all be brought down again, the straw tumbled out and the special straw put in. "There," he said, with one of his grand gestures, as we lads tramped wearily up the stairs with the refilled bags and as mother stood smiling—a little resentfully perhaps, but still smiling; "there, you kids, try sleeping on that. There is nothing on earth too good for my kids."

LET us, however, return to father and the tale he is telling as he sits in the farmhouse on the winter's evening. I am too good a son of my father to leave such a tale hanging forever thus, in the air.

As it turned out on that night, when it rained and when he in his young manhood stood just outside the door of that southern mansion house of his childhood, and when his mother, that proud woman of the Southland, spat at him and his companions in misery, so that a white speck of her spittle landed on his beard— where, as he said, it lay like a thing of fire burning into his soul—on that night, I say, he did, by a stroke of fortune, escape the fate that seemed to have him in its clutches.

Dawn was just beginning to break when the two Confederate officers came out at the door of the house and marched their prisoners away.

"We went off into the gray dawn, up out of the valley and over the hills, and then I turned to look back," father explained. Gray and weary and half dead with starvation, he turned to look. If he dropped dead from starvation and weariness on his way to the prison pen, what did it matter now? The light of his life had gone out. He was never again to see any of his own people, that he knew.

But even as he looked he did see something. The

57

company had stopped to rest for a moment and stood where a sharp wind blew over them, just at the crest of a hill. Down in the valley the dawn was just breaking and, as father looked, he could see the gray of the old house and against the gray of it, on the front veranda, just a fleck of white.

That would be his young and innocent sister, come out of the house, you will understand, to look along the road taken by the prisoners, whose evident misery had touched her young heart.

For father it would be, as he would so elaborately explain, a very high spot in his iife, perhaps the highest spot he was to reach in all his weary march to the grave.

He stood there on the hillside, quite cold and miserable—in just that utterly miserable and weary state when one is sometimes most alive—the senses, that is to say, are most alive. At the moment he felt, as any man must feel sometime in life, that an invisible cord does extend from the innermost parts of himself to the innermost parts of some other person. Love comes. For once in a lifetime a state of feeling becomes as definite a thing as a stone wall touched with the hand.

And father had that feeling, at that moment on the hill; and that the person for whom he had it was a woman and his own sister, made it even more an assured thing. He might have expressed the feeling by saying that, as by a miracle, the hill dropped away and he stood on dry level ground in the very presence of his younger sister, so close to her in fact that he might very easily have put out his hand and touched her. So strong was the feeling that he lost for the

58

moment all sense of his presence among the prisoners, all sense of the cold hunger and weariness of the hour and—exactly as the thing might be done, quite ridiculously, by a second-rate actor in the movies— he did in fact step out from among the ranks of prisoners and, with his hands extended before him and his eyes shining, took several steps down the hillside, only to be stopped by an oath from one of the guards.

In the farmhouse, as he told of that moment he would get out of his chair and actually take several steps. He would at bottom be always a good deal of an actor as well as a story-teller, as every story-teller worth his salt inevitably is.

And then came the oath from the guard and an up-raised gun, the heavy butt of a gun, ready to swing down upon his head, and back he goes into the ranks of prisoners. He mutters some excuse: "I just wanted to have a look"—and is thus jerked down from the high place, to which his imagination had suddenly lifted him, and back into the weariness of his apparently hopeless journey. Gone, he thought at the moment, was the sister he loved, his boyhood with its memories, all his past life, but it wasn't quite true.

Father did make an escape. How many escapes he, in fancy, made from the hands of the enemy during that Civil War! He lived, you will understand, in a rather dull farming community and loved at least some air of probability hanging over his tales.

And so the Civil War became for him the canvas, the tubes of paint, the brushes with which he painted his pictures. Perhaps one might better say his own imagination was the brush and the Civil War his paint

59

pot. And he did have a fancy for escapes, as I myself have always had. My own tales, told and untold, are full of escapes—by water in the dark and in
a leaky boat, escapes from situations, escapes from
dullness, from pretense, from the heavy-handed
seriousness of the half artists. What writer of tales
does not dote upon escapes? They are the very
breath in our nostrils.

It is just possible that upon that occasion, father
would have put it to his audience, that the sight, or the
imagined sight, of his sister that morning had given
him new hope. She was a virgin and there was something catholic about father.

Very well, then, off he goes down the road with
his head held high, thinking of the possible schemes
for escape and of his sister. He had been given
something, a new flair for life. A ray of new hope
had come into the black night of his situation. He
walked more stoutly.

> Stout Cortes—
> Silent upon a peak in Darien.

It was just that stout way in which he now walked
that gave him his opportunity for escape—that time.
All that day the other prisoners went with hanging
heads, tramping through the deep mud of the southern
roads in winter, but father walked with his head up.

Another night came and they were again in a forest,
on a dark and lonely road, with the guards walking at
the side and sometimes quite lost in the shadows cast
by the trees—the prisoners a dark mass in the very
centre of the road.

Father stumbled over a stick, the heavy branch of

a tree, quite dead and broken off by the wind, and, stooping down, picked it up. Something, perhaps just the impulse of a soldier, led him to sling the stick lightly over his shoulder and carry it like a gun.

There he was, stepping proudly among those who were not proud—that is to say, the other prisoners—and not having any plan in mind—just thinking of his virginal sister back there, I dare say; and one of the two officers of the guard spoke to him kindly.

"Don't walk in there so close to the Yanks, in the deep mud, John," the officer said; "it's better going out here. There is a path here at the side. Get in here back of me."

By his very pride, lifted up out of the ranks of the prisoners, father's mind acted quickly and with a muttered thanks he stepped to the side of the road and became as one of the guards. The men came out on the crest of another low hill and again, in the valley below, there was the faint light of a farmhouse. "Halt!" one of the officers gave command; and then—the younger of the two officers having been told by his superior to send a man down into the valley to the farmhouse to see if there was a chance for the guard and prisoners to rest for a few hours and to get food—he sent father. The officer touched him on the arm. "Go on you," he said. "You go down and find out."

So off father went, down a lane, holding the stick very correctly, like a gun, until he was safely out of sight of the others, and then he threw the stick away and ran.

The devil! He knew every inch of the ground on which he now stood. What an opportunity for escape! One of his boyhood friends had lived in the very house, toward which he was supposed to be going, and often, in his young manhood and when he had come home for vacation from the northern school, he had ridden and hunted along the very path his feet now touched. Why, the very dogs and "niggers" on the place knew him as they might have known their master.

And so, if he ran madly now, he ran knowing the ground under his feet. Ah, he would be sure! When his escape was discovered dogs might be set on his trail.

He plunged downward, getting clear of the trees, running across a field—the soft mud clinging to his feet—and so skirted the house and got to where there was a small creek down which he went for a mile in the darkness, walking in the cold water that often came up to his waist. That was to throw dogs off his trail, as any schoolboy should know.

By making a great circle he got back into the road, by which he and the other prisoners had been marched from his own father's house. They had come some twelve miles during the day and early evening, but the night was still young and, after he had gone three or four miles, he knew a short cut through the woods by which several miles could be cut off.

And so, you see, father went back again to his old home after all and once again saw the sister he loved. The dawn was just breaking when he arrived, but the dogs knew him and the negroes knew him. The very negro who had held the light while his mother spat at the prisoners hid him away in the loft of a barn and brought him food.

Not only food was brought, but also a suit of his own clothes that had been left in the house.

And so he stayed hidden in the loft for three days, and then another night came when it rained and was dark.

Then he crept out, with food for the needs of his journey, and knowing that, when he had walked for a mile along the road that led back toward the distant Union camp, a negro would be standing in a little grove with a good horse saddled and bridled for him. The negro, in the late afternoon, had gone off to a distant town, ostensibly for mail and was to be bound to a tree where he would be discovered later by a party of other negroes sent in search of him. Oh, all was arranged—everything elaborately planned to ward off, from his helpers, the wrath of the mother.

There was the night and the rain, and father, with a dark cloak now about his shoulders, creeping from the stables and toward the house. By the window of one of the rooms downstairs his young sister sat playing an organ, and so he crept to the window and stood for a time looking. Ah; there was moving-picture stuff for your soul! Why, oh why, did not father live in another and later generation? In what affluence might we not all have flourished! The old homestead, a fire burning in the grate, the stern and relentless parent, and outside in the cold and wet father, the outcast son, the disowned, the homeless one, about to ride off into the night in the service of his country—never to return.

On the organ his sister would have been playing "The Last Link is Broken," and there stands father with the great tears rolling down his cheeks.

63

Then to ride away into the night, to fight again for the flag he loved, and that to him meant more than home, more than family—ah! more than the love of the woman who was long afterward to come into his life, and to console him somewhat for the fair sister he had lost.

For he did love her, quite completely. Is it not odd, when one considers the matter, that the fair sister—who would have been my aunt, and who never perhaps existed except in father's fancy, but concerning whom I have heard him tell so many touching tales— is it not odd that I have never succeeded in inventing a satisfactory name for her? Father never—if I remember correctly—gave her a name and I have never succeeded in doing so.

How often have I tried and without success! Ophelia, Cornelia, Emily, Violet, Eunice. You see the difficulty? It must have a quaint and southern sound and must suggest—what must it not suggest?

But father's tale must have its proper dénouement. One could trust the tale-teller for that. Even had he lived in the days of the movies and had the dénouement quite killed his story—for movie purposes, at least in the northern towns, which would have been the best market—even in the face of all of such difficulties which he fortunately did not have to meet, one could be quite sure of the dénouement.

And he made it splashy. It was at the dreadful battle of Gettysburg, late in the war and on the third of July too. The Confederates had such a dreadful way of getting off on just the wrong foot on the very eve of our national holiday. Vicksburg and Gettysburg for Fourth of July celebrations.

Surely it was, what, during the World War, would have been called, "bad war psychology."

There can be no doubt that father had been a soldier of some sort during the Civil War and so, as was natural, he would give his tale a soldier's dénouement, sacrificing even the beloved and innocent younger sister to his purpose (to be brought back to life—oh, many, many times later, and made to serve in many future tales).

It was the second day of that great, that terrible battle of Gettysburg, father had picked upon to serve as the setting for the end of his yarn.

That was a moment! All over the North the people stood waiting; farmers stopped working in the fields and drove into northern towns, waiting for the click of the little telegraph instruments; country doctors let the sick lie unattended and stood with all the others in the streets of towns, where was no running in and out of stores. The whole North stood waiting, listening. No time for talk now.

Ah! that Confederate General Lee—the neat quiet Sunday-school superintendent among generals! One could never tell what he would do next. Was it not all planned that the war should be fought out on southern soil?—and here he had brought a great army of his finest troops far into the North.

Everyone waited and listened. No doubt the South waited and listened too.

No Lincoln and Douglas debates now. "A nation cannot exist half slave and half free."

Now there is the rattle of the box, and the dice that shall decide the fate of a nation are being thrown. In an obscure farmhouse, far in the North, long after

65

the battle of those two terrible days was fought and half forgotten, father also has got his hands on the dice box. He is rattling words in it now. We poor tellers of tales have our moments too, it seems. Like great generals sitting upon horses upon the tops of hills and throwing troops into the arena, we throw the little soldier words into our battles. No uniforms for us, no riders springing away into the gray smoke-mist of battle to carry out orders. We must sit in lonely farmhouses or in cheap rooms in city lodging houses before our typewriters; but if we do not look like generals, we at least feel like that at moments anyway.

Father dropping his little rattling words into the hearts of the farmer, the farmer's wife, Tilly's heart too. At Gettysburg a nation in the death grapple. The innocent sister, fair virgin of the South, cast in too.

Look at the eyes of that stoic Aldrich. They are shining now, eh? Ah! he has been a soldier too. In his youth he also stood firmly amid shot and shell, but ever after, poor dear, he had to be satisfied with mere blank dumbness about it all. At the best he could but turn the crank of a magic-lantern machine or join the G. A. R., and march with other men through the streets of an Ohio town on Decoration days, when the real question in the minds of all the onlookers was as to whether Clyde or Tiffin, Ohio, would win the ball game to be played at Ame's field that afternoon.

A poor sort Aldrich, being able to do nothing but fight. On Decoration days he marched dumbly through the dust to a graveyard and listened to an address made by a candidate for Congress, who had

66

made his money in the wholesale poultry business. At best Aldrich could but speak in low tones to another comrade, as the file of men marched along. "I was with Grant at the Wilderness and before that at Shiloh. Where were you? Oh, you were with Sherman, one of Sherman's bummers, eh?"

That and no more for Aldrich—but for father, ah!

The second day at Gettysburg and Pickett's men ready for their charge. Was that not a moment? What men—those fellows of Pickett's—the very flower of the Southland—young bearded giants, tough like athletes, trained to the minute.

It is growing late on that second day of the fight and Pickett's men are to decide it all. The sun will soon be going down behind the hills of that low flat valley—the valley in which, but a few short days ago, farmers were preparing to gather the grain crops. On the slope of one of the hills a body of men lies waiting. It is the flower of the Union army too. Father is among them, lying there.

They wait.

They are not trembling, but back of them in a thousand towns men and women are both waiting and trembling. Freedom itself waits and trembles—liberty is trembling—"You can't fool all of the people all of the time" is trembling like a broken reed. How many grand passages, words, Decoration day addresses, messages to Congress, Fourth of July addresses of the next two hundred years, not worth eight cents on the dollar at the moment!

And now they come—Pickett's men—down through the valley, in and out of groves of trees and up the little slope. There is a place, known to history as "the bloody angle." There the men of the South rush straight into a storm of iron. A hailstorm of iron swept also in among the men of the North waiting for them.

That wild Rebel yell that broke from the lips of Pickett's men is dying now. The lips of Pickett's men are turning white.

The voice of Meade has spoken and down through the valley go the Union men in their turn—father among them.

It was then that a bullet in the leg dropped him in his tracks, and in memory of that moment he stops the telling of his tale in the farmhouse long enough to pull up his pants leg and show the scar of his wound. Father was a true naturalist, liked to pin his tales down to earth, put a spike of truth in them—at moments.

He pitched forward and fell and the men of his company rolled on to a victory in which he could have no part. He had fallen in what was now, suddenly, a little, quiet place among trees in an old orchard, and there close beside him was a confederate boy, mortally wounded. The two men roll uneasily in their pain and look directly into each other's eyes. It is a long, long look the two men give each other, for one of them the last look into the eyes of a fellow before he goes on, over the river.

The man lying there, and now dying, is just that young man who, as a boy, was father's best friend and comrade, the lad to whose place—some twelve miles from his own father's plantation—he used to ride for days of sport. What rides they had taken

68

together through the forests, a pack of dogs at their heels, and what talks they then had!

You will understand that the young man now dying lived in that very house, far back from the road, toward which father went that night when he escaped the Rebel guard. He had marched off with the stick over his shoulder, you will remember, and had then cut off across fields to his own home where he was concealed by the negroes until the night of his final escape.

And he had gone away from his own home on that dark night, dreaming of a return, some time when the cruel war was over and the wounds it had made were healed; but now he could never return. He was condemned to remain alone, a wanderer always on the face of this earth.

For the lad now dying beside him on the field of Gettysburg was, in his death hour, telling a fearful and tragic story.

Father's family had been entirely wiped out. His father had been killed in battle as had also his brothers.

And now, from the lips of his old comrade, he was to hear the most fearful tale of all.

A party of northern foragers had come to the southern plantation house on just such another dark, rainy night as the one on which he was taken there as a prisoner. They marched as the confederate troops had marched, along the driveway to the front of the house, and stood on the lawn. A northern officer's voice called as the southern officer had called on that other night, and again the tall young negro came to the door with a light, followed by that fiery woman of the Southland.

The negro held the light above his head so that, even in the darkness, the blue coats of the hated northern troops could be seen.

The old southern woman came to stand at the edge of the porch. She understood for what purpose the northern men had come, and she had sworn that not a bite of food, raised on that plantation, should ever pass the lips of a Yank.

Now she held a shotgun in her hand and, without a word or without any sort of warning, raised it and fired into the mass of the men.

There was a cry of rage, and then many guns were raised to shoulders. A sudden roar of the guns and a hundred leaden bullets cut through the front of the house. It wiped out all of father's family—except just himself—and deprived his sons, too, of a proud southern ancestry; for, just in the moment, before the shower of bullets came, father's young and innocent sister—realizing with that sure instinct that, everyone understands, all women inevitably possess—realizing, I say, that death was about to call her mother—the young girl had rushed panic-stricken out of the door and had thrown her arms about her mother's body, just in time to meet death with her. And so all that was left of the family—except just father—fell there in a heap. The captain of the northern troops—a German brewer's son from Milwaukee, Wisconsin, cried when later he looked down into the white silent face of the young girl, and all his life afterward carried in his heart the remembrance of the dead, pleading young eyes; but, as father so philosophically remarked, what was done was done.

And with that fall there was father—a man left to

70

wander forever stricken and forlorn through life. Later he had, to be sure, married and he had children whom he loved and treasured, but was that the same thing? To the heart of a southerner, as every American understands, ancestry means everything.

The purity of a southern woman is unlike any other purity ever known to mankind. It is something special. The man who has been under the influence of it can never afterward quite escape. Father didn't expect to. He declared always, after he had told the above story, that he did not ever expect to be gay or happy again.

What he expected was that he would go on for the rest of his days doing just what he was doing at the time. Well, he would try to bring a litttle joy into the hearts of others—he would sing songs, dance a little dance—he would join an old comrade in arms, one whose heart he knew was as true as steel, and give a magic-lantern show. Others, for an hour anyway, would be made to forget that element of sadness and tragedy in life that he, of course, could never quite forget.

On that very night, lying half dead on the field of Gettysburg beside the dead comrade of his youth, he had made up his mind to spend the remaining days of his life bringing what sweetness and joy he could into the lacerated hearts of a nation torn by civil strife. It had been two o'clock in the morning before he was picked up by a squad of men sent out to gather in the wounded, and already the news of the great victory and the triumph of the cause of freedom was sweeping over the northern land. And he had lain looking at the stars and had made his resolution. Others

71

might seek for the applause of the world, but, as for himself, he would go into the dusty highways and byways of life and bring to the lowly and forgotten the joy of a little fun at the schoolhouse.

NOTE V

As for the show father and Aldrich put on, that is another matter.   One may, without too much injustice, reserve judgment on the show.   I myself never saw one of their performances, but one of my brothers once did and always, quietly and with commendable firmness, refused to speak of it afterward.

Fancy will, however, serve.   Aldrich would show his pictures of McKinley, Grover Cleveland and the others, and then father would sing and do one of his dances. There would be more pictures and another song and dance and after that the picture of the flag, in colors. If the night were fair forty or even fifty people, farmers, their wives, the hired men and the children, would gather in the schoolhouse.   The show only cost ten cents.   Too much injustice was not done them.

It is, however, rather a shame they did not let father tell stories instead.   Perhaps in all his life it never occurred to him they might have been written. Poor father! As a public figure, he had to content himself with the exercise of an art in which he was as bad, I fancy, as any man who has ever lived.

And it is his singing and dancing that remains like a scar in my memory of him.   In the late fall, before Aldrich and he started out on their adventure, father used to rehearse upstairs in our house.

The evening meal would have been out of the way

73

and we children would be sitting by the stove, about the table in the kitchen. Mother had washed clothes during the day and now she was doing an ironing. Father walked about, his hands clasped behind his back as though in deep thought, and occasionally he raised his eyes to the ceiling, while his lips moved silently.

Then he went out of the room and we heard him go upstairs into a bedroom above. None of us, in the kitchen below, looked at each other. We pretended to read books, to get our school lessons, or we looked at the floor.

At that time the humor of America—of which we Americans were so inordinately proud—expressed itself in the broader and less subtle jokes of Mark Twain, Bill Nye and Petroleum V. Nasby, and there was a book, commonly read by both children and grown-ups, and reputed to be very funny, called, "Peck's Bad Boy." It told, if I remember correctly, of the doings of a certain quite terrible youngster who put chewing gum or molasses on the seats of chairs, threw pepper into people's eyes, stuck pins into school-teachers, hung cats over clotheslines by their tails, and did any number of other such charmingly express-ive things.

This terrible child was, as I have said, reputed to be very funny and the book recounting his doings must have sold tremendously. And father, having read it, had written a ballad concerning just such an-other youngster. This child also made life a hell for his fellows, and his father was very proud of him. When the child had done something unusually shocking the father tried, one gathered, to share in the honor.

At any rate the refrain of father's song was:

"You grow more like your dad every day."

Evening after evening these words rang through our house. They made all of us children shiver a little. Father sang them, danced a few halting steps, and then sang them again.

In the kitchen, as I have already said, we others sat with our eyes on the floor. One could not hear the words of the verses themselves, but the spirit of the song was known to all of us. Am I right? Were there—sometimes—tears in mother's eyes as she bent over the ironing board?

Of that, after all, I cannot be too sure. I can only be everlastingly sure of the refrain:

"You grow more like your dad every day."

.   .   .   .

And, however that may be, there is always one consoling thought. As a showman, and on stormy nights, there must sometimes have been but slight audiences at the schoolhouses and the takings for Aldrich and father must have been thin. One fancies evenings when eighty cents might cover all the receipts at the door.

One thinks of the eighty cents and shudders, and then a consoling thought comes. Of one thing we may be quite sure—father and Aldrich would not have gone hungry, and at night there must always have been comfortable beds into which they could

75

crawl. Father had promised Aldrich he would see to the matter of bed and board.

And no doubt he did.

Even though the farmer and the farmer's wife should have proved hard-hearted one remembers the number of Tillies in the farmhouses of Ohio. When everything else failed the Tillies would have taken care of the troubadours. Of that one may be, I should say, very very sure.

NOTE VI

To the imaginative man in the modern world something becomes, from the first, sharply defined. Life splits itself into two sections and, no matter how long one may live or where one may live, the two ends continue to dangle, fluttering about in the empty air.

To which of the two lives, lived within the one body, are you to give yourself? There is, after all, some little freedom of choice.

There is the life of fancy. In it one sometimes moves with an ordered purpose through ordered days, or at the least through ordered hours. In the life of the fancy there is no such thing as good or bad. There are no Puritans in that life. The dry sisters of Philistia do not come in at the door. They cannot breathe in the life of the fancy. The Puritan, the reformer who scolds at the Puritans, the dry intellectuals, all who desire to uplift, to remake life on some definite plan conceived within the human brain die of a disease of the lungs. They would do better to stay in the world of fact to spend their energy in catching bootleggers, inventing new machines, helping humanity—as best they can—in its no doubt laudable ambition to hurl bodies through the air at the rate of five hundred miles an hour.

In the world of the fancy, life separates itself with slow movements and with many graduations into the

77

ugly and the beautiful. What is alive is opposed to what is dead. Is the air of the room in which we live sweet to the nostrils or is it poisoned with weariness? In the end it must become the one thing or the other.

All morality then becomes a purely æsthetic matter. What is beautiful must bring æsthetic joy; what is ugly must bring æsthetic sadness and suffering.

Or one may become, as so many younger Americans do, a mere smart-aleck, without humbleness before the possibilities of life, one sure of himself—and thus one may remain to the end, blind, deaf and dumb, feeling and seeing nothing. Many of our intellectuals find this is the more comfortable road to travel.

In the world of fancy, you must understand, no man is ugly. Man is ugly in fact only. Ah, there is the difficulty!

. . . .

In the world of fancy even the most base man's actions sometimes take on the forms of beauty. Dim pathways do sometimes open before the eyes of the man who has not killed the possibilities of beauty in himself by being too sure.

Let us (in fancy) imagine for a moment an American lad walking alone at evening in the streets of an American town.

American towns, and in particular American towns of the Middle West of twenty years ago, were not built for beauty, they were not built to be lived in permanently. A dreadful desire of escape, of physical escape, must have got, like a disease, into our father's brains. How they pitched the towns and cities together! What an insanity! The lad we have together invented, to walk at evening in the streets of such a town, must of necessity be more beautiful than all the hurriedly built towns and cities in which he may walk. True immaturity of the body and the spirit is more beautiful than mere tired-out physical maturity: the physical maturity of men and women that has no spiritual counterpart within itself falls quickly into physical and ugly decay—like the cheaply constructed frame houses of so many of our towns.

The lad of our fancy walks in the streets of a town hurriedly thrown together, striving to dream his dreams, and must continue for a long time to walk in the midst of such ugliness. The cheap, hurried, ugly construction of America's physical life still goes on and on. The idea of permanent residence has not taken hold on us. Our imaginations are not yet fired by love of our native soil.

The American boy of our mutual imaginative creation is walking in the streets of an Ohio town, after the factories have begun coming and the day of the hustlers is at hand, the houses of the town pushed up quickly, people swarming into the town who have no notion of staying there—a surprising number of them will stay, but they have, at first, no intention of staying.

Before the boy's day how slow the growth of the towns! There were the people of an older generation, coming out slowly to the Middle West, from New York state, from Pennsylvania, from New England—a great many to my own Ohio country from New England. They had come drifting in slowly, bringing traces of old customs, sayings, religions, prejudices. The young farmers came first, glad of the rich free soil and the friendlier climate—strong young males that were to come in such numbers as to leave New England, with its small fields and its thinner, stonier soil, a place of aging maiden ladies—that old-maid civilization that was, nevertheless, to be the seat of our American culture. An insane fear of the flesh, a touch of transcendentalism, a reaching always up into the sky. In the ground underfoot there is only fear, poverty, hardship. One must look upward, always upward.

What of the sensual love of life, of surfaces, words with a rich flavor on the tongue, colors, the soft texture of the skin of women, the play of muscles through the bodies of men?

The cry of fear—"that way lies sin."

In the new land, in that older time, too much maleness. Deep mud in the streets of the little towns, built in the forest along rivers or on the stage roads. Bearded, rough-handed men gathered about the saloons. Abe Lincoln proving his manhood by lifting a barrel of whisky and drinking from the bunghole. The ruffian of the frontier, father of the modern gunman of our cities, proving his manhood by murder—Blinky Morgan of Ohio, Jesse James of Missouri, Slade of the Overland Route to the gold and silver camps of the Far West—these the heroes of that life.

A slow culture growing up, however—growing as culture must always grow—through the hands of workmen.

In the small towns artisans coming in—the harness-maker, the carriage-builder, the builder of wagons, the smith, the tailor, the maker of shoes, the builders of houses and barns too.

As Slade and James were to be the fathers of the modern gunmen, so these the fathers of the artists of the generations to come. In their fingers the beginning of that love of surfaces, of the sensual love of materials, without which no true civilization can ever be born.

And then, like a great flood over it all the coming of the factories, the coming of modern industrialism.

Speed, hurried workmanship, cheap automobiles for cheap men, cheap chairs in cheap houses, city apartment houses with shining bathroom floors, the Ford, the Twentieth Century Limited, the World War, jazz, the movies.

The modern American youth is going forth to walk at evening in the midst of these. New and more terrible nerve tension, speed. Something vibrant in the air about us all.

The problem is to survive. If our youth is to get into his consciousness that love of life—that with the male comes only through the love of surfaces, sensually felt through the fingers—his problem is to reach down through all the broken surface distractions of modern life to that old love of craft out of which culture springs.

THE end of the second year after mother's death was at hand and our family was at the point of falling to pieces. No more sitting by the fire in the kitchen through the long fall and winter evenings with mother at the ironing board. The kitchen of our house was cold and cheerless. The spirit of the household had fled. It had gone down into the ground with the body of the woman out of whose living body had come five strong sons.

Mother had died swiftly, mysteriously, without warning. It was as though she had got out of bed on a fall morning and had taken a long look at her sons. "It's about the time when they will have to push out into the world. Any influence I may have on their lives has already been exerted. There is no time to think of any other purpose in life for myself, and anyway, I am too tired. Having lived out my life, now I shall die."

It was as though she had said something of the sort to herself, and had then laid down her life as one might lay down a finished book. On a rainy dismal day in the fall there she was, coming in at the kitchen door from hanging a wash out on the line, temporarily strung up in our woodshed, smiling quietly, making one of her quick soft ironic observations, sweetening always the air of the room into which she came with her presence.

On such a rainy morning in the fall she was like that, as she will live always in the memory of her sons, and then, on another equally wet dismal fall day two or three weeks later, she was dead.

What there had been of family life among us was going to pieces. It was sure that father was not one to hold it together. No one could think of him as destined to hold that or any other fort. That surely wasn't his line.

There was a period of waiting. The older son had already found his place in life. He had already become what he was to remain to the end, an American artist, a painter. The making of little designs for the gravestones of village merchants was for him a passing phase. Perhaps it was, at that time, the only form of expression one, having a tendency toward the plastic arts, could find in our towns.

And so there was his destiny fixed—but what of us others? We did not often speak openly of the matter among ourselves, but it was obvious something had to be done and soon. In the few talks we had concerning the matter in our broken household, while the one remaining daughter (destined to die before her life could be really developed) was acting as our temporary housekeeper, father held out strongly for the learning of one of the trades. He talked of long years of apprenticeship to some craft, and it was characteristic of him that as he talked he became in fancy himself such a craftsman. One was trained slowly and surely in one's craft. Then one became a journeyman and went on his travels, going from shop to shop, watching the master craftsmen. "It's something at your back," father said, "something that can be depended upon. It makes a man able to stand up as a man before his fellows."

Did it? We boys listened and thought our own thoughts. As for father—he had picked up a smattering knowledge of several crafts; and how eloquently he, dear word fellow, could speak of them, sling the jargon of the crafts! He had at various times been a harness-maker, house-painter, sign-writer of a feeble sort, such an actor as I have described, the tooter of a cornet in the village band.

In reality he was a tale-teller, but that was no craft among us. No union had been formed among tale-tellers. The Authors' League, the Pen Women, the Poet's Club, etc., had not yet been formed or, if there were such organizations in existence, they at any rate did not reach down into mid-American towns. At that time even the rumors of the vast sums to be made by turning out clever plot stories for the popular magazines or the movies had not been whispered about.

Other and more significant-seeming stories were floating however. A new kind of hero, tarnished somewhat later, filled the popular eye. As we boys went about in the main street of our town, citizens, feeling a kindly interest in the motherless sons, continually stopped us. Everyone was singing a new little song:

"Get on. Make money. Get to the top. A penny saved is a penny earned. Money makes the mare go."

"Save up your money, and save up your rocks.
And you'll always have tobacco in the old tobacco box,"

sang Sil West, the smith, who was shoeing a horse in the alleyway back of the stores on our main street.

The factories were calling. One went into a factory, did his work with care and skill, became foreman, superintendent, part owner, married the banker's daughter, got rich and went off to Paris to sin the sins neglected during so busy a youth and early manhood.

It sounded reasonable and possible. Learning a craft was slow business and one was in a hurry. "Hurry" was the battle cry of the day.

And the time of the factories was just at hand. At that time they were coming into Ohio, and into all the mid-American states in great numbers, and no town was without hope of becoming an industrial centre. The bicycle had come, followed by the automobile, and even the quiet country roads were taking on the new spirit of speed.

Something was in the air. One breathed a new spirit into the lungs. The paradise, later to be represented by the ford, the city apartment building with tiled bathroom floors, subways, jazz, the movies— was it not all just at hand? I myself and long afterward tried a little, in a novel of mine called, "Poor White," to give something of the feeling of life in our towns at that time.

Oil and gas were spurting out of the ground in Ohio and the discovery of oil and gas meant the coming of factories, it meant the New Age, prosperity, growth going onward and upward. "Death to everything old, slow and careful! Forward the Light Brigade! Theirs not to ask the reason why! Theirs but to do or die"—the light brigade in our particular town consisting of every merchant, doctor, workman, lawyer, who had saved a few pennies that could be invested. In our ears rang stories of the Lima Boom, the Gibsonburg boom, the Finley boom.

And was it not simple? One bored a hole deep down into the ground and out came wealth—oil and gas, followed by the coming of the factories. If we, in our town, did not quite "cut it," did not "make the grade," could not become later another fragrant Akron or blissful Youngstown, Ohio, it wasn't because we didn't try.

A hole was being bored at the edge of the town in a field near a grove of hickory trees where we lads had formerly gone for nuts and squirrel shooting on the fall days. In the field—a meadow—there had also been a baseball diamond, and sometimes visiting circuses set up their tents there; but now the hole had gone far down below the usually required depth and nothing had happened. Rumors ran through the streets. The well-drillers had come from over near Gibsonburg. Only a week or two before a stranger had got off a train, had walked about through the streets, and had then visited the place where the drilling was going on. He had been seen to speak with the drillers. No doubt our drillers were in "cahoots" with the Rockefellers, the Morgans, or some of that crowd. Perhaps John D. himself had been pussyfooting about. One couldn't tell. Stranger things than that had happened. Were we to be caught napping? It was decided to do what was called "shooting the well."

Surely here was something for a boy to take into account. Mysterious whisperings among our elders on the streets in the evening; plot and counterplot;

86

dark doings among the capitalists—"stand back, villain, unhand the fair figure of our hopes and dreams"—ah! an explosion at the mysterious hour of dawn, far down in the bowels of Mother Earth. Old Mother Earth to be given an emetic of a stirring sort. Forth would flow wealth, factories, the very New Age itself.

One didn't ask oneself how a participating interest in all these new glories was to be achieved, and in the whole town no man was more excited than father who had never owned a share of stock in anything. He ceased speaking of the crafts and only shook his head in sorrow. "I'd just like to be alive two hundred years from now," he said. "Why, I'll tell you what; there'll be a vast city right here—right on the very spot on which I am now standing there'll be, why there'll be a huge office building, like as not."

So sure was he of all this that the wealth of the future became in his fancy a thing of the present, even of the past. He felt himself magnificently wealthy and, one day when he had been drinking and when, because of what we thought his lack of dignity, we youngsters had treated him to a rather thorough snubbing, he grew angry. Night came and it rained. He went up into the garret of the house in which we then lived and presently came down with a package of papers in his hand. Were they old love letters, from the ladies he had known in his youth, or unpaid grocery bills? It is a mystery that may never be solved.

He went into the little back yard of the house and, making a pile of the papers, burned them solemnly. We boys crowded to the kitchen window to watch.

87

There was the little flare of the flame and above it, and leaning over, father's stern face—and then darkness.

Back he came into the house and before he went away, to spend the rest of the evening whispering of the wealth of the future with other men in the barrooms, he told us what had happened. "Do you know what those papers were?" he asked sharply. "They were deeds to the whole business section of the City of Cincinnati. I have been concealing from you the fact that I had such papers, intending to leave them to you as an inheritance but—

"Well, you have not seen fit to treat me with respect and I have burned them," he declared, tramping out of the house.

. . . .

Romance and mystery. There was the imagined figure of the shooter of wells. The thing was done with nitro-glycerine. One put "nitro" and "glycerine" together, one fancied, and there was this terrible result. One did not know what "nitro" was, but had seen and felt "glycerine." "Ah! chemistry. You wait and you'll see what will be done with chemistry," said father.

And so there was this mysterious stuff frozen into solid cakes and carted through the night, along unfrequented roads, by the heroic well-shooter.

Now, there was a man to suit a boy's fancy, that well-shooter, a fellow going nonchalantly along with the frozen cakes in the wagon behind him. Is he worried? Not at all! He lights his pipe. He looks at the stars. He sings a little ditty. "My bonny lies over the ocean. My bonny lies over the sea. My

88

bonny lies over the ocean—Oh, bring back my bonny to meeeeeee."

In the wagon back of him that stuff. A jar, a sudden jolt of the wagon, the breaking of a wagon axle and then—

We boys whisper about it when we meet on the streets. One of the boys holds up his thumb. "You see that thumbnail?" he asks. "Well, a little bit of that stuff, no more than would cover that thumbnail, would blow him and his wagon to smithereens." The question asked was, how much farther would, say a ton of the stuff, blow the outfit? Was there a land as far beyond smithereens as the stars from earth, to which the fellow might be sent, in the wink of an eye?

A glimpse of the infinite added to all the other excitement and mystery.

My first glimpse of the Industrial Age—with one of my brothers I got out of bed one morning, before dawn, and crept away into the darkness to lie in a grove of trees near the meadow and see the well shot. Several other boys came. The father of one of our town boys, who had stock in the gas-well company, had let slip the carefully hoarded secret of the hour when the fearful thing was to happen.

And so, there we were, ten or twelve of us, lying concealed in the wood. Dawn began to break. Birds and squirrels awoke in the trees over our heads. On the road that came out from town buggies and surreys appeared. The visitors tied their horses far away, by an old sawmill, near the town's edge, and came afoot to the field.

Now it was quite light and we could begin to recognize the men of the party, solid respectable men, with money in the bank. There was Penny Jacobs, who kept a little candy store; Seth McHugh, cashier of the bank; Wilmott the lawyer, a dozen others. No doubt Em Harkness was there. Of that I cannot be quite sure. He was a man of our town, who ran a small general store and brother, I believe, to that other Harkness who later became a man of vast wealth and a figure in the Standard Oil Company. His money built the Harkness Memorial at Yale, and if our town did not achieve the prominent position in the Industrial Age of which we all at that moment dreamed, we had at least among us the kin of royalty. We were not entirely left in the cold outside world. A Harkness was a Harkness and we had a Harkness.

But to return to that significant moment in the field. As we lads lay in the wood, well concealed from the eyes of our elders, we were silent. Solemnity lay like a frost over our young souls. Even the giggling and whispering that had gone on among us died now. The well-shooter was there and he had turned out to be just an ordinary looking teamster with whiskers, but that did not matter.

Greater and more significant things were astir. Even the birds stopped singing and the squirrels chattered no more.

A long tube, containing no doubt the nitro-glycerine, had been lowered into the hole in the ground and the honored guests of the occasion ran quickly across the field and stood among the trees near our hiding place.

They were dressed, these serious-minded citizens, as for a wedding or a funeral. Even Penny Jacobs had put on what was called among us "a boiled shirt."

What an occasion! Now we were, all of us, as we

stood or lay under the trees—we were all one thing; and presently there would be a terrific explosion, far down in the earth, below our bellies as we lay sprawled in the wet grass—there would be this explosion, and then would we not all, at that moment, become something else?

"Bang!" we would go into the New Age—that was the idea. In the presence of our elders, who now stood in silence very near us, we lads all felt a little ashamed of our ragged clothes and our unwashed faces. Perhaps some of us had been to Sunday school and had heard the parable of the virgins who did not keep their lamps trimmed and filled.

In shame we hid our faces before the glory of the vision before us. There we were, sons of house-painters, carpenters, shoemakers, and the like. Our fathers had worked with their hands. They had soiled their clothes and their faces with common labor. Poor, benighted men! What did they know of what Mark Twain called, "the glorious, rip-roaring century, greatest of all the centuries?" A man could make a wagon that would stand up, or shoe a horse, or build a house slowly and well, but what was that?

Shucks! There would be this terrific rumble in the bowels of the earth, and then the little cunning machines would come. Men would walk about smoking twenty-five-cent cigars; they would put their thumbs in the armholes of their vests and laugh at the past. Men would fly through the air, dive under the sea, have breakfast in Cleveland, Ohio, and lunch in London. A fellow couldn't tell what would happen now.

Why, no one would work at all maybe—well, that

is to say, not really work. Some of our fathers had read a book called "Looking Backward" and had talked about it in the homes and in the stores. Then we lads had talked. Well, a fellow would maybe roll downtown from his country home in the late morning and turn a few cranks or pull a few levers. Then he would go and play, make love to some beautiful female or take an afternoon's ride over to Egypt to see the Pyramids, or visit the Holy Land. A fellow had to get up an appetite for dinner, dang it all!

Anyway, that was that, and there we were. The well-shooter dropped a heavy weight down the hole and cut out for the woods. When he was halfway across the meadow the rumbling explosion occurred, down in the earth.

And into the bright morning air shot a great fountain of mud and muddy water. The derrick over the hole was covered with it, the grass in the meadow was covered and much of it fell down like rain on us in the wood. The front of Penny Jacobs' boiled shirt was covered with it.

The mud fell on us lads, too, but that didn't matter so much. None of us had put on Sunday clothes. Our elders, who represented among us the capitalistic class, went over and stood about the well for a time, and then went sadly off up the road to unhitch their horses and drive back to town.

When we lads emerged from the woods no one was left but the well-shooter, and he was suspect, and grumpy as well, not having breakfasted. Those of us whose fathers had no money invested were inclined to take the whole matter as rather a delicious joke, but were overruled. We stood about for a time, staring at the well-shooter, who was engaged in gathering his paraphernalia together, and then we also moved off toward town.

"I'll bet that well-shooter's a crook," said one of my companions. He had, I remember, a great deal of mud in his hair and on his face. He kept complaining as we went along. "He could have stuck that nitro-glycerine only halfway down, and then set it off, that's what he could have done." The idea, later taken up enthusiastically by the entire community, pleased us all. It was so apparent the well-shooter was not the hero we had hoped. He didn't look like a hero. "Well, my dad says he knows him. He lives over by Monroeville and he gets drunk and beats his wife, my dad says so," another lad declared.

It was rather a good solution of our difficulty. If one can't have a hero, who wants just a teamster?

It was infinitely better to have a villainous well-shooter about whose Machiavelian machinations one's imagination could linger in happiness.

NOTE VIII

IT must have been about this time that my own imaginative life began to take form. Having listened to the tales told by my father, I wanted to begin inventing tales of my own. At that time and for long years afterward, there was no notion of writing. Did I want an audience, someone to hear me tell my tales? It is likely I did. There is something of the actor in me.

When later I began to write I for a time told myself I would never publish, and I remember that I went about thinking of myself as a kind of heroic figure, a silent man creeping into little rooms, writing marvelous tales, poems, novels—that would never be published.

Perhaps it never went quite that far. They would have to be published sometime. My vanity demanded that. Very well—I had died and had been buried in some obscure place. In my actual physical life I had been a house-painter, a workman in a factory, an advertising writer—whatever you please. I had passed unnoticed through the throng, you see. "I say, John, who is that fellow over there?"

"Oh, I don't know. I've seen him about. He looks like a movie actor or a gambler to me."

You see, I dreamed of something like that—dead

94

and buried away—and then one day a man is snooping about in a garret in an old empty house. He finds a pile of papers and begins looking them over, lazily, without much interest. But look! "Hello here! Say, here is something!"

You get the notion. I'll not go into it further. It might have been a good card had I found within myself the courage to play it, but I didn't.

As to that first tale of mine and its invention. It grew out of dissatisfaction with my father and a desire to invent another to take his place. And professional jealousy may have had something to do with it. He had been strutting about long enough. "Get out from under the spotlight for a time, daddy. Give your son a chance to see what he can do," I perhaps really wanted to say.

It was fall and father had taken me with him to do a house-painting job in the country. The year was growing old and bad rainy weather had come. Perhaps we could not finish the painting job we were about to begin, but, as father had explained to the farmer who had just built a new house, we could at least put on a priming coat.

If the worst happened and we lost a good deal of time, waiting about—"well," said father winking at me, "you see, kid, we'll eat."

The farmer came for us in the early morning, driving in a spring wagon into which was to be packed the ladders, pots and other materials of our trade, and by the time we had got to his place the rain, that had persisted for several days, began again. The carpenters were still at work inside the house, so that nothing could be done there, and father went off to

95

the old cabin in which the farmer and his family were living until the new house could be finished. He would spend the day gossiping with the women folk or perhaps reading some book he had found in the house. The farmer had a barrel of hard cider in his cellar. The day promised to be not too depressing for father.

As for myself, I made the acquaintance of the farmer's son, a lad my own age, and we decided to go squirrel hunting in the near-by woods. "You wait 'til father drives down into the new clearing. He's going to bring up some fence posts. Then we'll take the gun and cut out. If he gets onto us he'll give me some job, make me wheel out manure, or whitewash the hen-house, or something like that."

We spent the morning and early afternoon tramping through muddy fields to visit the wood lots on neighboring farms and came home too late for the noon meal, but my new-found friend managed to get some sandwiches, made of huge slices of bread and cold meat, and bring them to the barn.

We were tired and wet and had got no squirrels and so we crawled up into the hay loft and burrowed down into the warm hay.

When we had finished eating our lunch and had got ourselves comfortably warm my companion, a fat boy of perhaps sixteen, wanted to talk.

We talked as young males do, of hunting and what naturally good shots we were but that we were not used to just the kind of gun we had been handling. Then we spoke of riding horses and how nice it would have been had we both been cowboys, and finally of the girls we had known. What was a fellow to do? How was he to get close to some girl who wasn't too hoity-toity. The fat boy had a sister of about his own age that I wanted to ask about but didn't dare. What was she like? Was she too hoity-toity?

We spoke vaguely of other girls we had been seated near at school, or had met at boy-and-girl parties. "Did you ever kiss a girl? I did once," said the fat boy. "Kiss, eh? Is that all you've done?" I answered, feeling the necessity of maintaining a kind of advantage, due to my position as a town boy.

The hay into which we had burrowed deeply, so that just our heads were in the outer air, was sweet to the nostrils and warm and we began to grow sleepy. What was the use of talking of girls? They were silly things and had in some queer way the power to un-man a boy, to make a fellow act and feel nervous and uneasy.

We lay in silence, thinking each his own thoughts, and presently the fat boy closed his eyes and slept.

Father came upon the floor of the stable with his employer the farmer, and the two men pulled boxes to the door looking out into the barnyard and began to talk.

The farmer explained that he had come into our country from New England, from Vermont, when he was a young man, and had gone into debt for two hundred acres of land, when land could be had cheap. He had worked and he had achieved. In time the farm had been paid for and fifty additional acres bought. It had taken time, patience, and hard labor. Much of the land had to be cleared. A man worked day and night, that's how he managed to get on.

And now he was building a new house. "Well," he had said to his wife; "Mary, you have been a good wife to me and I want you to have every comfort." The house was to have a bathroom and a bathtub. It would cost money and maybe it would be all foolishness, but he wanted his wife to have it. When a man was young he didn't mind splashing about in a washtub in a woodshed on Saturday evenings, but when he got a little older and had, now and then, a touch of rheumatism, well, he thought his wife deserved to have a bathtub in the house if she wanted it, no matter what it cost.

Father agreed with his host. (It is perhaps as well to think of him as our host and ourselves as guests since we stayed two weeks and worked but two days.) He said that he had always felt just that way himself. Women were the weaker sex and a man had to take that into consideration. "You take a woman, now, that is like a horse and I don't like her," said father. He spoke of mother as though she had been a weak, gentle thing, entirely dependent upon the strength in himself in getting through her life. "I married my wife up in your own state, up in Vermont," father said, indulging in one of his characteristic quick imaginative flights.

And now that he had got a start I knew there was no telling where his flight might end and I listened for a time, and then, turning away in disgust, I began working my way downward into the hay. My mother, now dead, was something I prized. He had just said she was born in Vermont of an old decayed English gentle family. She wasn't very strong but would have children. They were born one after the other, but, thank God! because of his own great natural strength his boys were strong.

"The one I have out here with me now was born in Kentucky," he said. "I took my wife down there on a visi. to my own father's place and he was born during the visit. I thought his mother would die that time, but she didn't—I saved her. Night and day I stayed in her sick room, nursing her."

Now he had got himself launched and I knew the farmer would have no more chance to do his own bragging. Father would invent another decayed, gentle family in Kentucky to match the one he had just so lightly brought into existence in the cold barren hills of Vermont.

But I was getting deeper and deeper down into the hay now and the sounds of his voice grew faint, words could no longer be distinguished. There was only a gentle murmuring sound, far off—like a summer breeze just stirring the leaves of a forest; or, better yet, like the soft murmur of some southern sea. Already, you see, I had begun reading romances and knew, in fancy, just how the seas of the South murmured and beat upon coral islands; and then how the fearful hurricane came ramping along and swept the seas clear of ships. No one reads as a boy reads. The boy gives himself utterly to the printed page and perhaps the most blessed of all the tribe of the ink-pots are those who write what we used to call "dime novels"—blessed in their audience, I mean, to be sure.

So there I was, sunk far down into a mythical Southland, my own Southland, product of my own imaginings—not father's. One could go deep down into the hay and still breathe. All sounds became faint, even the gentle sound of the snoring of the fat boy some ten feet away. One closed the eyes and stepped off into a fragrant new world. Mother was in that new world, but not father. I had left him out in the cold.

I considered the matter of births—my own birth in particular. The idea of being born in Kentucky—the result of a union between two decaying, gentle families—did not strike my fancy, not much.

The devil! Even then I felt myself a little the product of a new age and a new land. Could I then have had all the thoughts I am now about to attribute to myself! Probably not. But these notes make no pretense of being a record of fact. That isn't their object. They are merely notes of impressions, a record of vagrant thoughts, hopes, ideas that have floated through the mind of one present-day American. It is likely that I have not, and will not, put into them one truth, measuring by the ordinary standards of truth. It is my aim to be true to the essence of things. That's what I'm after.

And haven't we Americans built enough railroads and factories, haven't we made our cities large and dirty and noisy enough, haven't we been giving ourselves to surface facts long enough? Let us away with the fact of existence, for the moment at least. You, the reader, are to imagine yourself sitting under a tree with me on a summer afternoon; or, better yet, lying with me in the sweet-smelling hay in an Ohio barn. We shall let our fancies loose, lie to ourselves if you please. Let us not question each other too closely.

There is America, now. What is America? Whee! I say, now, don't begin with such a gigantic question as that.

Let's think a little about what it isn't. It isn't English, for one thing, and—isn't it odd?—the notion persists that it is. If we are ever to have a race of our own here—if the melting pot we are always talking about ever really melts up the mass—how English, how German, how Puritanic will it be? Not very much, I fancy. Too many Slavs, Poles, Wops, Chinese, Negroes, Mexicans, Hindoos, Jews, whatnot, for the old influences to hold in the end.

But is it not odd how that old notion persists? A few English came and settled in that far-away frozen northeast corner—New England—and their sons did the book-writing and the school-teaching. They did not get themselves—physically—as breeders—very deeply into the new blood of the land, but they made their notion of what we are and of what we are to be stick pretty well.

In time, however, the basic cultural feeling of the land must change too. Mind cannot persist without body. Blood will tell.

And in my own time I was to see the grip of the old New England, the Puritanic culture, begin to loosen. The physical incoming of the Celts, Latins, Slavs, men of the Far East, the blood of the dreaming nations of the world gradually flowing thicker and thicker in the body of the American, and the shrewd shop-keeping money-saving blood of the northern men getting thinner and thinner.

But I run far, far ahead of myself. Did my own fancy, even then, as a boy, lying in the hay in the

101

barn, did it run ahead of my own day and my own time? Of that I cannot say, but of one thing I am quite certain—in all my life I have never for a moment subscribed to the philosophy of life as set forth by the *Saturday Evening Post,* the *Atlantic Monthly, Yale,* "Upward and Onward," "The White Man's Burden," etc.

There was always within me a notion of another aspect of life—at least faintly felt—a life that dreamed a little of more colorful and gaudy things— cruelty and tragedy creeping in the night, laughter, splashing sunlight, the pomp and splendor of the old tyrants, the simple devotion of old devotees.

Had I not seen and did I not then sharply remember that old grandmother from the southeast of Europe, she with the one eye and the quick, dark and dangerous temper! There were possibilities of cruelty in her. Once she had tried to kill my sister with a butcher knife, and one could think of her as killing with a laugh on her lips. Having known her one could easily conceive of the possibility of a life in which cruelty had its place too.

At that moment as I lay deeply buried in the warm hay and when the fancy of my own flesh-and-blood father, down on the floor of the barn, was giving me a birthright of decaying Germanic gentlefolk the dark old woman who was my grandmother was more in my line.

And no doubt the warmth of the hay itself may have had something to do with the setting and the mood of my first invented tale, as you will perceive as you read of it. Cruelty, like breadfruit and pineapples, is a product, I believe, of the South.

By the tale, told me by my parents, I had myself been born in a place called Camden, Ohio, and in the articles touching on my birthplace that have appeared in newspapers that town has always been named. It was one of the towns through which father and mother had trekked when they were first married.

Father must have had a little money at that time, as there is a tradition of his having been a merchant, and of course there were not, at that time, so many children. One could get up and out more easily. Moving, perhaps at night, from town to town, to escape bill collectors, was not so difficult. And then I fancy that, at first his own people, from time to time, sent him money. However, I know little of his people and only have the notion because I cannot conceive of his having earned it or of his having made it by his shrewdness.

And so he was a merchant then, the grandest thing one could be in a small Ohio town at that time. He kept shop in places known as Camden, Morning Sun and Caledonia, Ohio. I believe he and President Harding once played in the same brass band at Caledonia.

He was in the saddlery and harness business and you cannot fail to catch the flavor of that. There would be a little shop on the town's main street with a leather horse collar hanging on a peg over the sidewalk before the door. Inside there would be shiny new harness hanging on the shop walls and, in the morning when the sun crept in, the brass and nickel buckles would shine like jewels.

Young farmers coming in with great work harnesses on their shoulders and throwing them with a great rattle and bang on the floor—the rich pungent smell of leather—an old man, a workman, a harness-maker, sitting on his horse and sewing a strap—on the floor by the stove a wooden box filled with sawdust into which the workmen and the visiting farmers, all of whom would chew tobacco, could spit—

Father prancing about—the young merchant then, with the young merchant's heavy silver watch and gold chain—a prospective Marshall Field, a Wanamaker, a Julius Rosenwald, in his own fancy, perhaps.

"Hello, you, Ted. When you go'en a get that trace sewed up? These new fangle factory harnesses ain't worth a tinker's dam. How's wheat looking out your way? No, the frost ain't all out of the ground yet. What do you think of elections, eh? D'you hear what that fellow said—'all Democrats ain't horse thieves, but all horse thieves is democrats'? Do you think Frank Means will make it for sheriff?"

That—in just that tone—and in a small frame house on a side street of the town myself waiting to be born.

What is a birth? Has a man no rights of his own?

NOTE IX

Such a birth in an Ohio Village—the neighbor women coming in to help—rather fat women in aprons.

They have had children of their own and are not too excited, but stand about, waiting and indulging in gossip. "If the men had to have the babies there would never be more than one child in a family. What do men know about suffering? It's the women who have to do all the suffering in life, I always said— I said a woman feels everything deeper than a man— don't you think so? A woman has intuition, that's what it is."

And then the doctor coming hurriedly, father having run for him. He would be a large man with side whiskers and large red hands. Well; he is a doctor of the new school, a modernist, like the child he is about to help into the world. What he believes in, is fresh air. Wherever he goes, and no matter what the disease he is treating, he always says the same things. Modernists sometimes are like that. "Clean and fresh air—that's what I believe in. Throw open the doors and the windows. Let's have some fresh air in here."

While the child is being born he tells his one joke. One might as well be cheerful. Cheerfulness is a great healer, and what he believes in is in making his patients smile in the midst of suffering. "Do you want to know why I'm so strong on cleanliness?" he asks. "It's because I'm a damned sinner, I guess, and I don't go to church, and I've heard that cleanliness is next to Godliness. I'm trying to slip into Heaven on a cake of soap—ha! that's what I'm up to."

A quick nervous laugh from the lips of father. He goes out of the house to tell the story to a neighbor he has seen raking leaves in a near-by yard. It is September now. He is a little unstrung. Under such conditions a man feels faintly guilty. People conspire to give him the feeling. It is as though all the women of the town were pointing accusing fingers and as though all the men were laughing, "greasy-eyed married men," Bernard Shaw once called them. One will have to set up the cigars to the men, darn 'em. As for the women—they are saying, half jokingly, half in earnest: "There, you devil; see what you have done—this is your doings."

Father stands beside the fence telling the doctor's joke to the neighbor, who has heard it many times before but who, out of sympathy, now laughs heartily. As though drawn toward each other by some invisible cord they both sidle along the fence until they are standing close together. It is a moment of masculine obscurity. Men must stand shoulder to shoulder. The women have the centre of the stage—as father would have said later, when he became an actor and loved to sling the actor's jargon, they were "hogging the footlights."

Not quite succeeding however. This is the moment for me to come upon the stage. The two men stand closely together, father fingering nervously the heavy gold watch chain—he is soon to lose it with all his other property in one of his frequent business failures —and from the house comes a faint cry. To the two men standing there it sounds not unlike the cry of a puppy inadvertently stepped on by a careless master, and father jumps suddenly aside so that his neighbor laughs again.

And that is myself—just being actually born into the world.

.   .   .   .

Which is one thing, but sometimes one's fancy wants something else. As I lay, deep buried in the hay in the barn on another fall day, and as the resentment—born in me through having been made the son of two decaying, gentle families—grew deeper and deeper, and also as the grateful warmth of the departed summer—captured and held by the hay—stole over my body, cold from the day of tramping in the wood in a cold rain in pursuit of the squirrels—as the warmth took hold of my body, the scene of my actual birth hour, just depicted, faded. I fled from the field of fact and into the field of fancy.

Upon the sand on a desolated coast far down on the Gulf of Mexico an athletic looking man of perhaps thirty lies looking out over the sea. What cruel eyes he has, like the eyes of some cunning beast of prey.

He is perhaps thirty years of age, but one can see well enough, just by looking at him casually, that he has retained all the youthful strength and elasticity of his splendid body. He has a small black mustache and black hair and his skin is burned to a deep brown. Even as he lies, relaxed and listless, on the yellow sand a glow of life and of strength seems to emanate from him.

As he lies thus one can tell, any schoolboy could tell, that he is physically made to be the very ideal of American romance. He is a man of action—young and strong—there can be little doubt he is a man of daring. What might not be done with such a man! Throw him back into the days of the early pioneers and he will turn you out another Daniel Boone. He will creep through hundreds of miles of forests, never disturbing a grass blade, and bring you back the fair daughter of the English nobleman, traveling in this country, whose daughter inadvertently went for an afternoon's stroll in the wood and was captured by a skulking Indian; or he will shoot you a squirrel in the eye at five hundred yards with his faithful rifle, called, playfully, "Old Betsy." Move him up a little now. Let, say Bret Harte, have him. There he is, fine and dandy. He is a gambler in a Western mining camp now, wearing a silk shirt and a Stetson hat. He will lose you a whole fortune without the bat of an eye, but his personal associates are a bit rough. He is always being seen about with Black Peg, who runs a house of prostitution, and with Silent Smith, the killer.

Until, well, until one day when a New England school-teacher comes into the rough mining camp. One night she is set upon and is about to be outraged by a drunken miner. Then he, the associate of Black Peg, steps forward and shoots the miner. Ten minutes before, he was drunk and lying in the gutter, so drunk in fact that flies had been using his eyeballs as sliding places, but the danger to the school-teacher had sobered him instantly. He is a gentleman now. He offers the school-teacher his arm and they walk to her cabin discussing Emerson and Longfellow, and then our central figure of romance leaves her at her cabin door and goes to a lonely spot in the mountains. He sits down to wait until winter and the deep snows come, in order that he may freeze to death. He has realized that he loves the New England lady and is, in the language of the Far West, as set forth in all the best books, "not fitten for her."

The truth is that father, that is to say, my fanciful father, might well have been used by any one of a dozen of our American hero-makers. He is in the goods. That is the idea. In the hands of a Jack London he might have been another Sea Wolf or a musher trudging through the deep snow of the frozen North, cornering some fair virgin in an isolated cabin, only to let her off at the last moment out of respect for her dead mother, who expected something quite different of her. Then later he might have gone to Yale, and after that become a stock broker, taking daring chances with railroad stocks, married a woman who loved only the glare and shine of social life, chucked her, failed in business, gone farming, and turned out a clean man after all, say in the pages of the *Saturday Evening Post*. It could have been done.

Where my fanciful father was unfortunate, however, was in that he had to live in the fancy of a boy in a hay barn—one who had as yet had little or no experience with heroes.

And then there is no doubt he, from the first, had

certain weaknesses. He wasn't always kind to old women and children and, as you will see in the sequel, he wasn't to be trusted with a virgin. He just wouldn't behave himself, and when it comes to this matter of virgins, perhaps the least said about any man's attitude toward them—except, to be sure, in novels and in the movies—the better. As Mr. Howells once pointed out, "it is better to present to the readers only the brighter and more pleasant aspects of our common lives."

However, let us return to the man lying on the sand. There he is, you see, and it was sure he had been all his life, at any rate, a man of action. The Civil War had just come to an end a few years before and during the war he had been rather busily engaged. He had gone into the war as a spy for the Federal government and when he had got into the South had managed to engage himself as a spy for the Confederate side also. This had permitted him to move rather freely back and forth and to do well carrying contraband goods. When he had no special information to give to one or the other of his employers he could invent information —during a war that is always easy. He was, as I have said, a man of action. He aimed to get results, as they say in the advertising profession.

The war at an end, he had gone into the South, having several projects in mind and, at the time we meet him first, he was waiting on the lonely coast to sight a ship that was to bring some business associates of his. In a bayou, near the mouth of the river, some ten miles away, there was a ship, manned by his own men, awaiting his return. He was engaged in the business of smuggling firearms to various revolutionary parties in

South American republics and was now only waiting for the coming of a man who was to hand over to him certain monies.

And so the day passed and the evening came and at last an hour before darkness settled down over the lonely sand dunes a ship appeared. My mythical father arose and, fastening a cloth to the end of a stick, waved it back and forth over his head. The ship drew near and two boats were lowered. Some ten or twelve men were coming ashore and with them a woman. When they had got into the boats the ship did not wait but immediately steamed away.

The man on the beach began gathering a great pile of sticks and bits of driftwood, preparative to building a fire, and now and then he turned his head to look toward the approaching boats. That there was a woman among his visitors bothered him. Women were always interfering with business. Why had they wanted to bring a woman? "To the deuce with women!" he growled, making his way through the deep sand with a great pile of sticks in his arms.

Then the boat had landed and there was the old Harry to pay. A revolutionary party in one of the South American republics had gone to pieces and nearly all its members had been arrested and were to be executed. There was no money to pay for the firearms that were to have been shipped, and the little band of men, now standing on the lonely beach and facing the smugglers, had barely escaped with their lives. They had rowed out to sea in two boats and had been picked up by a steamer, and one among them had in his possession money enough to bribe the steamer captain to bring them to this spot, where they were to have landed, just at this time, under quite different circumstances.

Different circumstances indeed!

The lady of the party—well, she was something special—the daughter of one of the wealthiest sugar planters of her native land, she had given her young soul to the cause of the revolution and when the smash came had been compelled to fly with the others. Her own father disowned her in a moment of cowardice and the death sentence was out against her. What else could she do but flee?

If they had brought nothing else, they had brought food ashore from the ship, and the party might as well eat, since they would, in any event, have to spend the night on the beach. In the morning, it was the hope expressed by the leader of the party, that the firearms smuggler would guide them inland. They had friends in America but had they landed at a regular port of entry it might well have turned out that their own government would have asked the American government to send them home—to face the consequences of their folly.

With a grim smile on his cruel lips my fanciful father had heard them out in silence and now began building a fire. Night came and he moved softly about. A strange and new impulse had come into his hard and cruel heart. He had fallen instantly in love with the young female leader of revolution from the foreign land and was trying to figure out how he could get away from the others and have a talk with her.

At last when food had been prepared and eaten, he spoke, agreeing to perform all that had been asked of him, but declaring that the young woman could not be compelled to spend the night in such a place. Speaking in the Spanish language—with which he was marvelously conversant—he commanded the others to stay by the fire while he took the young woman inland to where, some two miles away, he declared he had some horses concealed in the stable of an oyster thief, a friend of his who lived up the bay.

The others consenting, he and the young woman set off. She was very beautiful and, as they had all been seated about the fire, she had kept her eyes almost constantly upon the American.

He was of the type of which American heroes are made, you see, and she had, in her young girlhood, read American novels. In American novels, as in American plays—as everyone knows—a man can, just as well as not, be a horse thief, a desperado, a child-kidnapper, a gentleman burglar, or a well-poisoner for years and years, and then, in an instant, become the sweetest and most amiable fellow possible, and with perfect manners too. It is one of the most interesting things about us Americans. No doubt it came to us from the English. It seems to be an Anglo-Saxon trait and a very lovely one too. All anyone need do is to mention in the presence of any one of us at any time the word "mother," or leave one of us alone in the darkness in a forest in a lonely cabin on a mountain at night with a virgin.

With some of us—that is to say, with those of us who have gone into politics—the same results can sometimes be had by speaking of the simple and humble laboring man, but it is the virgin that gets us every shot. In bringing out all the best in us she is a hundred per cent. efficient.

In the presence of a virgin something like a dawn among mountains creeps over the spirit of the Anglo-Saxon and a gentle light comes into his eyes. If he has a dress suit anywhere about he goes and puts it on. Also he gets himself a shave and a hair cut, and you would be surprised to see how everything clears up after that.

.   .   .   .

I, however, digress. In my enthusiasm for my fellows I jerk myself too violently out of my boyhood. No boy could so whole-heartedly appreciate or understand our national traits.

The story I had set myself down to tell was that of my own birth into the world of fancy—as opposed to the rather too realistic birth already depicted—and that, as I have explained, took place in Camden, Ohio.

Very well, then, a year has passed and I am being born a second time, as it were, but this second birth is quite different from the one in the Ohio town. There is more punch to it. Reading of it will lift you, who have been patient enough to follow me so far, out of your common everyday humdrum existences.

And if you have read Freud you will find it of additional interest that, in my fanciful birth, I have retained the very form and substance of my earthly mother while getting an entirely new father, whom I set up—making anything but a hero of him—only to sling mud at him. I am giving myself away to the initiated, that is certain.

But be that as it may, however, there is mother lying in bed in a lonely cabin on another long sandy beach, also on the Gulf of Mexico. (In my fanciful

life I have always had a hunger for the warm South.)
Mother has been honorably married to my fanciful
father on that very evening when she went with him
from among her fellow-countrymen, sitting by the fire
on that other beach, and after just such a metamorphosis of his character as she had come to expect
through having read American novels and through
having seen two or three American plays produced in
the capital of her native land.

After having secured the horses from the stable of
the oyster thief they had ridden off together and had
come at last into a deep forest of magnolia trees in
blossom. A southern moon came up into the sky and
so soft was the night, so gentle the breezes from the
now distant sea, and so sweet the hum of insect life
under their horses' feet, that mother found herself
speaking of her lost home and of her mother.

To my fanciful father the combination—the deep
forest, the scent of the magnolia blossoms and the
word "mother"—together with the fact that he was
alone in a dark place with a virgin, an innocent one,
these things were all irresistible to him. The metamorphosis spoken of above took place, and he pro-
poses marriage and on the spot proposed to live a
better life.

And so they rode together out of the forest and
were married, but, in his case, the metamorphosis did
not hold.

Within a few months he had gone back to his old
life, leaving mother alone in a strange land until the
time should come when I, having been born, could take
up the task of being her protector and guardian.

And now I am being born. It is late in the after-

noon of a still hot day and I, having just been ushered
into the world by the aid of a fisherman's wife, who
also does duty as a midwife in that isolated place and
who has now left to return again late at night—I, having been so born, am lying on the bed beside mother
and thinking my first thoughts. In my own fancy I
was, from the very first, a remarkable child and did
not cry out as most newly born infants do, but lay
buried in deep thought. In the little hut it is stifling
hot, and flies and other winged insects of the warm
South are buzzing in the air. Strange insects of gigantic size crawl over the walls and, from far-away
somewhere, there comes the murmur of the sea.
Mother is lying beside me, weak and wan.

We lie there for a long time and, young as I am, I
realize that she is tired and discouraged about life.
"Why has not life in America turned out as it always
did in the novels and plays?" she is asking herself;
but I, having at that time still retained all my young
courage and freshness of outlook, am not discouraged.

There is a sound outside the cabin, the swishing
sound of heavy feet dragged through the hot dry
sands, and the low moaning sound of a woman crying.

Again a steamer, from foreign parts, has visited
that lonely coast and again a boat has been lowered.
In the boat is my fanciful father accompanied by four
of his evil henchmen and accompanied also by another
woman. She is young and fair, another virgin; but
now, alas, father has become hardened on that subject!

The strange woman is terribly afraid but is at the
same time in love with her captor (owing to the
strange natures of women, this, you will understand,
is entirely possible), and father has had the cruel im-

pulse to bring the two women together. Perhaps he
wants to see them suffer the pangs of jealousy.

But he will get no such pangs from mother. With
her son beside her she lies silently waiting.

For what? That is the question that, try as he
would, the son could not answer.

And so the two lie there in silence on the poor bed
in the hut while that strange monster of a man drags
another woman across the yellow sands and in at the
door of the hut. What has happened is that he has
gone back to his old wicked life and, with his comrade,
has joined another revolutionary party in another
South American republic, and this time the revolution
has been successful and he and his partners have helped
sack a South American city.

At the forefront of the invaders was my fanciful
father and—whatever else may be said of him it can
never be said that he lacked in courage—it was from
him, in fact, that I got my own courage.

Into the invaded city he had rushed at the head of
his men and, when the city was being sacked, he demanded riches for his men but took none for himself.
For his own portion of the loot he had taken the virginal daughter of the leader of the Federal forces and
it was this woman he was now dragging in at the door
of our hut.

She was very beautiful and perhaps, had I been
older, I should not have blamed father, but at that
time the love of right was very strong in me.

When father saw that I had already been born he
staggered back for a step and leaned against the wall
of the cabin, still however clinging to the hand of his
new-found woman. "I had hoped to arrive before or

at the very hour of birth, I had counted on that," he muttered, cursing under his breath.

For a moment he stood looking at mother and myself and both of us looked calmly at him.

"Birth—the birth hour—is the test of womanhood," he said, taking hold of the shoulder of his new woman and shaking her violently, as though to fix her attention. I wanted you to see how the women of my own race meet bravely all such trying situations; for, as you must know, by the customs of my country, the woman who marries an American becomes instantly an American, with all the American virtues. It is our climate, I dare say, and it happens to people very quickly.

"At any rate there it is. The woman you see before you I really love, but she has become Anglo-Saxon, through having married me, and is therefore above me, as far above me as the stars.

"I cannot live with her. She is too good, too brave," said my fanciful father, staggering through the door and dragging his woman after him. Outside the door I heard him still talking loudly to his new woman as they went away. "Our Anglo-Saxon women are the most wonderful creatures in the world," I heard him saying. "In a few years now they will run the world."

. . . .

It was growing dark in the hayloft in the barn in the state of Ohio. Did I, as I lay deeply buried in the warm hay, really imagine the absurd scene depicted above? Although I was very young I had already read many novels and stories.

In any event the whole silly affair has remained in my fancy for years. When I was a lad I played with such fanciful scenes as other boys play with brightly colored marbles. From the beginning there has been, as opposed to my actual life, these grotesque fancies. Later, to be sure, I did acquire more or less skill in bringing them more and more closely into the world of the actual. They were but the raw materials with which the story-writer must work as the worker in woods works with trees cut in a forest.

As for the fancies themselves, they have always seemed to me like trees that have grown without having been planted. Later, after the period in my own life of which I am now writing, I worked for many years as a laborer in many places, and gradually as I stood all day beside a lathe in some factory, or later went about among business men trying to sell some article, in which I was myself not interested, I began to look at other men and to wonder what absurd fancies went on in secret within them. There was that curiosity and there was something else. I had perhaps, as I have no doubt all people have, a great desire to be loved and a little respected. My own fancies rule me. Even to-day I cannot go into a movie theatre and see there some such national hero as, say, Bill Hart, without wishing myself such another. In the theatre I sit looking at the people and see how they are all absorbed in the affairs of the man on the stage. Now he springs lightly off a horse and goes toward the door of a lonely cabin. We, in the theatre, know that within the cabin are some ten desperate men all heavily armed with guns and with them, bound to a chair, is a fair woman, another virgin got off the

119

reservation, as it were. Bill stops at the door of the cabin and takes a careful look at his guns, and we, in the audience, know well enough that in a few minutes now he will go inside and just shoot all of those ten fellows in there to death, fairly make sieves of them, and that he will get wounded himself but not seriously—just enough to need the help of the virgin in getting out of the cabin and onto his horse—so he can ride to her father's ranch house and go to bed and get well after a while, in time for the wedding.

All these things we know, but we love our Bill and can hardly wait until the shooting begins. As for myself I never see such a performance but that I later go out of the theatre and, when I get off into a quiet street alone, I become just such another. Looking about to see that I am unobserved, I jerk two imaginary guns out of my hip pockets and draw a quick bead on some near-by tree. "Dog," I cry, "unhand her!" All my early reading of American literature comes into my mind and I try to do a thing that is always being spoken of in the books. I try to make my eyes narrow to pin points. Bill Hart can do it wonderfully in the pictures and why not I? As I sat in the movie house it was evident that Bill Hart was being loved by all the men women and children sitting about and I also want to be loved—to be a little dreaded and feared, too, perhaps. "Ah! there goes Sherwood Anderson! Treat him with respect. He is a bad man when he is aroused. But treat him kindly and he will be as gentle with you as any cooing dove."

. . . .

As a boy lying buried in the hay I presume I had

some such notion as that, and later as a man standing by a lathe in some factory some such notion must have still been in my mind. I wanted then to be something heroic in the eyes of my own mother, now dead, and at the same time wanted to be something heroic in my own eyes too.

One could not do the thing in actual life, so one did it in a new world created within one's fancy.

And what a world that fanciful one—how grotesque, how strange, how teeming with strange life! Could one ever bring order into that world? In my own actual work as a tale-teller I have been able to organize and tell but a few of the fancies that have come to me. There is a world into which no one but myself has ever entered and I would like to take you there; but how often when I go, filled with confidence, to the very door leading into that strange world, I find it locked! Now, in the morning, I myself cannot enter the land into which all last night, as I lay awake in my bed, I went alone at will.

There are so many people in that land of whom I should like to tell you. I should like to take you with me through the gate into the land, let you wander there with me. There are people there with whom I should like you to talk. There is the old woman accompanied by the gigantic dogs who died alone in a wood on a winter day, the stout man with the gray eyes and with the pack on his back, who stands talking to the beautiful woman as she sits in her carriage, the little dark woman with the boyish husband who lives in a small frame house by a dusty road far out, in the country.

These and many other figures, all having a life of

their own, all playing forever in the field of my fancy. The fanciful shadowy life striving to take on flesh, to live as you and I live, to come out of the shadowy world of the fancy into the actuality of accomplished art.

When I had grown to be a man, and had begun to try a little to organize this inner life, I wondered often if a woman, being pregnant, and walking about through the streets, past factory doors, in the "loop district" of Chicago, let us say, if such a woman being conscious of something alive within—that is, at the moment a part of herself, flesh of her flesh, and that will presently come out of herself to live its own life, in a world her eyes now see passing before her—if such a woman does not have dreadful moments of fear.

To the tale-teller, you must understand, the telling of the tale is the cutting of the natal cord. When the tale is told it exists outside oneself and often it is more living than the living man from whom it came. The imagined figure may well live on and on in the fanciful life of others after the man from whose lips it came, or whose fingers guided the pen that wrote the tale, long after he is forgotten, and I have myself had some curious experiences of this sort. A public speaker, in speaking of my Winesburg tales, praised me as a writer but spoke slightingly of the figures that lived in the tales. "They weren't worth telling about," he said; and I remember that I sat at the back of the room, filled with people, hearing him speak, and remember sharply also just the sense of horror that crept over me at the moment. "It is a lie. He has missed the point," I cried to myself. Could the man not understand that he was doing a quite unpermissible thing? As well go into the bedroom of a woman during her lying-in and say to her: "You are no doubt a very nice woman, but the child to which you have just given birth is a little monster and will be hanged." Surely any man can understand that, to such a one, it might be permitted to speak at any length regarding her own failings as a woman, but—if the child live— surely this other thing must not be done. "It must not be condemned for the failings of the mother," I thought, shivering with fright. As I sat listening certain figures, Wing Biddlebaum, Hugh McVey, Elizabeth Willard, Kate Swift, Jesse Bentley, marched across the field of my fancy. They had lived within me, and I had given a kind of life to them. They had lived, for a passing moment anyway, in the consciousness of others beside myself. Surely I myself might well be blamed—condemned—for not having the strength or skill in myself to give them a more vital and a truer life—but that they should be called people not fit to be written about filled me with horror.

However, I again find myself plunging forward into a more advanced and sophisticated point of view than could have been held by the boy, beginning to remake his own life more to his own liking by plunging into a fanciful life. I shall be blamed. Those of my critics who declare I have no feeling for form will be filled with delight over the meandering formlessness of these notes.

It does not matter. My point is that, in the boy, as later in the man into whom the boy is to grow, there are two beings, each distinct, each having its own life and each of importance to the man himself.

The boy who lives in the world of fact is to help his

father put a priming coat on a new house built by a prosperous Ohio farmer. In my day we used a dirty yellow ochre for the purpose. The color satisfied no sensual part of myself. How I hated it! It was used because it was cheap and later was to be covered up, buried away out of sight. Ugly colors, buried away out of sight, have a way of remaining always in sight in the consciousness of the painter who has spread them.

In the hayloft the fat boy was awake now. Darkness was coming fast and he must bestir himself, must if possible escape the wrath of his father for the day wasted in entertaining me. He crawled up out of his own hole and, reaching down, put a fat hand on my shoulder and shook me. He had a plan for his own escape which he whispered to me as my head came up into sight in the dim evening light in the loft.

He was an only son and his mother was fond of him —she would even lie for him. Now he would creep away unseen to the house and frankly tell his mother he has been fooling about with me all day long. She would scold a little but, after a time, when his father came into the house for supper and when in harsh tones he asked what the boy had been doing, the gentle little lie would come. "It won't really be a lie," the fat boy declared stoutly, defending the virtue of his mother. "Do you expect me to do all the housework and the churning as well?" the farm woman would ask her husband sharply. She, it seemed, was a person of understanding and did not expect a boy to do a man's work all the time. "You'd think dad never was a kid," he whispered to me. "He works all the time and he wants me to work all the time too. I wouldn't never have no fun if it wasn't for ma. Gee, I only wish I had a dad like your'n. He's just like a kid himself, isn't he now?"

In the gathering darkness the farm boy and I crept down a ladder to the floor of the barn and he ran away to the farmhouse, his feet making no sound in the soft mud of the farmyard. The rain persisted and the night would be cold. In another part of the barn the farmer was doing his evening chores, assisted by father—always the accommodating one—who held the lantern and ran to get ears of corn to throw into the horses' feed-boxes. I could hear his voice, calling cheerfully. Already he knew all the farm horses by name and spoke of them familiarly. "How many ears for old Frank? Does Topsy get five ears too?"

Outside the barn, as I stood under the eaves, there was still a faint streak of light in the western sky, and the new house we were to give the priming coat, built close down to the road, could still be seen. Little strings of water fell from the roof above and made a tiny stream at my feet. The new house had two full stories and an attic. How magnificent to be a man, to be rich and to be able to build such a house! When the fat boy grew into manhood he would inherit the house and many broad acres. He also would be rich and would have a great house, with bathrooms and perhaps electric lights. The automobile had come. No doubt he would have one. How magnificent a house, a farm, an automobile—a beautiful wife to lie with him at night! I had been to Sunday school and had heard the stories of the magnificent men of old, Jacob and David and that young man Absalom, who

125

had everything in the world to look forward to but who nevertheless did unspeakable things.

And now the voices of the men inside the barn seemed far away. The new house was in some queer way a menace to me. I wondered why. The older house, the one the young New Englander had builded when he had first come into the new land, stood far away from the road. One went, from the barns, along a path to the right. The path lay beside an apple orchard, and at the orchard's end there was a bridge over a small stream. Then one crossed the bridge and started climbing the hill against the side of which the house had been built. It had been built of logs, very solidly, on a small terrace, and as the farmer had begun to prosper wings had been added. Back of the house stood forest trees, some the same trees that had been there when the first room of the cabin was built. The young farmer, with some of his neighbors, had felled the trees for his house on the very ground on which it now stood, and then during the long winter he had felled many other trees in the flat plain below, where his farming land was to lie, and, on a certain day, there had no doubt been a log-rolling, with other young farmers and their women coming from far and near. A whole forest of magnificent trees had been rolled into a great pile and burned—there had been feastings, tests of physical strength among the young men, a few unmarried fellows about, looking shyly at the unmarried girls, game on the table, talk in the evening of the possibilities of a war with the slave-holding farmers of the South.

All these things the older house had seen as it crouched on the side of the hill, and now it seemed to have crept away out of sight in the darkness, hidden itself among the trees still left standing on the hill; but even as I stood looking lights began to appear at its windows. The old house seemed smiling and calling to me. Now, myself and my brothers had no home—the house in which we at that time lived was not a home—for us there could be no home now that mother was not there. We but stayed temporarily in a house, with a few sticks of furniture—waiting—for what?

The older people of our native town had gone out of themselves, warmly, toward us. How many times had I been stopped on the street by some solid citizen of our town, a carpenter, Vet Howard, a wheelwright, Val Voght, a white bearded old merchant, Thad Hurd. In the eyes of these older people, as they talked to me, there was something, a light shining as the lights now shone from the farmhouse among the trees. They knew father—loved him, too, in a way—but well they knew he was not one to plan for his sons, help his sons in making their own plans. Was there something wistful in their eyes as they stood talking to the boy on the village street? I remember the old merchant spoke of God, but the carpenter and the wheelwright spoke of something else—of the new times coming. "Things are on the march," they said, "and the new generation will do great things. We older fellows belong to something that is passing. We had our trades and worked at them, but you young fellows have to think of something else. It is going to be a time when money will count big, so save your money, boy. You have energy. I've watched you. Now you are a little wild after the girls and going to dances. I saw you going down toward the cemetery with that little Truscan girl last Wednesday evening. Better cut that all out. Work. Save money. Get into the manufacturing business if you can. The thing now is to get rich, be in the swim. That's the ticket."

The older fellows had said these words to me, somewhat wistfully, as the old house, hidden now in the darkness, seemed to look at me. Was it because the men who said the words were themselves not quite convinced? Did the old American farmhouse among the trees know the end of its life was at hand and was it also calling wistfully to me?

One remains doubtful and, as I now sit writing, I am most doubtful of all the veracity of this impression I am trying to give of myself as a boy standing in the darkness in the shelter of the barn's eaves.

Did I really want to be the son of some prosperous farmer with the prospect ahead of some day owning land of my own and having a big new house and an automobile? Or did my eyes but turn hungrily toward the older house because it represented to my lonely heart the presence of a mother—who would even go to the length of lying for a fellow?

I was sure I wanted something I did not have, could never (having my father's blood in me) achieve.

Old houses in which long lives have been lived, in which men and women have lived, suffered and endured together—a people, my own people, come to a day when entire lives are lived in one place, a people who have come to love the streets of old towns, the mellow color of the stone walls of old houses.

Did I want these things, even then? Being an American in a new land and facing a new time, did I want even what Europe must have meant in the hearts of many of the older men who had talked to the boy on the streets of an Ohio town? Was there something in me that, at the moment, went wandering back through the blood of my ancestors, through the blood of the ancestors of the men about me—to England, to Italy, Sweden, Russia, France, Germany— older places, older towns, older impulses?

The new house, the farmer was having built, stood clear of the forest and directly faced the dirt road that led into town. It had instinctively run out to meet the coming automobile and the interurban car—and how blatantly it announced itself! "You see I am new, I cost money. I am big. I am bold," it seemed to be saying.

And looking at it I crouched for a moment against the wall of the barn, instinctively afraid.

Was it because the new house was, for all its size, cheaply constructed and at bottom ugly? Could I have known that even as a boy? To make such a declaration would, I am sure, be giving myself an early critical instinct too much developed. It would be making something of a little monster of the boy crouching there in the darkness by the barn.

All I can say is that I remember how the boy who, on that evening long ago, went slowly away from the barn through the mud of the barnyard, turned his back on the new house, and stopped for a moment on the bridge leading to the old house, sad and frightened. Before him lay a life of adventures (imagined if not actually experienced), but at the moment he went not toward the future but toward the past. In the older house there was, to be sure, a meal to be had without labor—in this case a meal prepared at the hands of a kindly faced woman—and there was also a warm bed into which the boy could crawl to indulge all night long undisturbed in his dreams; but there was something else. A sense of security? It may be, after all, just the sense of security, or assurance of warmth, food, and leisure—most of all leisure—the boy wanted on that evening, that, for some reason I cannot explain, marked the end of boyhood for him.

BOOK TWO

I WAS rolling kegs of nails out of a great sheet-iron warehouse and onto a long platform, from where they were to be carted by trucks, down a short street, out to a wharf and aboard a ship. The kegs were heavy but they were not large, and as they were rolled down a slight incline to the platform the rolling could be done with the foot. Like practically all modern workmen my body had plenty to do but my mind was idle. There was no planning of the work, no scheming to make the day's work fit the plan. The truckmen, four heavy and good-natured Swedes, loaded the trucks, and that also required no skill. The kegs were so heavy that a few of them only could be put on a truck at one time and the trucks did not have to be loaded skillfully.

As for the nails themselves, they came pouring out of machines somewhere back in the factory at the edge of which the warehouse stood.

The warehouse had two platforms, one at which cars were loaded and our own for the loading of trucks, and I could hear voices on the other platform —an oath, a broken laugh—but never did I see the men employed there.

On our side we had a little life of our own. My single fellow-workman, who all day long ran in and out of the warehouse with me, was a short, stocky young man who on Saturday afternoons played baseball and, in the winter, hockey. He continually boasted of his prowess in games and when the warehouse foreman was not about—he seldom appeared on our platform—the athlete stopped work to tell one of the teamsters a story.

The stories all concerned one impulse in life, and as I had grown unspeakably weary of hearing them and indeed doubted the man's potency, he was so insistent about it, I did not stop working but rolled kegs busily. The teamster laughed heavily. "There was a fat woman, hanging out clothes, on a line. Two stray dogs came along," etc. The story-teller himself laughed as he told his tale and sometimes glared at me because I did not stop to listen. "You ain't afraid of your job, are you?" he asked, but I did not answer. The horses hitched to the trucks were quiet beasts with broad flanks, and as he talked, telling his tales, they switched their tails slowly back and forth, driving flies away. Then they turned their heads to look at me, running out of the warehouse and down the incline behind one of the flying kegs. "Don't be in a hurry. You ain't afraid of your job, are you?" they also seemed to be saying.

My legs and arms, my body had enough to do but my mind was idle. During the year before I had been with race horses, going with them about Ohio to the fairs and race meetings, and then I had given up that life, although I loved it well, because I wanted something from men I did not think I could find at the tracks. The life of the sporting fraternity had color and the horses themselves, beautiful temperamental things, fascinated me, but I hungered for something of my own. At the tracks one received a succession of thrills and was kept on the alert but the emotions aroused were all vicarious.

"No Wonder," a gray pacer, was on the track for his morning workout and I, being unoccupied at the moment, leaned over a wooden fence to watch. He had been jogged slowly around the track and now his driver was about to do what we called "setting him down." His flanks flattened and he seemed to spring into his stride, and what a stride it was! He fairly flew over the ground and the boy by the fence, half asleep but a moment before, was now all attention. He leaned far over the fence to watch and wait. Now the gray was making the upper turn and soon he would be headed directly down the home stretch. By leaning far forward the boy could see just the play of the muscles over the powerful breast. Oh, the flying legs, the distended nostrils, the sobbing whistle of the wind in and out of the great lungs!

But all vicarious after all, all something outside myself. I rubbed the legs of the horses and later walked them slowly for miles, cooling them out after a race or after a workout. Plenty of time to think. Could I, in time, become a Geers, a Snapper Garrison, a Bradley, a Walter Cox, a Murphy? Something whispered to me that I could not. There was required of a successful horseman something I did not have. Either the trotting or the running tracks required a calm, a seemingly indifferent exterior I could not achieve. A track negro with whom I worked had spoken discouraging words. "You're too excitable, too flighty," he said. "A horse, that wanted to, would know how to bluff you. You ain't made to get all they is outen a horse."

Restlessness had taken hold of me and I had left the tracks to go visit certain cities.

The work, I found, did not tire me and after the longest and hardest day I went to my room, bathed, took off my sweaty clothes and was a new man, quite refreshed and ready for adventure.

At the warehouse a kind of understanding between myself and the Swedish teamsters, had already been achieved. When they returned with the empty trucks along the short street between our warehouse and the wharf they stopped at a saloon to have filled the tin pails for beer they carried on the trucks, and the athlete and myself had also provided ourselves with pails which they had filled for us. Aha! the athlete might boast of his prowess on the baseball field or at playing hockey in the winter, but I could outdrink him and in the eyes of the teamsters that made me the better man. How foolish the athlete! Had he declined to have anything to do with drink all might have been well with him, but as the ability to "carry your liquor" was an accepted standard among us he foolishly accepted it. On hot days and in the late afternoon the pails were sent frequently to the saloon and the athlete became worried. "Ah, let's cut it out," he said to me coaxingly and the teamsters laughed. "Why, Eddie, we haven't had any at all yet," they said; but he insisted, was compelled to insist. Already he staggered a little as he rolled the kegs out of the warehouse and now it was my turn to loiter with the teamsters while he worked. No more story-telling now. "I have a kind of headache today," he said, while the teamsters and I drank six, eight, sometimes ten or twelve of the generous portions of strong beer, flauntingly. As the beer was paid for from a fund collected from all, we were drinking, in part at least, at the athlete's expense. I drank and drank, enjoying the discomfiture of my fellow-worker, and something happened inside my head. My legs remained steady and I could roll the kegs more rapidly and accurately than ever—they became like corks and I fairly whirled them along the warehouse floor and down the incline and to the trucks—but at the same time all reality became strangely colored and overlaid with unreality inside myself. Beyond the roadway, in which the trucks stood, there was a vacant lot and this now became the centre of my attention. The vacant lot was in reality filled with rubbish, rusty tin cans, piles of dirt, broken wagon wheels and wornout household utensils, and among all this foul stuff dirty-faced children played and screamed; but now all this unsightliness was wiped off the surface of my vision. I talked to the teamsters and together we laughed at Eddie who kept scolding and saying apologetically that the beer we had been drinking was rotten stuff and gave him a headache, while all the time the most marvelous things took place in the vacant lot before my eyes.

First of all an army of soldiers appeared and marched back and forth directed by a man on a magnificent horse. He was many years older but at the same time looked strangely like myself and wore a long, flowing purple mantle. And also he had a golden helmet on his head while his soldiers, who obeyed his slightest wish, were also richly dressed. First there came a file of men dressed in light green and with bright yellow plumes flying from their helmets, and these were followed by others dressed in blue, in flaming red and in uniforms combining all these colors.

The men marched for what seemed a long time in the vacant lot while I dreamed of becoming a great general, a world conqueror perhaps, but continued meanwhile sending the kegs whirling down the incline. Eddie and I had a race to see who could roll kegs most accurately and rapidly—an hour before he could have beaten me easily, but now I could roll six to his five and land them just so, standing upright on the platform below—while at the same time there was this other life, outside myself, going on before my eyes.

I raised my eyes and looked at the vacant lot and the soldiers went through quick and accurate manœuvres. Then they marched away along a near-by street and the place became a great canvas over which colors played. The surface was brown, a soft velvety glowing brown, now other colors appeared, reds, golden yellows, deep purples. The colors stole swiftly out across the open place and designs were formed. I will be a great painter, I decided; but now the vacant lot had become a carpet on which walked beautiful men and women. They smiled at me, beckoned to me, and then they paid me no more attention and became absorbed in each other. "Very well; if you prefer to roll kegs, go your own way," they seemed to be saying, and when they laughed there was something derisive in their laughter.

Was I a little insane? Had I been born a little insane? I rolled the kegs of nails, drank innumerable pails of beer, the sweat rolled from my body and soaked my clothes and presently quitting time came and I returned along a street with hundreds of other workers—all smelling equally vile—to a rooming house where I lived with many other laborers, Hungarians, Swedes, a few Irish, several Italians and, oddly enough, one English Jew.

The house was run by a worried-looking woman of forty who had one daughter, a young woman of nineteen, who had taken a kind of fancy to me. Her father, a laborer like myself, had deserted her mother when the child was but four or five years old and had never been seen again. As for the daughter, she had a strong body, clear blue eyes, thick lips and a large nose, and like myself she had Italian blood in her veins, her father having been an Italian.

Toward her mother she was loyal, staying in the house and doing the work of a chambermaid for very little pay when she might have made a great deal more money at something else; but her loyalty was tempered by a sturdy kind of independence that nothing could shake. During the spring, before I came to live at the house, she had become engaged to marry a young sailor, an engineer's assistant on a lake boat, but, although later I spoke to her of the danger, she did not let the fact of her engagement to another interfere with her relationship with me.

Our own relationship is a little hard to explain. When I came from the warehouse and climbed the stairs to my room I found her there at work, making my bed, which had been allowed to air all day, or changing the sheets. The sheets were changed almost daily and her mother constantly scolded about the matter. "If he wants clean sheets every day let him pay for them," the mother said, but the daughter paid no attention, and indeed I was no doubt responsible for more than one quarrel between mother and daughter. Among laboring people a girl engaged is taboo and the other men in the house thought I was doing an unfair thing to her absent lover. Whether or not he knew what was going on I never found out.

What was going on? I came into the house, climbed the stairs and found her at work in my room. At the foot of the stairs I had met her mother, who had scowled at me, and now the other workers, trooping in, attempted to tease. She kept on working and did not look at me and I went to stand by a window that looked down into the street. "Which one is she going to marry?—that's what I want to know," one of the workers on the floor below called to another. She looked up at me and something I saw in her eyes made me bold. "Don't mind them," I said. "What makes you think I do?" she replied. I was glad none of the men who worked at our warehouse roomed at the house. "They would be shouting, laughing and going on about it all day," I thought.

The young woman—her name was Nora—talked to me in whispers as she did the work in the room, or she listened and I talked. The minutes passed and we stayed on together, looking at each other, whispering, laughing at each other. In the house all, including the mother, were convinced I was working to bring about Nora's ruin and the mother wanted to order me out of the house but did not dare. Once as I stood in the hallway outside my door late at night I had overheard the two women talking in the kitchen of the house.

"If you mention the matter again I shall walk out of the house and never come back."

Occasionally in the evening Nora and I walked along the street, past the warehouse where I was employed, and out upon the docks, where we sat together looking into the darkness and once—but I will not tell you what happened upon that occasion.

First of all I will tell you of how the relationship of Nora and myself began. It may be that the bond between us was brought into existence by the beer I drank at the warehouse in the late afternoons. One evening, when I had first come to the house, I came home, after drinking heavily, and it was then Nora and I had our first intimate conversation.

I had come into the house and climbed the three flights of stairs to my room, thinking of the vacant lot covered with the soft glowing carpet and of the beautiful men and women walking thereon, and when I got to my room it seemed unspeakably shabby. No doubt I was drunk. In any event there was Nora at work and it was my opportunity. For what? I did not quite know, but there was something I knew I wanted from Nora and the beer drinking had made me bold. I had a sudden conviction that my boldness would overawe her.

And there was something else too. Although I was but a young man I had already worked in factories in several cities and had lived in too many shabby rooms in shabby houses in factory streets. The outer surface of my life was too violently uncouth, too persistently uncouth. Well enough for Walt Whitman, Carl Sandburg and others to sing of the strength and fineness of laboring men, making heroes of them, but already the democratic dream had faded and laborers were not my heroes. I was born fussy, liked cleanness and orderliness about me and had already been thrown too much into the midst of shiftlessness. The socialists and communists I had seen and heard talk nearly all struck me as men who had no sense of life at all. They were so likely to be dry intellectual sterile men. Already I had begun asking myself the questions I have been asking myself ever since. "Does no man love another man? Why does not some man arise who wants the man working next to him to work in the midst of order? Can a man and a woman love each other when they live in an ugly house in an ugly street? Why do working men and women so often seem perversely unclean and disorderly in their houses? Why do not factory owners realize that, although they build large, well-lighted factories, they will accomplish nothing until they realize the need of order and cleanliness in thinking and feeling also?" I had come into the midst of men with a clean strong body, my mother had been one who would have fought to the death for order and cleanliness about her and her sons. Was it not apparent that something had already happened to the democracy on which Whitman had counted so much? (I had not heard of Whitman then. My thoughts were my own. Perhaps I had better be more simple in speaking of them.)

I had come out of a messy workplace along a messy street to a messy room and did not like it and within me was the beer that made me bold.

And there were the visions I had seen in the vacant lot. It may be that I thought then that all my fellows lived as I did, having quite conscious and separate inner and outer lives going on in the same body that they were trying to bring into accord. As for myself I saw visions, had from boyhood been seeing visions. Moments of extreme exaltation were followed by times of terrible depression. Were all people really like that? The visions were sometimes stronger than the reality of life about me. Might it not be that they were the reality, that they existed rather than myself —that is to say, rather than my physical self and the physical fact of the men and women among whom I then worked and lived, rather than the physical fact of the ugly rooms in ugly houses in ugly streets?

Was there a consciousness of something wrong, a consciousness we all had and were ashamed of?

There was the vacant lot in which an hour before I had seen the marching soldiers and the beautifully gowned men and women walking about. Why might that not exist as really as the half-drunken teamsters, myself, the irritated athlete and the piles of unsightly rubbish?

Perhaps it did exist in all of us. Perhaps the others saw what I saw. At that time I had a great deal of faith in a belief of my own that there existed a kind of secret and well-nigh universal conspiracy to insist on ugliness. "It's just a kind of boyish trick we're up to, myself and the others," I sometimes told myself, and there were times when I became almost convinced that if I just went suddenly up behind any man or any woman and said "boo" he or she would come out of it and I would come out of it, and we would march off arm in arm laughing at ourselves and everyone else and having really quite a wonderful time.

I had decided to try to say "boo" to Nora, I fancy. There I was in the room with her (I had been in the house about three days and had only seen her and heard her name spoken once before, when she was sweeping out the hallway by my door), and now she was throwing the covers back over the soiled sheets on my bed and there was dust on the window panes and streaks along the wall paper, while the floor of the room had been given but two or three careless whisks with a broom. Nora was making the bed and back of her head, as she leaned over to do the job, there was a picture on the wall, a picture of five or six water lilies lying on a table. There was a streak of dust down across the white face of the lilies and at that moment a cloud of dust, stirred up by the heavy trucks now going homeward along the street, floated just outside the window.

"Well, Miss Nora," I suddenly said after I had been standing in the room for a moment, silently and boldly staring at her. I began advancing toward her and no doubt my eyes were shining with enthusiasm. I dare say I was pretty drunk but I am sure I walked steadily. "Well," I cried in a loud voice, "what are you up to there?"

She turned to stare at me and I went on, still speaking rapidly, with a kind of hurried nervous stuttering manner brought on by the liquor and a fear that if I stopped speaking I should not be able to start again. "I refer to the bed," I said, going up close to her and pointing at it. "You see, don't you, that the sheets you are putting on the bed are soiled?" I pounded on my own chest, much in the manner of the primitive hero in Mr. Eugene O'Neill's play "The Hairy Ape";

144

and no doubt had I at that time seen the play I might at that moment have begun saying in hoarse, throaty tones: "I belong. I belong."

I did not say anything of the sort because I am not primitive and had not then seen the play, nor did I whine or complain because of the soiled sheets on the bed. I talked, I am afraid, rather like a Napoleon or a Tamerlane to poor Nora who was already appalled by my sudden descent upon her.

Pounding on my chest and descending upon her I made a speech something in the following manner: "My dear Nora, you are a woman and no doubt a virgin, but you may not always be one. Have hopes. Some day a man will come along who will admire your person and will ask your hand in marriage." I looked at her somewhat critically. "You will not refuse him," I declared, with the air of a soothsayer delivering himself of a prophecy. "You will accept the marriage state, Nora, partly because you are bored, partly because you will look upon the opportunity as a means of escape from your present way of life, and partly because you will find within yourself an instinct telling you that any kind of marriage will bring you something you want.

"But we will not discuss you. We will discuss myself," I declared. I continued pounding myself on the chest and so great was my momentary enthusiasm that later my breast was somewhat sore. "Nora, woman," I said, "look at me! You cannot see my body and I dare say if I did not have on these soiled clothes your maidenly modesty would compel you to run out of this room. But do not run. I do not intend to take off my clothes.

145

"Very well, we will not speak any more of my body," I said in a loud voice, wishing to reassure her since I could see she was becoming a little alarmed. No doubt she thought me insane. She had grown slightly pale and had stepped away from me so that her back was against the wall and the soiled water lilies were just above her head. "I am not speaking of my own body in relation to your body, do not get that entirely feminine notion into your head," I explained. "I am speaking of my body in relation to yonder soiled sheets."

And now I pointed toward the bed and stopped pounding my own chest which was becoming sore. Stepping quite close to her, so close in fact that my face was within a few inches of her own, I put one hand against the wall and tried to quiet my own loud, blustering tones, and to assume a tone of great ease, or rather, of nonchalance. I took a cigarette from my pocket and succeeded in lighting it without burning my fingers, a feat requiring a good deal of concentration under the circumstances. The truth is, that I had bethought myself that in a moment more Nora would either hit me with the broom, that stood close at her hand, or would run out of the room thinking me insane.

As I had a notion I wanted to put over to her while I could and while my beer-born courage lasted I now tried to be more at my ease. A little smile began to play about the corners of my mouth and I thought of myself at the moment as a diplomat—not an American or an English diplomat, let me say, but an Italian diplomat of, we will suppose, the sixteenth century.

In as light and bantering a tone as I could assume

under the circumstances—my task was the more difficult because a workman, hearing my speech from a neighboring room, had come along the hallway and was now standing at the door with a look of astonishment on his face—assuming, I say, a light bantering tone, I now rapidly explained to Nora the notion that had been in my head when I interrupted her bedmaking. She had been about to reach for the broom and with it to drive me from the room, but now the words streaming from my lips caught and held her attention. With a fluency in words that never comes to me when I am writing and that only comes to my lips when I am slightly under the influence of strong drink I explained myself. To the astonished young woman I compared the bed she had been making to a suit of clothes I might be about to put on my body after I had bathed the aforesaid body. Talking rapidly and enunciating my words very distinctly so she should lose nothing of my discourse (and I might here explain to you, my readers, that in ordinary conversation I am rather given to the slovenly dragging of words so common to the people of the Middle West. We, you must know, do not say "feah," as a New Englander might, nor "fear," as an Italian-American might, that is to say, pronouncing distinctly the "r," but "feehr"), going on very clearly and distinctly I told Nora she was not to judge me by the smell that came from my clothes, that under my clothes lived a body I was about to wash clean as soon as she had finished her work in the room and had gone away. Leaving both her and the workman outside the door standing and staring at me I walked to the window and threw it up. "The cloud of dust you see floating up from the street below," I explained, "does not represent all the elements of the atmosphere even in an American industrial city." I then tried, as best I could, to explain to my limited audience that air, normally, might be a clean thing to be cleanly breathed into the lungs and that a man like myself, although he might wear dirty, soiled clothes in order to earn money to keep his body alive might also at the same time have a certain feeling of pride and joy in his body and want clean sheets to put it between when he laid it down to sleep at night.

To Nora, standing there and staring at me, half in wonder, half in anger, I tried to explain a little my habit of having visions and sketched for her, as rapidly and briefly as I could, the marvelous sights I had in fancy seen in the vacant lot near the warehouse in the late afternoon, and also I preached her a kind of sermon, not, I assure you, with the object of changing her own character but rather to carry out the plan that had formed in my rather befuddled brain, a plan for bullying her—that is to say of bending her to my own purpose if possible.

Being by nature a rather shrewd man, however, I did not put the case to her directly but pursuing the method common to preachers who always try to conceal their own wants under the mask of the common good, so that a man who is apparently always trying to get others into Heaven is really only afraid he will not manage to get there himself, pursuing valiantly this method, I pointed to the soiled water lilies above Nora's head. An inspiration seized me. At that time, you must remember, I did know that Nora was engaged to be married to an engineer's assistant on a lake steamer. I chanced at that moment to see the picture of the water lilies and thought of the little quiet back waters of Sandusky Bay where as a boy I had sometimes gone fishing with a certain charming old country doctor who for a time had employed me, ostensibly as a stable boy but really as a companion on long country drives. The old doctor had been a talkative soul and loved to speculate on life and its purposes and we often went fishing on summer afternoons and evenings, not so much for the purpose of catching fish as to give the doctor the opportunity to sit in a boat on the bank of some stream and pour wisdom into my willing young ears.

And so there I was, in the presence of Nora and that wondering workman, standing with one arm raised and pointing at the cheap chromo on the wall and being as much the actor as I could. Even though my brain was somewhat befuddled I was watching Nora, waiting and hoping that something I might say would really arrest her attention, and now I thought, as I have said, of quiet sweet back waters of bays and rivers, of suns going down in clean evening skies, of my own white bare feet dangling in warm pellucid waters.

To Nora I said the following words, quite without definite thought, as they came flowing from my lips: "I do not know you, young woman, and have never until this moment thought of you and your life but I'll tell you this: the time will come when you will marry a man who now sails on the seas. Even at this moment he is standing on the deck of a boat and thinking of you, and the air about him is not like this air you and I for our sins are compelled to breathe.

"Ah ha!" I cried, seeing by a look in Nora's eyes that my chance shot had hit home and shrewdly following up the advantage that gave me. "Ah ha!" I cried; "let us think and speak of the life of a sailor. He is in the presence of the clean sea. God has made clean the scene upon which his eyes rest. At night he lies down in a clean bunk. Nothing about him is as it is about us. There is no foul air, no dirty streaks on wall paper, no unclean sheets, no unclean beds.

"Your young sailor lies in bed at night and his body is clean, as I dare say also is his mind. He thinks of his sweetheart on shore and of necessity, do you see, all about him is so clean, he must think of her as one who in her soul is clean."

And now to my readers I must stop a moment to explain that I speak at length in this way of my conversation with Nora, my triumph with her, as I may I think legitimately call it, because it was a purely literary feat and I am writing, as you know, of the life of a literary man. I had never, when all this occurred, been at sea nor had I ever been aboard a ship, but I had, to be sure, read books and stories regarding ships and the conduct of sailors aboard ships, and in my boyhood I had known a man who was once mate on a river boat on the Mississippi River. He to be sure had spoken more often of the gaudiness rather than the cleanliness of the boats on which he had worked but, as I have said, I was being as literary as I could.

And realizing now that I had by good fortune stumbled upon the right note I went on elaborating the romantic side of the life of the sailor aboard ship, touching upon the hopes and dreams of such a man and pointing out to Nora that it was a great mistake on her part not to have one room in the great house of so many rooms, upon the care of which she could pour some of the natural housewifely qualities with which her nature was, I was certain, so richly endowed.

I saw, you understand, that I had her but was careful not to press my advantage too far. And then, too, I had begun to like her, as all literary men like inordinately those who take seriously their outpourings.

And so I now quickly drove a bargain with Nora. Like herself, I explained, I was lonely and wanting companionship. Strange thoughts and fancies came to me that I would like to tell to another. "We will have a friendship," I exclaimed enthusiastically. "In the evenings we will walk about together. I will tell you of the strange notions that come into my head and of the marvelous adventures that sometimes occur to me in the life of my fancy. I will do that and you—well, you see, you will take extra good care of my room. You will lavish upon it some of the affection natural to your nature, thinking as you do so, not of me but of your sailor man at sea, and of the time to come when you may make a clean warm nest for him ashore.

"Poor man," I said, "you must remember that he is buffeted often by storms, often his life is in danger and often too he is in strange ports where but for his constancy to the thoughts of you, he might get into almost any kind of a muddle with some other woman."

I had succeeded, you see, by a purely literary trick, in getting myself into Nora's consciousness as in some way connected with her absent lover.

"But I must not press the matter too far," I

151

thought, and, stepping back, stood smiling at her as genially as I could.

And then another thought came. "There will be a kind of wrath in her soul at this moment and I must direct it quickly toward someone other than myself." The workman who, attracted by my loud words at the beginning of my discourse, had come along the hall-way and who now stood at the door of my room looking in, did not speak English very well and I was sure had not understood much of my long speech.

Going to the open window I now said, over my shoulder: "I am silly saying all these things to you, Nora, but I have been lonesome and to tell the truth I am a little drunk. Forgive me. You know yourself that the other men in this house are stupid fellows and do not care at all in what shape their rooms are kept. They work like dogs and sleep like dogs and do not have thoughts and dreams as you do and as I and your sailor man do.

"There is that man listening to our little conversation, there now, by the door," I said straightening up and pointing; but my speech got no further. As I had conjectured within myself, Nora had for some minutes been anxious to hit someone with the broom that stood close at hand and she now, suddenly and quite unreasonably, decided to hit the workman. Grabbing the broom in her hand she flew at him screaming with wrath. "Can't we have a little talk, my friend and I, without your sticking in your nose?" she cried, and the workman fled down the hallway with Nora at his heels, striking vigorously at him with the broom.

NOTE II

ONE who like myself could not, because of circumstances, spend the years of his youth in the schools must of necessity turn to books and to the men and women directly about him; upon these he must depend for his knowledge of life and to these I had turned. What a life the people of the books led! They were for the most part such respectable people, with problems I did not have at all or they were such keen and brainy villains as I could never hope to become. Being a Nero a Jesse James or a Napoleon I often thought would suit me first rate but I could not see how I was going to make it. In the first place I never could shoot very well, I hadn't the courage to kill people I did not like and to steal on any grand scale involved the risk of prison—or at least I then thought it did. I later found that only petty thieves were in danger but at that time, long before I myself became a schemer in business, I knew only petty thieves. At the race tracks some of my friends were always being marched off to prison or I heard of some man I had known being nabbed and taken away and prisons frightened me. I remembered vividly a night of my boyhood and myself going through an alleyway and past our town jail and the white face of a man staring out at me from behind iron bars. "Hey kid, get me

153

an iron bar or a hammer and pass it up here to me and I'll give you a quarter," he said in harsh throaty tones but I was frightened at the sight of his white drawn face in the moonlight and at the thoughts of the grim silent place in which he stood. A murderer, a crazed farmer who had killed his wife and hired man with an ax, had once been lodged in the jail and I had got the notion into my head that all men who passed into its doors were terrible and dangerous. I ran quickly away and got out of the alleyway into a lighted street and always afterward I remembered that moment, the stars in the sky, the moonlight shining on the faces of buildings, the quick sharp laughter of a girl somewhere in the darkness on the porch of a house, the sound of a horse's hoofs in a roadway, all the sweet sounds of free men and women walking about. I wanted to spend my life walking about and looking at things, listening to words, to the sound of winds blowing through trees, smelling life sweet and alive, not put away somewhere in a dark ill-smelling place. Once later when I was working at Columbus, Ohio, I went with a fellow—he had a sickening kind of curiosity about such places and kept urging and urging—to the state prison on visiting day. It was at the hour when the prisoners take exercise and many of them were in a large open place between high walls, on which guards with guns walked up and down. I looked once and then closed my eyes and during the rest of our pilgrimage through the place I carefully avoided looking into the prisoners' faces or into the cells before which we stopped but looked down instead at the stone floors until we were again outside in the sunlight.

As I have said the books were mostly about respectable people with moral problems, with family fortunes that must be saved or built up, daughters safely married, hints at a possible loss of virtue on the part of some woman and the terrible consequences that were to follow. In the books the women who grew familiar with men, to whom they were not married, were always having children and thus giving themselves away to all and I did not know any such women. The kind of women among whom life at that time threw me were much wiser and pretty much seemed to have children or not as they chose and I presume I thought the other kind must be a rather foolish sort and not worth bothering or thinking about.

And then there was the grand life in the big world, the life of the courts, the field, camp and palace, and in the America of Newport, Boston and New York. It was all a life far away from me but it seemed to occupy the attention of most of the novelists. As for myself I did not think at that time that I would ever see much of such life and I am afraid it did not much tempt me.

However, I read greedily everything that came into my hands. Laura Jean Libbey, Walter Scott, Harriet Beecher Stowe, Henry Fielding, Shakespeare, Jules Verne, Balzac, the Bible, Stephen Crane, dime novels, Cooper, Stevenson, our own Mark Twain and Howells and later Whitman. The books—any books —have always fed my dreams and I am one who has always lived by his dreams and even to-day I can often get as much fun and satisfaction out of a dull book as out of a so-called brilliant or witty one. The books like life itself are only useful to me in as much as they feed my own dreams or give me a background upon which I can construct new dreams.

Books I have always had access to and I am sure there is no other country in the world where people in general are so sentimentally romantic on the subject of books and education. Not that we read the books or really care about education. Not we. What we do is to own books and go to colleges and I have known more than one young man without money work his way patiently through college without paying much attention to what the colleges are presumed to teach. The fact of having got through college and of having managed to get a degree satisfies us and so the owning of books has become in most American families a kind of moral necessity. We own the books, put them on the shelves and go to the movies and the books, not being read and sitting dumbly there on the shelves in the houses, fairly jump at anyone who cares for them. It was so also in my own youth. Wherever I went someone was always bringing me books or urging me to come to some house and help myself and having got into most houses I could have helped myself, if books were not offered, simply by rearranging the shelves so there was no gaping hole left. I did it sometimes but not often.

As for the owners, they were interested, absorbed in the great industrial future just ahead for all Americans. We were all to have college degrees, ride in automobiles, come by some kind of marvelous mechanical process into a new, more cultured and better age. "Clear the track! Come on! Get in the swim!" was the cry and later I was to take up the cry myself and become one of the most valiant of the hustlers but for a time—for several years—I stayed in the backwaters of life and looked about.

My companions for the time being were flash men, the sharpshooters and touts at the race tracks. How many such fellows as Sit-still Murphy, Flatnose Humphrey of Frisco, Horsey Hollister and others of that stripe I knew at that time! And there were also gamblers, a politician or two and most of all a strange kind of sensitive and foot-loose man or woman, unfitted for the life of a hustler, not shrewd, usually lovable and perplexed, feeling themselves out of touch with the mood of the times and often spending life getting drunk, wandering about and loving to talk away long hours on bridges in cities, on country roads and in the back rooms of little saloons, which for all the evil they are presumed to have brought upon us I thank my gods existed during my youth. How often have I said to myself: "What kind of a world will this be when we are all moral and good people, when there are no more rascals to be found among us and no places left where rascals may congregate to speak lovingly of their rascalities?"

Of the rascals I met at that time there was one of a far different sort than the others who did much to educate me in the ways of the world. I found him in a town of northern Ohio to which I had drifted and in which I had got a job in a stable run by a man named Nate Lovett, who owned several race horses and who also kept a livery barn. Nate had a stallion, a fast trotter named "Will you Please" and got most of his income by taking him about to neighboring towns to serve mares but he had also some ten or twelve half-wornout old driving horses that were let to the young men of the town when they wanted to take some girl to a dance or for a drive in the country. These I took care of, working all day and sleeping on a cot in what we called the office but having my evenings free. A gigantic and goodhearted Negro took care of the racing horses and stayed in the office from eight until eleven in the evening. "Go on child. I ain't got no folks in this town and I don't want none here neither," he said.

Lovett, a man of the English jockey type, had lost one eye in a fight but was a quiet enough fellow, never losing his temper except when someone spoke favorably of the Irish or of the Catholic religion. He had a fixed notion that the Pope at Rome had made up his mind to get control of America and had filled the land with crafty spies and agents who worked tirelessly night and day to accomplish his ends and when he spoke of the Irish Catholics he lowered his voice, put his hand over his mouth, winked, scowled and acted in general like one creeping stealthily through some mountainous country, infested with desperadoes, and in which every tree and stone might conceal a deadly enemy.

At the stable during the long quiet winter afternoons there was little to do so we all gathered in the office, a room some fifteen by twenty with a large stove in the centre. There certain citizens of the town came daily to visit us.

In the room there would be at one time Bert the Negro; Lovett, sitting on a stool and tapping the floor with a driver's whip; myself, taking in everything and sometimes with my nose in a book; Tom Moseby, who had been a gambler on a Mississippi River boat in his young days and who always wore a large dirty white collar with a black stock; Silas Hunt, a lawyer who had no practice nor seemed to want any and who was said to be writing a book on the subject of constitutional law, a book that no one ever saw; a fat German, who was a follower of Karl Marx and who owned a large farm near the town, but who, for all his anti-capitalistic beliefs, was said to cheat ruthlessly all who had any sort of dealings with him; Billy West, who owned two race horses himself and whose wife ran the town millinery store and who was himself something of a dandy and, last of all, Judge Turner.

The judge was a short fat neatly-dressed man with a bald head, a white Vandyke beard, cold blue eyes, soft round white cheeks and extraordinarily small hands and feet. In his younger days he had a cousin, at one time a quite powerful political figure in Ohio, and after the Civil War the judge, an unsuccessful young lawyer, had managed through the cousin to get himself sent South on some sort of financial mission, to settle, I believe, certain claims covering cotton corn and other stores requisitioned or destroyed by the conquering Union armies.

It had been the great opportunity of the judge's life and he had taken shrewd advantage of it, had come near being shot in two or three southern cities but had kept his head and had, it was whispered about, well feathered his own and the cousin's nest. After it was all over and the cousin had fallen from power he had come back to his native place—after three or four years spent in Europe, lying low in fear of a threatened investigation of his operations—and had bought a large brick house with a lawn and trees and had imported a Negro man-servant from the South. He spent his time reading books and listening during the afternoon to the talk of the men of our little circle, flattering women rather grossly, drinking a good deal of raw whisky and delivering himself of rather shrewd observations on life and the men he had known and seen.

The judge had never married and indeed cared nothing for women although he fancied himself in the rôle of a gallant who could do with women as he pleased, a notion constantly fed by the reactions to his advances of the women with whom his life in the town threw him into contact—the wife of the grocer from whom he bought the supplies for his home, a fat girl with red cheeks who clerked in the dry-goods store, Billy West's wife, and several others. To all these women he was elaborately courteous, bowing before them, making pretty speeches and when no one was watching even boldly caressing them with his little fat hands. In the grocery he even pressed the hand of the merchant's wife while her lord was engaged, with his back turned, in getting a package down off a shelf, and even sometimes pinched her hips, laughing softly while she shook her head and scowled at him, but to me, for whom he had taken a fancy born of my predilection for books, he spoke of women always with contempt.

"My dislike of them is however but a peculiarity of my own nature and I would not have it influence you in the least," he explained. "The French, among whom I once lived and whose language I speak, make an art of this matter of love-making between men and women and I admire the French exceedingly. They are a wise and shrewd people and not much given to the talking of tommyrot I assure you."

The judge had, early in our acquaintance, invited me to his house where I later spent many of my evenings during that spring, drinking his whisky, listening to his talk and smoking cigarettes with him. It was the judge in fact who taught me to smoke cigarettes, a habit much looked down upon in American towns at that time, being taken as an indication of weakness and effeminacy. The judge was, however, able to carry off his own devotion to the habit because he had been in Europe, spoke several languages and most of all because he was reported to be educated. In the saloons of the town, when men congregated before the bar in the evening, the subject of cigarette smoking was often discussed. "If I ever caught a son of mine smoking one of those coffin nails I'd knock his fool head off," said a drayman. "I agree with you for all except maybe Judge Turner now," said his companion. "For him it's all right. He sets a bad example maybe, but looket! Ain't he been to college and to Paris and London and all them places? Lord, I only wish I had his education, that's all I wish."

I am in the judge's house and it is dark and stormy outside. I have dined with the Negro Bert at six in the kitchen of Nate Lovett's house and now, although it is but shortly past seven, the judge has also dined and is ready for an evening of talk. There is a large stove of the sort known as a baseburner in the room and the walls are lined with books. We sit by a small table and there is a decanter of whisky upon it. Although I am but eighteen the judge does not hesitate to invite me to help myself to the whisky. "Drink all you want. If you are the kind of a fool who makes a pig of himself you might as well find it out."

The judge talks as we drink and his talk is something new to my ears. These are not the words or thoughts of the towns, the city factories or the sports of the race tracks. All of the judge's talk is a laughing, half-cynical, half-earnest kind of confession. Were the things the judge told me of himself true? They were no doubt as true as these confessions of myself and my own relations to life I am setting down here. What I mean is that he was at least trying to inject into them the essence of truth.

I drank of the whisky sparingly, not so much through fear of being convicted of piggishness by getting drunk as from a desire to hear all the judge might have to say.

At the barn when he came there to loaf with the others during the winter afternoons the judge usually remained silent and managed always to achieve an effect of wisdom by the good-natured but cynical expression of his face and eyes. He sat with his fat white hands folded over his round neatly-waistcoated paunch and looked about with the cold little eyes that were so amazingly like the eyes of a bird. My employer, Nate Lovett, was upon his everlasting theme. "Now you just look at it. I wish the people would begin to do some thinking in this country. Why, there were six Catholics elected to this last Congress and people just sit still and say there's no harm in a Catholic." The horseman was a regular subscriber to a weekly paper that attributed all the ills of society to the growth in America of the Catholic faith and read

162

it eagerly—it was the only thing he did read—
that his own pet prejudice be properly fed and nour-
ished, and no doubt there was published somewhere a
paper that carried on an equally earnest campaign
against the Protestants. My employer went to no
church but the notion of six Catholics in the national
Congress alarmed him. The horseman declared that
the Catholics would in a short time come into absolute power in America and drew a black enough picture of the future when all of the things he so feared
had come to pass. The wheels of the factories would
stop turning, streets of towns would be unlighted,
men and women would be burned at the stake, there
would be no schools, no books accessible to the general public, we would have a tyrant king instead of a
Congress and no man who did not bow his knee to
the Pope in Rome would be safe in his bed at night.
The horseman declared he had once read a book show-
ing just the condition of affairs when the Catholics
were in power—that is to say in the Middle Ages.
Pointing the butt of his driving whip at Judge Turner
he pleaded, and never in vain, for a more learned and
scholarly substantiation of his theory. "Ain't I right
now, Judge?" he asked pleadingly. "Mind you, I
ain't setting myself up before a man who knows more
than I do and has read all the books and been everywhere, even in Rome itself, but I'll tell you something. That king, that Englishman, of the name of
Henry the Eighth, who first told the Pope at Rome
to go back to his Dago town and mind his own business was some man now, wasn't he, eh?"

And now Nate had got himself warmed up and lit
into his theme. "They say he was too free with

163

women, that King Henry. Well, what if he was?"
he cried. "I knew a man once, Jake Freer it was,
from over near Muncie Indiana, who could get more
out of a bum horse in a hard race than any man you
ever set your eyes on and he was the darndest woman-
chaser in ten states. Why, he couldn't get near a
skirt, old or young, without prancing around like a
two-year-old stud and he was forty-five if he was a
day but put him in a hard race and then you'd see the
stuff come out in him. He'd be laying back in second
or third place, let us say. Well, they gets to the upper turn and he knows he ain't got the speed to outstep
'em. What does he do? Does he give up? Not
he. He lets on to go crazy and begins to swear and
rip around. Such language! Lord a'mighty, how
he could swear! It was wonderful to hear him. He
tells them other stiffs of drivers, laying in there ahead
of him, that he's going to kill 'em or punch their eyes
out and the first you know he slides his old skate of
a horse out in front and once in front he stays there.
They don't dast to try to pass him. He scares his
own horse too I suppose but anyway he sure scares
them other drivers. Down he sails to the wire looking back over his shoulder making threats and switch-
ing his long whip around. He was a big fine-looking
man that had had his cheek laid open with a razor
in a fight with a nigger and was an ugly looking man
to see. "I'm going to whip hell outen you," he keeps
saying over his shoulder, just loud enough so the
judges can't hear him up in the stand. But them other
drivers can hear him all right.

"And then what does he do? As soon as the heat
is finished he hurries up to the stand, to the judges'

164

stand you see, pretending to be mad as a wildcat and he claims the other drivers put it up between them to foul him. That's what he does, and he talks so hard and so earnest that he half makes the judges believe it and he gets away with maybe hitting one of the other horses in the face with his whip at the upper turn and throwing him off his stride or something like that.

"Now, Judge, I ask you, wasn't he all right, if he was a woman-chaser? And that Henry the Eighth was just like him. He told the Pope to go hang himself and I'm an Englishman and once I told two Catholic stiffs the same thing. They banged out this here eye of mine but you bet I gave 'em what for, and that's just what Henry did to the Pope, now ain't it?"

At the livery barn the judge had smilingly agreed with Nate Lovett that Henry the Eighth was one of the great and noble kings of the world and had expressed unbounded admiration for Jake Freer, adding that, as far as his own reading and traveling had carried him, he had never been able to find that the Catholics when they were in absolute power all over the world had ever done anything for racing or to improve the trotting or pacing-horse breeds. "All they did," he remarked, quietly "except perhaps Francesco Gonzago, Marquis of Mantua, who did rather go in for good horses, was to build a lot of cathedrals like Chartres, Saint Mark's at Venice, Westminster Abbey, Mont St. Michel and others and to inspire the loveliest and truest art in the world. But," he said smilingly, "what good does all that do for a man like you Nate, or for anyone here in this town? You didn't know Francesco, who had a knack for fast horses, and forty cathedrals would never get you another mare for 'Will you Please' or help either you or Jake Freer to win one race, and there is at present little doubt in my own mind that the future of America lies largely with just such men as you and Jake."

At his own house as we sat together in the evenings, the judge paid me the rare compliment, always deeply appreciated by a young man, of assuming I was on the same intellectual level with himself. He smoked cigarettes and drank surprising quantities of whisky, holding each glass for a moment between his eyes and the light and making a queer clicking sound with his thin dry lips as he sat looking at it.

The man talked on whatever subject came into his mind and I remember an evening when he got on the subject of women and his own attitude toward them and the queer feeling of sadness that crept over me as he talked. Much of what he had to say I did not at that time understand but I sensed the tragedy of the man's figure as he drew for me a picture of his life.

His father had been a Presbyterian minister and a widower in the town to which the son came later to lead his own solitary life and the judge said that in his youth he remembered his father chiefly as a silent figure given to long solitary walks in fields and on country roads. "He loved my mother I fancy," the judge said. "Perhaps he was one of those rare men who can really love."

The boy had grown up, himself rather drawn away from the life of the town, and had been sent later to a college in the East, and during his first year in college his father died. There was a suspicion of suicide, although little was said about it, the man having taken an overdose of some sort of medicine given him by one of the town physicians.

It was then that the politician cousin appeared and after the funeral he talked to the younger man, telling him that a few days before his death the father had come to him and talked of the son, securing from the politician a promise that in case of his own sudden death, the lad would be looked after and given a fair chance in life. "Your father killed himself," said the cousin, a rather downright fellow who was fifteen years older than the young man he addressed. "He was in love with your mother and was also a man who believed in a future life. What he did was to spend years in prayer. He was always praying, day and night as he walked around, and in the end he convinced himself that his untiring devotion had won him so high a place in God's esteem he would be forgiven for doing away with his own life and would be admitted into Heaven to live throughout eternity with the woman he loved."

After his father's funeral young Turner had gone back to the eastern college and there the tragedy that had been long awaiting him suddenly pounced.

During his boyhood, he explained, he had been rather a solitary, spending his time in reading books and in playing on a piano that had belonged to his mother and that his father, who was also devoted to music, had taught him to play. "The boys of the town," he said, in speaking of that portion of his life, "were not of my sort and I could not understand them.

167

At school the larger boys often beat me and they encouraged the younger boys in treating me with contempt. I could not play baseball or football, physical pain of any sort made me ill, I would begin crying when anyone spoke harshly to me, and then I developed a kind of viciousness in myself too. Being unable to beat the other boys with my fists and having even at that early age read a great many books, particularly books of history, with which my father's library were filled, I spent my days and nights dreaming of all sorts of sly deviltry.

"For one thing," the judge went on, laughing and rubbing his hands together, "I thought a great deal of poisoning some of the boys at the school. At the recess time we were all gathered in a large yard given over to the boys as a playground. There was the yard without any grass and at one side, by a high board fence, a long wooden shed into which we went to perform certain necessary functions of the body. The board fence separated our play place from one given over to the recreation of the girls.

"The walls of our own shed and our side of the fence itself were covered with crude drawings and scrawled sentences expressing the sensual dreams of crude and adolescent youth and these were allowed by the authorities to remain. The place filled me with unspeakable revulsion as did also much of the talk of the boys and I shall remember always something that happened to me there. A great loutish boy is standing at the door of our shed into which I am at that moment forced by nature to go and is gazing at the sky over the high board fence that separates us from

168

the playground of the girls. His eyes are heavy with stupid sensuality. From beyond the fence comes the shrill laughter of the little girls. Suddenly, as I am about to pass—a small creature I was then with delicate hands and at that time I believe with small delicate features—suddenly and quite without apparent cause he raises a large heavy hand and strikes me full in the face, so that the blood runs in a stream from my nose, and then, without a word to me, shrinking in terror against the fence on which the horrible pictures and words are scrawled and mingling my blood with tears, he goes calmly away. He is quite cheerful in fact, as though some deep want of his nature had suddenly been satisfied.

"I had been reading a history of Italy; a most flam-boyant book it was, filled with the doings of vicious and crafty men—I now suppose they must have been, vicious and crafty but then how I delighted in them! My father's being a minister had I presume turned my mind to the Church and how I wished he had been a great and powerful cardinal or a pope of the fifteenth century instead of what he was! I had dreamed of him as a Cosmo de Medici and myself as that Duke Francisco who succeeded Cosmo.

"What a grand time in which to live I thought that must have been and how I loved the book in my father's library that described the life of those days. In the book were such sentences! Some of them I remember even to this day and in my bed at night, even yet sometimes, I lie laughing with delight at the thought of the fanfaronading march of the words across the pages of that book. 'Italian vitality had subsided into the repose of the tomb. The winged arrow of death entered his heart. The hour of vengeance had struck.'

"I will read you something from the book itself," said the judge, pouring himself another glass of whisky, holding it for a moment between his eyes and the light and then, after drinking, going to a shelf from which he took a book in a red cover. After turning the pages for a few minutes and having lighted himself a fresh cigarette he read: "'The emperor Charles the Fifth placed Cosmo de Medici on the ducal chair of Florence and Pope Pius Fifth granted him the title of grand duke of Tuscany. He was a cruel and perfidious tyrant.

"'Cosmo was succeeded by Francisco, a duke who governed through the instrumentality of the poisoned cup and the dagger, and who lapped blood with the greed of a bloodhound. He married Bianca Cabello, the daughter of a nobleman of Venice. She was the wife of a young Florentine. Francisco saw her, and, inflamed by her marvelous beauty, invited her and her husband to his palace, and assassinated her husband. His own wife died at just that time, probably by poison, and the grand duke married Bianca. His brother, the Cardinal Ferdinando, displeased with the union, presented them each with a goblet of poisoned wine, and they sank into the grave together.'

"Aha!" cried Judge Turner, looking over the top of the book at me and laughing gleefully. "There you are, you see. That was myself in my boyhood, that young Francisco. In my fancy I succeeded, when there was no one about, when I was walking alone along the sidewalks of this very town or when I had got into my bed at night, I succeeded I say in making the great metamorphosis. In the books in my father's library were many pictures of the streets of old Italian and Spanish cities. There was one I sharply remember. Two young bloods, with cloaks over their shoulders and with swords swinging at their sides, are approaching each other along a street. Two or three monks, a man seated on the back of a donkey going along a narrow roadway, a great stone bridge in the far distance, a bridge spanning perhaps a deep dark gulf between high mountain peaks, peaks faintly seen amid clouds and in the foreground, near the two young men and dominating the whole scene, a great cathedral done in the glorious Gothic style that I myself later, in my real flesh and blood life, so loved and bowed down before at Chartres in France.

"And there was I, in fancy you understand, one of the two young men walking in that glorious street and not frightened little Arthur Turner, son of a sad and discouraged Presbyterian minister in an Ohio town. There was the metempsychosis. I was Francisco before he had succeeded Cosmo and had become himself the great and charmingly wicked duke sitting in his ducal chair, and long before he became enamored of the lovely Bianca. Every day I went into my own little room in my father's house and got out a sword of wood I had fashioned from a lath and buckled it on. I had got one of my father's coats from a closet and this, serving me as a cloak, I imagined it of the finest Florentine stuff, a cloak of such stuff as would become the shoulders of one who belonged to the great Medici family and who was to sit in the proud ducal chair of Florence. Up and down the room I went

171

and below my father, the sad long-faced man, had become in my fancy the great Cosmo himself. We were in our ducal palace and cardinals in their red cloaks, princes, captains of armies, ambassadors and other princely personages were waiting at the door for a word with the great Cosmo.

"Welladay! My own time would come. For the present I was concerning myself with the study of poisons. On a little table in my room I had a collection of various small receptacles, an old saltcellar with a broken top, two small teacups, an empty baking-powder can and other small vessels, found in the street or stolen from our kitchen, and into these I had put salt, flour, pepper, ginger and other spices taken also by stealth from the kitchen. I mixed and remixed, making various colored powders which I folded into small packets or dampened and rolled into little balls which I concealed about my person, and then went forth into the street, to visit in fancy other palaces or to poison, or run through with my sword, people who were enemies of our house. What beautifully wicked men and women all about me and with what suavity we greeted each other! How deeply we loved and served—to the very death—our friends and how quietly crafty and urbane we were with our enemies! Oh, I loved then the word urbane. What a glorious word, I thought. At that time, as the young Francisco, I was determined that if my craftiness could raise me to the great office of pope I would take for myself the name Urbane, adding the 'e' to a name already taken by some of them.

"These were my dreams, and then, well I was compelled to go to the town school and sit sometimes in

that horrible shed facing the crude and terrible scrawl-
ings on the walls and to become also the victim of the
crude outbreaks of my companions.

"Until one day in the spring. I had gone for a
walk with my father in the late afternoon after school
was dismissed and we were botanizing, as my father
was fond of doing, both for his own edification and
also I suppose in order to further his son's education.
In a meadow at the edge of a strip of woodland into
which we were passing I found a white mushroom
with which I ran to father. 'Throw it away,' he
cried. 'It is an Amanita Phalloides, the Destroying
Angel. A bit of it no larger than a mustard seed
would destroy your life.'

"We returned to our own house and sat down for
the evening meal with the words 'Amanita Phalloides'
ringing in my ears and with the round bell-like shape
of the Amanita Phalloides dancing before my eyes.
It was white, of a strange glowing whiteness, sug-
gesting I thought not the death of some common man
of low degree but that of a prince or a great duke. It
was so Francisco and Bianca must have looked, I
thought, when in the words of the flamboyant writer
of the book in my father's library, they 'sank into the
grave together.' There must have been just that very
white metallic pallor on their cheeks. What a picture
of that sinking I had in my fancy. It was not just a
grave, a mere dirty hole scooped out of the ground,
as graves were wont to be in our Ohio town. No
indeed! An opening had been made in the earth it
is true but this had been entirely rimmed with flowers
and was filled with a liquid, a soft purple perfumed
liquid. And so into the grave went the bodies of my-

173

self as Francisco and of my lovely paramour, Bianca. The weight of our golden robes made us sink slowly into the soft purple flood and as we sank from sight music from the lips of all the fair children of the aristocracy of Florence was wafted far over fair fields, while back of the massed children in white stood also— upon a kind of green eminence at the foot of a majestic mountain—all the great lords, dukes, cardinals and other dignitaries of our imperial city.

"It was so that, as the grown-up Francisco, I was to die but I was yet alive and there was the Amanita Phalloides—later when I grew older I laughed to myself and told myself it should have been a Phallus Impudicus—there it was lying on the grass in the meadow at the edge of the wood. I had placed it carefully there at the command of my father and had, oh very carefully, marked the spot. One went along the main road leading out of town, to the south, to a certain bridge and across a meadow by a cowpath, climbed a fence, walked a certain number of steps along a rail fence beside a young wheat field, where elders grew, crossed another meadow and came to the edge of the wood. There was a stump near which grew a bush and even as I sat with father at our evening meal and as our housekeeper, a fat silent old woman with false teeth that rattled sometimes as she talked, even as she served the evening meal I was repeating to myself a certain formula I had made on our homeward journey. One hundred and nineteen steps along the cowpath in the meadow, ninety-three steps along the fence in the shadow of the elders, two hundred and six steps across the second meadow to the stump and my prize.

"I had determined to get the Amanita Phalloides on that very night after my father and our housekeeper had gone to sleep and although I was terribly frightened at the prospect of the tramp along lonely country roads and across fields, that I imagined were at night infested by strange and ferocious beasts lying in wait ready to destroy, I did not think of giving up for that reason.

"And so in fact in the middle of that very night, when all in our house and in the town were asleep, I went. Buckling on my wooden sword and creeping silently downstairs I let myself out at the kitchen door, having first supplied myself with matches and two or three bits of candle from a kitchen shelf.

"Oh, how I suffered on that journey and how determined I was! When I had got out from among the silent terrifying houses and had come nearly to the place where I was to turn off the highroad two men on horseback passed and I hid myself, lying on my belly, white and silent, in a ditch at the side of the road. 'They are desperadoes going forth to kill,' I told myself.

"And then they were gone and I could no longer hear the tramp of their horses and there was the trip to be made across the fields, recounting the steps as I had counted them during the homeward journey that afternoon with my father. During the walk homeward that afternoon both father and myself were muttering to ourselves, he praying no doubt that when he had taken his own life God would admit him into Heaven and into the company of the woman he loved and I counting steadily 'eighty-six, eighty-seven, eighty-eight,' counting steadily the steps that would lead me again to the Amanita Phalloides, to the Destroying Angel, with which I dreamed I might take many lives.

"I got my prize by the aid of the matches and the bits of candle and after a good deal of nervous fumbling about, creeping on my hands and knees in the wet grass," said the old judge laughing in his peculiarly bitter and at the same time half-jolly way. "I got it and ran all the way home, imagining every bush and every deep shadow on the road and in the fields might contain man or beast lying in wait ready to destroy me. Then later I managed without the old housekeeper knowing to dry it on a small shelf at the back of our kitchen stove and after it was thoroughly dried I powdered it and putting the horrible powder I had concocted into papers, carried them off with me to school.

"Many of the boys of our school lived at a distance and carried their luncheons and I fancied myself going nonchalantly into the hallway where the luncheon pails were left standing in a row and sprinkling the powders over their contents. As for the boys who went home at the noon hour—well, you see I had read in one of the books in my father's library of a certain elegant lady of Pisa who once cut a peach, handing half of it to a gallant she wished to destroy and herself eating the other quite harmless half. I thought I might work out some such scheme, using an apple instead of a peach and working some of the poison under the skin of one side with a pin point."

The judge had been laughing, I thought in a somewhat nervous manner, as he told me the above tale of his youth. "To be sure I never really intended to poison anyone," he said. "Well now, did I or did I not? I really can't say. I had achieved however, through the accidental discovery of the qualities of the Amanita Phalloides, a certain new attitude toward myself. As I went about with the little poison packets in my pockets I felt suddenly a new kind of respect for myself. I felt power in myself and something quite new to the other boys must have crept at about this time into the expression of my eyes. I was no longer frightened and did not shrink away or begin crying when one of the bullies of the school approached me at the recess time now and—could it be true?—I felt they were suddenly afraid of me. The thought filled me with a queer sort of joy and I walked boldly about the school yard, not strutting but at the same time shrinking from no one. There was at that time a report current among the boys—I do not know where it came from but it was believed and I did not deny it—that I carried a loaded pistol about in my pocket."

The judge—and by the way his title was a quite spurious one given him by his fellow-townsmen late in his life because he had been a lawyer, because he had money, had been in the government service and had been to Europe—the judge now told me of his experience as a young man in college. Now that I come to think of it he no doubt did not tell me at one time all the things I am here setting down. During that winter and spring I spent a great many evenings in his company and he talked continuously of himself, of his cheating the men of the South to get money for himself and cousin, of his wanderings in Europe, of the men he had met at home and abroad and of what he had concluded concerning men's lives, their motives and impulses and what he thought it would be best for me to do to make my own life as happy as possible.

He had returned at the end of his own life to live out his days alone in his native place because, as he said, one had in the end to accept his own time, place and people, whatever they might be, and that one gained nothing by wandering about the earth among strangers. During his middle years he had thought he would live out his life in some European town or city, in Chartres where, while he lived there for some months, he was all tender with love and regard for the men of a bygone age who had built the lovely cathedral at that place; at Oxford where he had spent some months wandering filled with joy among the old colleges and under the great trees that line the river Thames; in London where he got to have a great respect for the half-stupid but as he said wholly dignified self-respect of the young Englishmen he saw walking in the Strand or along Piccadilly; or in some more colorful town of the south like Madrid or Florence. The French and Paris he declared he could not understand, although he wanted very much to understand and be understood by them, as he felt they were in a way more like himself than any of the others of the Europeans he had seen. "I learned to speak their language quite fluently," he said, "but they never really took me into their lives. The men I met, painters, writers and fellows of that sort, went about with me, borrowed my money and tried continually to sell me inferior paintings but I always realized they were laughing up their sleeves, and just what about I couldn't make out or perhaps I shouldn't have cared."

In the end the judge had come home to his Ohio town and had settled down to his books, his whisky and his companionship with such men as Nate Lovett, Billy West, and the others. "We are what we are, we Americans," he said, "and we had better stick to our knitting. Anyway," he added, "people are nice here as far as I have been able to observe and although they are filled with stupid prejudices and are fools, the common people, workers and the like, such as the men of this town, wherever you find them, are about the nicest folk one ever finds."

As for the judge's experience as a young college man and the sort of tragedy that then came and that no doubt set the tone of his after life, it was stupid enough. With his mind filled with the thoughts taken from the books in his father's library and after a boyhood of such loneliness and brooding as I have here described he went to college filled with high hopes but was there doomed to live as lonely an existence as he had lived in his home town. The young men of the college, given for the most part to the cultivation of athletic sports and to going about to parties and dances with the girls of a near-by city, did not take to young Turner and he did not take to them.

And then during his second year something happened. There was a young man in one of the upper classes, an athlete of note but at the same time an earnest student, toward whom the Ohio boy's fancy now turned. It was an entirely sentimental affair, as the man afterward explained and might have done him no harm had he been content never to give it any kind of expression.

He did however near the end of his second year try to give it expression. For weeks he had been going about, much like a young girl in love, thinking constantly of the athlete, of his splendid rugged figure fine eyes and quick active mind and of how wonderful it would be if he could have an intimate friendship with such a fellow. He dreamed of walks the two might take together in the evenings under the elms that grew on the campus. "I thought he would take my arm or I would take his and we would walk and talk," Judge Turner said, and I remember that as he spoke he got out of his chair and walked about the room and that his small white hands played nervously over the front of his coat. He seemed not to want to face me as he told the more vital part of his tale but going behind my chair walked up and down the room at my back, and I remember how, although I was then but a boy, I knew he suffered and wanted to put his arms about me as he talked but did not dare. My own heart was filled with sadness so that unknown perhaps to him tears came in my eyes and what part of his tragedy and his words I did not understand I am sure I did dimly sense the meaning of.

He had, it happened, gone about for months thinking of the older fellow of his college as one much like himself but blessed with a stronger body, greater ability to make his way in the world and no doubt also wanting to give something of himself, or something beautiful outside himself that would represent some spirit of himself, to another man. Once young Turner went to a near-by city and spent a whole afternoon going from shop to shop trying to find some bit of jewelry, a painting or something of the sort he himself thought lovely and that would be within the limits of his own slender means that he might in secret send to the man he so admired.

"For women I did not care," the judge said huskily. "To tell the truth I was afraid of women. In a relationship made with a woman one, I thought, risked too much. It might be quite altogether perfect or it might be just nothing at all. To tell the truth I did not then have and never have had enough assurance of fineness in myself to make it possible for me to approach a woman with the object of becoming her lover and I was not then and never have been a strong lustful man and I had, even at that time, put all thought of anything very definite ever happening between myself and a woman utterly aside.

"I had put the thought aside, and had taken up this other, you see. Between myself and the young athlete I had created in fancy a relation that would never attempt to come to any sort of physical expression. We would live, I dreamed, each his own life, each gathering what beauty might be possible from the great outer world and bringing it as a prize to the other. There would be this man I loved and of whom I asked nothing and toward whom my whole impulse would be forever just to give and give to the very top of my bent.

"You understand how it was, or rather of course you do not understand now but some day it may be you will," said the voice coming from the thin lips of the small fat man walking up and down the room behind me in the house in Ohio. "I did a foolish thing," said the voice. "One day I wrote a note to the man telling something of the dream that had been in my mind and as I had nothing else to send I went to a florist's and sent him a great bunch of beautiful roses.

"I got no answer to the note but later he showed it about and all during the rest of my days at the school —and out of a kind of blind determination I stayed on there until I graduated and had got my degree, my expenses after my father's death being paid by my cousin—during all the rest of my days at the school I was looked upon generally as a—perhaps you do not even know the meaning of the word—I was looked upon as a pervert.

"There was another and more vulgar word, a word I had seen on the walls of the shed and on the board fence when I was a schoolboy that was also shouted at me. Like my father before me I, in my trouble, took to walking in the streets and in lonely places at night. The word would be shouted at me from the darkness or from the steps of a house as I stumbled along in the darkness and I had not then, as I had when I was a lad, the satisfaction of thinking of myself as another Francisco, as one who could resort to poison powders to assert his own supremacy and to reëstablish himself with himself.

"I was simply determined I would finish my days in college and would not follow my father's footsteps in taking my own life—having then and always having had a queer sort of respect, do you see, for life as it manifested itself in my own body—that I would finish my days in that place and that I would then, at the first opportunity, get hold of enough money to make myself respected among the men with whom and in whose company I would in all likelihood have to live out my days.

"I conceived, do you see, of money-making as the only sure method to win respect from the men of the modern world and as for you, my lad, if you have sensibilities as I suppose you have or I should not have taken the trouble to invite you to my house—as for you, my lad, if an opportunity comes to you, as it did to me when my cousin got me sent South, you had better take advantage of it," said the judge, coming from behind my chair and standing before me to pour himself another glass of the whisky which he drank this time I noticed without the customary little ceremony of holding it for a moment between his eyes and the light.

I thought, or I may fancy I then thought, that the judge's bright birdlike eyes were clouded and looked tired as he said these last words and that his hands as he poured the whisky trembled a little but perhaps the notion but springs from my more mature fancy playing over a dramatic moment in life.

And at any rate he came to loaf away the next afternoon at the stable and was as he always had been, sitting in silence, listening to the talk that went round and folding his fat little hands over his neatly-waistcoated paunch. And when he spoke he, as always, concealed under so thick a coat of good-natured toleration what sarcasm may have lurked in his words that he won and seemed always to hold the respect of all of his hearers.

NOTE III

DEFINITION

*"A really high-class horse is one that is consistent,
game, intelligent, gentle, obedient, courageous, and
at all times willing and able to go any route with
weight up and maintain a high rate of speed and
overcome all ordinary difficulties under adverse
conditions.*

"Remember that horses are not machines."
—*Trainer and Cloeker's Handicap (strictly private).*

A NARROW beam of yellow light against the satin surface of purplish gray wood, wood become soft of
texture, touched with these delicate shades of color.
The light from above falls straight down the face of
a great heavy beam of the wood. Or is it marble
rather than wood, marble touched also by the delicate
hand of time? I am perhaps dead and in my grave.
No, it cannot be a grave. Would it not be wonderful
if I had died and been buried in a marble sepulchre,
say on the summit of a high hill above a city in which
live many beautiful men and women? It is a grand
notion and I entertain it for a time. What have I
done to be buried so splendidly? Well, never mind
that. I have always been one who wanted a great
deal of love, admiration and respect from others without having to go to all the trouble of deserving it.
I am buried magnificently in a marble sepulchre cut

into the side of a large hill, near the top. On a certain day my body was brought hither with great pomp. Music played, women and children wept and strong men bowed their heads. Now on feast days young men and women come up the hillside to look through a small glass opening left in the side of my burial place. It must be through the opening the yellow light comes. The young men who come up the hillside are wishing they could be like me, and the young and beautiful women are all wishing I were still alive and that I might be their lover.

How splendid! What have I done? The last thing I remember I was working at that place where so many kegs of nails had to be rolled down an incline. I was full of beer too. What happened after that? Did I save a besieged city, kill a dragon like Saint George, drive snakes out of the land like Saint Patrick, inaugurate a new and better social system, or what could I have done?

I am somewhere in a huge place. Perhaps I am standing in that great cathedral at Chartres, the cathedral that Judge Turner told me about when I was a lad and that I myself long afterward saw and that became for me as it has been for many other men and women the beauty shrine of my life. It may be that I am standing in that great place at midnight alone. It cannot be that there is any one with me for I feel very lonely. A feeling of being very small in the presence of something vast has taken possession of me. Can it be Chartres, the Virgin, the woman, God's woman?

What am I talking about? I cannot be in the cathedral at Chartres or buried splendidly in a marble sepulchre on a hillside above a magnificent city. I am an American and if I am dead my spirit must now be in a large half-ruined and empty factory, a factory with cracks in the walls where the work of the builders was scamped, as nearly all building was scamped in my time.

It cannot be I am in the presence of the Virgin. Americans do not believe in either Virgins or Venuses. Americans believe in themselves. There is no need of gods now but if the need arises Americans will manufacture many millions of them, all alike. They will label them "Keep smiling" or "Safety first" and go on their way, and as for the woman, the Virgin, she is the enemy of our race. Her purpose is not our purpose. Away with her!

The beam of wood I see is just a beam of wood. It was cut in a forest and brought to the factory to support a wall that had begun to give way. No one touched it with careless hurried hands and so it aged as you see, quite beautifully—as trees themselves age. All about me are broken wheels. In the factory the great steam-driven wheels are forever still now.

Broken dreams, ends of thoughts, a stifled feeling within my chest.

Aha, you Stephenson, Franklin, Fulton, Bell, Edison —you heroes of my Industrial Age, you men who have been the gods of the men of my day—is your day over so soon? "In the end," I am telling myself, "all of your triumphs come to the dull and meaningless absurdity, of say a clothespin factory. There have been sweeter men in old times, half forgotten now, who will be remembered after you are forgotten. The Virgin too, will be remembered after you are forgotten.

186

Would it not be amusing if Chartres continued to stand after you are forgotten?"

Is it not absurd? Because I do not want to work in a warehouse and roll kegs, because I do not want to work in a factory anywhere I must needs go getting gaudy and magnificent and try to blow all factories away with a breath of my fancy. My fancy climbs up and up.

Democracy shall spread itself out thinner and thinner, it shall come to nothing but empty mouthings in the end. Everywhere, all over the earth, shall be the dreary commercial and material success of, say the later Byzantine Empire. In the West and after the great dukes, the kings and the popes, the commoners —who were not commoners after all but only stole the name—are having their day. The shrewd little money-getters with the cry "democracy" on their lips shall rule for a time and then the real commoners shall come—and that shall be the worst time of all. Oh, the futile little vanity of the workers who have forgotten the cunning of hands, who have long let machines take the place of the cunning of hands!

And the tired men of the arts. Oh, the cunning smart little men of the arts of New York and Chicago! Painters making advertising designs for soap, painters making portraits of bankers' wives, story-tellers striving wearily to "make" the *Saturday Evening Post* or to be revolutionists in the arts. Artists everywhere striving for what?

Respectability perhaps—to call attention to themselves perhaps.

They will get—a Ford. On holidays they may go see the great automobile races on the speedway at

Indianapolis Indiana. Not for them the flashing thoroughbreds or the sturdy trotters and pacers. Not for them freedom, laughter. For them machines.

Long ago that Judge Turner had corrupted my mind. He played me a hell of a trick. I have been going about trying to have thoughts. What a fool I have been! I have read many books of history, many stories of men's lives. Why did I not go to college and get a safe education? I might have worked my way through and got my mind fixed in a comfortable mold. There is no excuse for me. I shall have to pay for my lack of a proper training.

In the next room to the one in which I am lying two men are talking.

FIRST VOICE. "He took straw, ground it, put it into some kind of rubber composition. The whole was mixed up together and subjected to an immense hydraulic pressure. It came out a tough kind of composition that can be made to look like wood. It can be grained like wood. He will get rich. I tell you he is one of the great minds of the age."

SECOND VOICE. "We shall have prohibition after a while and then you'll see how it will turn out. You can't down the American mind. Some fellow will make a drink, a synthetic drink. It won't cost much to make. Perhaps it can be made out of crude oil like gasoline and then the Standard will take him up. He'll get rich. We Americans can't be put down, I'll tell you that."

FIRST VOICE. "There is a man in New York makes car wheels out of paper. It is ground, I suppose, and made into a kind of mush and then is subjected to an immense hydraulic pressure. The wheels look like iron."

SECOND VOICE. "Do you suppose he paints them black like iron?"

FIRST VOICE. "It's a great age we live in. You can't down machinery. I read a book by Mark Twain. He knocked theories cold, I'll tell you what. He made out all life was just a great machine."

.　.　.　.　.　.　.　.

Where am I? Am I dreaming or am I awake? It seems to me that I am somewhere in a great empty place. I shall have one of my terrible fits of depression if I am not careful now. Sometimes I walk gayly along the streets and talk to men and women gayly but there are other times when I am so depressed that all the muscles of my body ache. I am like one on whose back a great beast sits. Now it seems to me I am in a huge empty place. Has the roof of a factory in which I was at work at night fallen in? There is a long shaft of yellow light falling down a beam of wood or marble.

Thoughts flitting, an effort to awaken out of dreams, voices heard, voices talking somewhere in the distance, the figures of men and women I have known flashing in and out of darkness. There is a tiny faint voice speaking: "The money-makers will grow weary and disgusted with their own money-making and labor shall have lost all faith, all sense of the cunning of the hand. The factory hands shall rule. What a mess it will be!"

.　.　.　.　.　.　.　.

Where am I? I am in a bed somewhere in a room in a workers' rooming house. Two young mechanics live in the next room and now they are getting out of bed and are talking cheerfully. Once on cold nights monks awoke in cold cells in monasteries and muttered prayers to God. Now in a cold room two young mechanics proclaim their faith in new gods.

Words in a brain trying to come into consciousness out of heavy sleep. "Service! They make a point of service," says one of the young men's voices. My brain, a voice in my own brain, chattering: "The woman who had been taken in adultery came to wash with her hands the tired feet of the Christ. She wiped his feet with her long hair and poured precious ointment upon them." A distorted thought born of the effort to awaken from a heavy dream: "Many men and women are going along a street. They all have long hair and bear vessels of precious ointment. They are going to wash the feet of a Rockefeller, of 'Bet a million' Gates, of a Henry Ford or the son of a Henry Ford, the gods of the new day."

And now the dream again. Again the great empty place. I cannot breathe. There is a great black bell without a tongue, swinging silently in darkness. It swings and swings, making a great arch and I await silent and frightened. Now it stops and descends slowly. I am terrified. Can nothing stop the great descending iron bell? It stops and hangs for a moment and now it drops suddenly and I am a prisoner under the great iron bell.

NOTE IV

WITH a frantic effort I am awake. I am in my laborers' rooming house and Nora, who is my friend, has been trying to clean the wall paper in my room. She takes bits of bread dough and rubs the walls. The paper on the walls was originally yellow but time and coal soot have made it almost black. Light is struggling in through a window, wiped clean by Nora but yesterday, but already nearly black again. The morning sun is playing on the wall.

Nora's lover does not come home although he writes whenever his ship comes to port. The ship carries ore from Duluth to Chicago and one may be quite sure he does not sleep much of the time in a clean berth nor smell in his nostrils the clean sea air, as I represented things to Nora when I wanted her to take better care of my room. Nora has tried. That idea of mine was a purely literary one but it has made Nora and myself friends.

She fancies the notion of having someone to care for, to do things for, and so do I. It is a literary triumph for me and I instinctively like literary triumphs. We are much together and as the time is a black one for me she makes life livable. Nora is a true modern, not fussy, not making a great brag and bluster about it as did so many of the "moderns" in the arts I was to see later in New York. In my day I was to see a time when if a man wrote ten honest paragraphs or painted three honest paintings he immediately set himself up as a persecuted saint and wept if Mr. Sumner of New York or the Watch and Ward Club of Boston did not descend upon him. Most "moderns" of the arts I was later to see regretted the day of the passing of the Inquisition. They did not hanker to be burned at the stake but would have loved having it done to them, as in the moving picture, with some sort of mechanical cold flame. As for Nora she wanted to know all I thought, all I felt. She was not afraid I would "ruin" her. She knew how to look out for herself.

In the evenings we went out to walk together, sometimes going to the docks and sitting together while the moon came up over the waters of the lake and sometimes going to what was called the better part of town to walk under trees in a park or along a residence street.

There was no love-making for Nora's mind was turned toward her sailorman and I was ill. My body was well and strong most of the time, but there was an illness within.

My mind dwelt too much of the time in darkness. I had already worked in a dozen factories and much of the time it had been with me as it was with Judge Turner when he was a boy in an Ohio town. Nature had compelled him to go into a vile shed on the walls of which were scrawled sentences that revolted his soul and the necessity of keeping my body going—a necessity I myself did not understand but that was there, in me—had compelled me, time and again, to go into the door of a factory as an employee.

I talked constantly to Nora of the thoughts in my mind. There was a kind of understanding between us. I did not try to come between her and her sailor-man and I had the privilege of saying to her what I pleased.

What a mixed-up affair! I was always pretending to Nora that I loved men and was a great mixer with men while at the same time I was dreaming of having a fight with my fists with the athlete at the warehouse.

In the late afternoon I went along a street home-ward bound, filled with beer and imagining a scene. In my wanderings I had known personally two fighters, Bill McCarthy, a lightweight, and Harry Walters, a heavy. Once I was second for Harry Walters in a fight with a Negro in a barn near Toledo, Ohio. Sports came out from the city to the barn near a river and when Harry began to lose I was shrewd enough to spread the alarm that the police were coming so that everyone fled and Harry was saved a beating at the hands of the black.

I remembered the blows Harry had struck and that the black had struck and the blows I had seen Billy McCarthy strike. The black had a feint and a cross that confused Harry and that landed the black's left every time full on Harry's chin. Each time it landed Harry became a little more groggy but he could not avoid the blow. And I remembered how the black smiled each time as it landed. He had two rows of gold-covered teeth and his smile was like Jack Johnson's golden smile.

I went along factory streets fancying myself the great black, possessing the knowledge of the black's feint and cross and with the athlete of the warehouse standing before me.

Aha! There is a slight rocking movement of the

body, just so. The head moves slowly and rhythmically like the head of a snake when it is about to strike. Oh, for a long row of yellow gold-crowned teeth to glisten in the mouth when one smiles the golden smile in factory streets, in factories themselves or, most of all, when in a fight, when about to knock an athlete who works with one on a certain platform, "for a goal," as we used to say among us fighters—an athlete on a platform and with three or four large heavy Swede teamsters standing looking on and smiling also their own slow smiles.

Patience now! One gets the body and the head moving just so, in opposite directions, with opposing rhythm—a sort of counterpoint, as it were—and then the golden smile comes and, quickly, shiftily, the feint with the right for the belly followed with lightning quickness by the left, crossed to the chin.

Oh, for a powerful left! "I would give freely and willingly all the chances I possess of being buried with great pomp in a marble sepulchre on a hillside above a magnificent city for a powerful left," I think each evening as I go home from work.

And all the time pretending to Nora and myself that I am one who loves mankind! Love indeed! Nora who wished to make happy the one man she understood and with whom she was to live was the lover, not I.

For me the athlete, poor innocent one, has become a symbol.

NOTE V

IN the many factories where I have worked most men talked vilely to their fellows and long afterward I was to begin to understand that a little. It is the impotent man who is vile. His very impotence has made him vile and in the end I was to understand that when you take from man the cunning of the hand, the opportunity to constantly create new forms in materials, you make him impotent. His maleness slips imperceptibly from him and he can no longer give himself in love, either to work or to women. "Standardization! Standardization!" was to be the cry of my age and all standardization is necessarily a standardization in impotence. It is God's law. Women who choose childlessness for themselves choose also impotence—perhaps to be the better companions for the men of a factory, a standardization age. To live is to create constantly new forms: with the body in living children; in new and more beautiful forms carved out of materials; in the creation of a world of the fancy; in scholarship; in clear and lucid thought; and those who do not live die and decay and from decay always a stench arises.

These the thoughts of a time long after the one of which I am now writing. One cannot think of the figure of a single man as being in himself to blame but as the man named Ford of Detroit has done more than any other man of my day to carry standardization to its logical end might he also not come to be looked upon as the great killer of his age? To make impotent is surely to kill. And there is talk of making him President. How fitting! Tamerlane, who specialized in the killing of men's bodies but who tells in his autobiography how he was always desirous that all living men under him retain their manhood and self-respect, was the ruler of the world in his age. Tamerlane for the ancients. Ford for the moderns.

In our age why should we not all have houses alike, all men and women clad alike (I am afraid we shall have a bad time managing the women), all food alike, all the streets in all of our cities alike? Surely individuality is ruinous to an age of standardization. It should at once and without mercy be crushed out. Let us give all workers larger and larger salaries but let us crush out of them at once all flowering of individualities. It can be done. Let us arise in our might.

And let us put at our head the man who has done in his own affairs what we are all so universally agreed should everywhere be done, the man who has made standardization the fetish of his life.

Books may be standardized—they are already almost that; painting may be standardized—it has often been done, and the standardization of poetry will be easy. Already I know a man who is working on a machine for the production of poetry. One feeds into it the letters of the alphabet and out comes poetry and one may pull various levers for the production of poems either of the *vers libre* sort or poetry in the classic style.

Arise, men of my age! Under the banner of the

new age we shall have a great machine moving slowly down a street and depositing cement houses to the right and left as it goes, like a diarrhœic elephant. All the young Edisons will enlist under the banner of a Ford. We shall have all the great minds of our age properly employed making car wheels out of waste newspapers and synthetic wines out of crude oils. I am told by intelligent men who were soldiers in the World War that in all the world before the war standardization had been carried to the highest pitch by the Germans but now the Germans have been defeated. May it not be that we Americans have all along been intended by God to be the nation that will carry highest the banner of the New Age?

NOTE VI

But I wander from my subject to leap into the future, to become a prophet, and I have no prophet's beard. In reality I am thinking of a certain young man who once came rushing, full of vitality and health, into a mechanical age and of what happened to him and to the men among whom he worked.

There was in the factories where I worked and where the efficient Ford type of man was just beginning his dull reign this strange and futile outpouring of men's lives in vileness through their lips. Ennui was at work. The talk of the men about me was not Rabelaisian. In old Rabelais there was the salt of infinite wit and I have no doubt the Rabelaisian flashes that came from our own Lincoln, Washington and the others had point and a flare to them.

But in the factories and in army camps!

Into my own consciousness, as I, a young man wishing vaguely to mature, walked in a factory street wishing childishly for a golden smile and a wicked left to cross over to the chin of some defender of the new age there was burned the memory of the last place in which I had worked before I had come to the warehouse to roll the kegs of nails.

It was a bicycle factory where I was employed as an assembler. With some ten or twelve other men I worked at a bench in a long room facing a row of win-

198

dows. We assembled the parts that were brought to us by boys from other departments of the factory and put the bicycles together. There was such and such a screw to go into such and such a screw hole, such and such a nut to go on such and such a bolt. As always in the modern factory nothing ever varied and within a week any intelligent quick-handed man could have done the work with his eyes closed. One turned certain screws, tightened certain bolts, whirled a wheel, fastened on certain foot pedals and passed the work on to the next man. Outside the window I faced there was a railroad track lined on one side by factory walls and the other by what had started to be a stone quarry. The stone of this quarry had not, I presume, turned out to be satisfactory and the hole was being filled with rubbish carted from various parts of the city and all day carts arrived, dumped their loads—making each time a little cloud of dust—and over the dump wandered certain individuals, men and women who were looking among the rubbish for bits of treasure, bottles I fancy and bits of cloth and iron that could later be sold to junk men.

For three months I had worked at the place and listened to the talk of my companions and then I had fled. The men seemed everlastingly anxious to assert their manhood, to make it clear to their fellows that they were potent men able to do great deeds in the realms of the flesh and all day I stood beside a little stand-like bench, on which the frame of the bicycle was stuck upside down, tightening nuts and screws and listening to the men, the while I looked from their faces out the window to the factory walls and the rubbish heap. An unmarried man had been on the evening

before to a certain house in a certain street and there
had happened between himself and a woman what he
now wished to talk about and to describe with infinite
care in putting in all the details.   What an undignified
stallion he made of himself!   He had his moment, was
allowed his moment by the others and then another,
a married man, took up the theme, also boastfully.
There were days as I worked in that place when I became physically ill and other days when I cursed all
the gods of my age that had made men—who in another age might have been farmers, shepherds or
craftsmen—these futile fellows, ever more and more
loudly proclaiming their potency as they felt the age
of impotency asserting itself in their bodies.

In the bicycle factory I had repeatedly told the other
men that I was subject to sick headaches and I used to
go often to a window, throw it open and lean out, closing my eyes and trying to create in fancy a world in
which men lived under bright skies, drank wine, loved
women and with their hands created something of lasting value and beauty and seeing me thus, white and
with trembling hands, the men dropped the talk that
so sickened me.   Like kind children they came and did
my work or, after the noon hour, brought me little
packages of remedies they had bought at the drug store
or had carried to me from their homes.

I had worked the sick headache racket to the limit
and then, feeling it had become wornout, had quit my
job and had gone to the place where I worked with the
young athlete I now wanted to beat with my fists.

And on a certain day I tried.   I had now convinced
myself that the feint, the cross and the golden smile
were all in good working condition and that no man,

least of all the young athlete who could not stand up to his drink, could stand up against me.

For weeks I had been as nasty as I could be to my fellow-workman. There was a trick I had learned. I gave one of the kegs I was rolling down the incline just a little sudden turn with my foot so that it struck him on the legs as he came into the house through a door. I hit him on the shins and when he howled with pain expressed the greatest regret and then as soon as I could, without arousing too much suspicion, I did it again.

We ceased speaking and only glared at each other. Even the dull-witted teamsters knew there was a fight brewing. I waited and watched, making my lips do the nearest thing possible to a golden smile, and at night in my room and even sometimes when I was walking with Nora and had come into a quiet dark street I practiced the feint and the cross. "What in Heaven's name are you doing?" Nora asked, but I did not tell her but talked instead of my dreams, of brave men in rich clothes walking with lovely women in a strange land I was always trying to create in a world of my fancy and that was always being knocked galley-west by the facts of my life. Regarding the queer sudden little movements I was always making with my shoulders and hands I tried to be very mysterious and once I remember, when we had been sitting on a bench in a little park, I left her and went behind a bush. She thought I had gone there out of a natural necessity but it was not true. I had remembered how Harry Walters and Billy McCarthy, when they were preparing for a fight, did a good deal of what is called shadow boxing. One imagines an opponent before oneself and advances and recedes, feints and crosses, whirls suddenly around and gives ground before a rushing opponent only to come back at him with terrific straight rights and lefts, just as his attack has exhausted itself.

I wanted, I fancy, to have Nora grow tired of waiting for me and to come look around the bush and to discover my secret—that I was not as she thought, a rather foolish but smart-talking fellow inclined to be something of a cloud man. Ah, I thought, as I danced about on a bit of grass back of the bush, she will come to peek and see me here in my true light. She will take me for some famous fighter, a young Corbett or that famous middleweight of the day called "The Nonpareil." What I hoped was that she would come to some such conclusion without asking questions and would go back to the bench to wait for my coming filled with a new wonder. A famous young prizefighter traveling incognito, not wanting public applause, a young Henry Adams of Boston with the punch of a Bob Fitzsimmons, a Ralph Waldo Emerson with the physical assurance of a railway brakeman—what painter, literary man or scholar has not had moments of indulging in some such dream? A burly landlord has been crude enough to demand instant pay for the room in which one is living, or some taxi driver, who has all but run one down at a corner, jerked out of his seat and given a thorough beating in the face of an entire street. "Did you see him pummel that fellow? And he such a pale intellectual looking chap, too! You can never tell how far a dog can jump by the length of his tail." Etc., etc.

Men lost in admiration going off along a street

talking of one's physical prowess. Oneself flecking the dust off one's hands and lighting a cigarette, while one looks with calm indifference at a red-faced taxi driver lying pale and quite defeated and hopeless in a gutter.

It was something of that sort of admiration I wanted from Nora but I did not get it. Once when I was walking in a street with her and had just gone through with my exercises she looked at me with scorn in her eyes. "You're a nice fellow but you're bug-house all right," she said and that was all I ever succeeded in getting out of her.

But I got something else at the warehouse.

The fight came off on a Wednesday at about three in the afternoon and the athlete and myself had two teamsters as witnesses to the affair.

All day I had been bedeviling him—being just as downright ugly and nasty as I could, clipping him on the shins with several flying kegs, making my apologies as insolently as possible and when he started telling one of his endless nasty tales to the teamsters starting a loud conversation on some other subject just as he was about to come to the nub of his story. The teamsters felt the fight brewing and wanted to encourage it. They purposely listened to me and did not hear the nub.

He thought, I dare say, that I would never be foolish enough to fight him and I must have taken his scorn of me for timidity for I suddenly grew very bold. He was coming in at the door of the house just as I was on my way out behind one of the kegs and I suddenly stopped it, looked him squarely in the eyes and then, with an attempt at the golden smile on my lips, sent the keg flying directly at him.

203

He leaped over the keg and came toward me in silence and I prepared to bring my technique into play. Really I had, at the moment, a great deal of confidence in myself and began at once rocking my head, making queer little shifting movements with my feet and trying to establish a kind of cross rhythm in my shoulders and head that would, I felt, confuse him.

He looked at me lost in astonishment and I decided to lead. Had I been content to hit him in the belly with my right, putting all my strength back of the blow and then had I begun kicking, biting and pummeling furiously, I might have come out all right. He was so astonished—no doubt, like Nora, he thought me quite bughouse—that the right would surely have landed, but that, you see, was not the technique of the situation.

The thing was to feint for the belly and then "pull one's punch" as it were, and immediately afterwards whip over the powerful left to the jaw. But my left was not powerful and anyway it did not land.

He knocked me down and when I got up and started my gymnastics again he knocked me down a second time and a third and a fourth. He knocked me down perhaps a dozen times and the two teamsters came to the door to watch and all the time there was the most foolish look on his face and on their faces. It was a look a bulldog attacked by a hen might have assumed —no doubt by my bullyragging I had convinced them, as I had myself, I could fight—but presently both my eyes were so swollen and my nose and mouth so bruised and cut that I could not see and so I got to my feet and walked away, going out of the warehouse in the midst of an intense silence on the part of all three of the spectators.

And so along a street I went to my room, followed by two or three curious children who perhaps thought I had been hit by a freight train and succeeded in also getting my door bolted against any sudden descent of Nora. My eyes were very evidently going to be badly discolored, my nose bled and my lips were badly cut, and so, after bathing my face in cold water, I put a wet towel over it and went and threw myself on the bed.

It was one of those moments that come, I presume, into every man's life. I was lying on my bed in my room, in the condition already described, the door was bolted, Nora was not directly about and I was out from under the eyes of my fellowmen.

I tried to think as one will at such moments.

As for Nora, I might very well have gone to my door and called to her—she was at work somewhere on the floor below and would have gladly come running to offer her woman's sympathy to my hurt physical self— but it was not my hurt physical self that I thought wanted attention. As far as that is concerned I was then, as I have been all my life, not so much concerned with the matter of physical discomfort or pain. Always it has been true of me that a framed water lily on a wall or a walk in a factory street can hurt me worse than a blow on the jaw and long afterward when I became a scribbler of tales I was able to take advantage of this peculiarity of my nature to do my work under conditions that would have disheartened a more physically sensitive man. As I was destined to live most of my life and do most of my work in factory towns and in little, ill-smelling, hideously-furnished rooms, freezing cold in winter and hot and cheerless in summer, it turned out to be a good and convenient trait in me and in the end I had so trained myself to forget my surroundings that I could sit for hours lost in my own thoughts and dreams, or scribbling oftentimes meaningless sentences in a cold room in a factory street, on a log beside some country road, in a railroad station or in the lobby of some large hotel, filled with the hurrying hustling figures of business men, totally unconscious of my surroundings, until my mood had worn itself out and I had sunk into one of the moods of depression common, I think, to all such fellows as myself. Never was such an almighty scribbler as I later became and am even now. Ink, paper and pencils are cheap in our day and I have taken full advantage of that fact and have during some years written hundreds of thousands of words which have afterward been thrown away. Many have told me, in print or by word of mouth, that all should have been thrown away and they may be right, but I am one who loves, like a drunkard his drink, the smell of ink, and the sight of a great pile of white sheets that may be scrawled over with words always gladdens me. The result of the scribbling, the tale of perfect balance, all the elements of the tale understood, an infinite number of minute adjustments perfectly made, the power of self-criticism fully at work, the shifting surface of word values and color in full play, form and the rhythmic flow of thought and mood marching forward with the sentences—these are things of a dream, of a far dim day toward which one goes knowing one can never arrive but infinitely glad to be on the road. It is the story I dare say of the "Pilgrim's Progress," and the sloughs and sink holes

206

on the road are many but the tale of that journey is known to other men than scribblers.

The consolation of ink and paper came, however, long after the time with which I am now concerned, and what a consolation it is! How much easier it is to sit in a room before a desk and with paper before one to describe a fight between oneself as hero of some tale and five or six burly ruffians than with the fists to dispose of one baseball player on the platform of a warehouse.

In the tale one can do any such job as it should be done and in the doing give satisfaction both to oneself and the possible reader, for the reader will always share in the emotions of the hero and gloat with him over his victories. In the tale, as you will understand, all is in order. The feint and the cross, the powerful left to the jaw, the golden smile, the shifting movements of the shoulders that confuse and disconcert the opponent, all work like well-oiled machines. One defeats not one baseball player or ruffian of the city streets but a dozen if the need arises. Oh, what glorious times I have had, sitting in little rooms with great piles of paper before me; what buckets of blood have run from the wounds of the villains, foolish enough to oppose me on the field of honor; what fair women I have loved and how they have loved me and on the whole how generous, chivalrous, open-hearted and fine I have been! I remember how I sat in the back room of a small bootlegging establishment at Mobile, Alabama, one afternoon, long after the time with which I am now concerned and while three drunken sailors discussed the divinity of Christ at a near-by table wrote the story of little, tired-out and crazed Joe

Wainsworth's killing of Jim Gibson in the harness shop at Bidwell Ohio, that afterward was used in the novel "Poor White"; and of how at a railroad station at Detroit I sat writing the tale of Elsie Leander's westward journey, in "The Triumph of the Egg," and missed my own train—these remain as rich and fine spots in a precarious existence.

But at the time of which I am speaking the consolation of ink and paper was a thing of the future and my bunged-up eyes and hurt spirits were facts.

> Adieu! the fancy cannot cheat so well
> As she is famed to do, deceiving elf.

I lay on my back on my bed, trying to get up courage to face facts. As for the throbbing of the hurt places, the pain was a kind of satisfaction to me at the moment.

There was the warehouse where I had been more or less a spiritual bully but where I would now have to eat crow. Well, I need not go back. The day before had been payday and I would, by never going near the place again, lose little money and save myself the humiliation of facing the teamsters. And when it came to the scratch, I thought, there was the city I was in, the state, the very United States of America itself—I could if I chose desert them all. I was young, had been well trained in poverty, had no family ties, no social position to uphold, I was unmarried and as yet childless.

I was a free man, I told myself, sitting on the bed and staring about the room through swollen eyelids. Was I free? Did any man ever achieve freedom? I had my own life before me. Why did I not, by some grand effort, begin to live a life?

I lay on the bed with the wet towel thrown aside thinking, trying to make plans. A faint suspicion of something permanently wrong with me had begun to creep into my consciousness. Was I, alas, a fellow born out of his place and time? I was in a world where only men of action seemed to thrive. Already I had noted that fact. One wanted a definite thing to go after, money, fame, a position of power in the big world, and having something definite of the sort in mind one shut one's eyes and pitched in with all the force of one's physical and mental self. I squirmed about trying to force myself to face myself. My body was strong enough for all practical purposes, when not scarred and bruised by the blows of an angry ball player, and I was not such a bad-looking fellow. I was not lazy and on the whole rather liked hard physical labor. Need I be what I at the moment seemed to myself to be, a useless and foolish dreamer, a child in a world filled with what I thought to be grown-up men? Why should I myself not also grow up, take the plow by the handle, plow vast fields, become rich or famous? Perhaps I could become a man of power and rule or influence many other men's lives.

There is a trick the fancy has. Start it in any direction and it goes prancing off at a great rate and that trick my own fancy now did.

Although my body ached as a result of my recent plunge into the field of action I, in fancy, plunged in again and began thinking of myself as holding the handle of a plow and plowing the fields of life, turning great furrows, planting perhaps the seeds of new ideas. Oho, for the smell of new-turned earth, the sight of the sower casting his seed!

I was off again. On that day Nora had done the work in my room early but now she was sweeping and dusting on the floor below and I could hear her moving about.

Why should I not first of all conquer Nora? That, I at that moment thought, was surely the beginning of manhood, to conquer some woman, and why not Nora as well as another? It would be something of an undertaking that was sure. Nora was not beautiful nor perhaps too subtle in her outlook on life but then was I myself subtle? She was direct and simple and had, I thought, a direct and simple mind and after I had conquered her, had bent her to my own will, what might we not do together? There was to be sure the sailor with whom she was to live and to whom she was promised but I brushed him aside. "I can cook his goose in some way," I thought to myself, much as I had thought I could easily dispose of the ball player by my feints and crosses.

We might, I thought, following up the fancy I had just had, begin by being tillers of the soil. We could go West somewhere and take up land. Already I had read many tales of the West and had a fancy for casting in my fortunes with the West. "Out where the smile lasts a little longer, out where the handclasp is a little stronger," etc. "Oho, for the land where men are men and gals are gals!" I thought my fancy running away like a wild horse broken out of its stall. I saw myself owning vast farms somewhere in the Far

West and saw, I am afraid, Nora doing most of the plowing, planting and the harvesting of crops, the while I rode grandly over the estate on a black stallion, receiving the homage of serfs.

But what would I do with my odd moments? I had tried talking to Nora of the things that interested me most, the play of light over a factory chimney, seen amid smoke as darkness came on, odd expressions caught from the lips of passing men and women, the play of the fancy over the imagined lives of men and women too. Had Nora understood or cared? Could I go on always talking and talking in the face of the fact that I knew she was not much interested?

With a rush of resolution I threw my doubts aside. Oh, to be one who made two blades of grass where but one had grown before! With Nora at my side I would in some field become great and powerful. I was at the moment but a bunged-up fellow lying on the bed in a cheap rooming house but what did that matter? All about me was the great American world rushing on and on to new mechanical and material triumphs. Teddy Roosevelt and the strenuous life had not yet come but he was implicit in the American mood. Imperialism had already come. It was time, I told myself, to be up and doing.

> Behind him lay the gray Azores,
> Behind the Gates of Hercules;
> Before him not the ghost of shores;
> Before him only shoreless seas.
> The good mate said, "Now must we pray,
> For lo, the very stars are gone.
> Brave Admr'l speak." "What shall I say?"
> "Why say: 'Sail on, sail on and on.'"

JUMPING off the bed I instantly began to try to prepare myself for new adventures. As I had been lying on the bed thinking the thoughts above set down and working myself up to new heights of fancied grandeur some time had passed. Perhaps I had slept and awakened. At any rate it was now dark in the room and I lighted a lamp. By its light and after I had bathed my face for some time it did not look so swollen although both eyes had turned a deep purple.

Undaunted I dressed in my best Sunday clothes and prepared to set out. I had engaged to walk with Nora on that evening and it was our custom on such occasions for me to pass quietly out of the house, tapping on the door of her room on the floor below and waiting for her on the front steps.

To tell the truth I had already got well going the new dramatization of myself as a man of action but was not sure of myself in the new rôle to want to face any of the workmen in the house. Nora I thought I could handle.

As I stood in the room dressed in my best clothes I counted my money and then decided I would not be a Western ranchman after all but a man of commerce, an empire builder perhaps. I had in my possession some ninety-eight dollars which seemed to me at the moment sufficient for a start in almost any undertaking.

It would support me for a few weeks while I looked about and then I would pitch in somewhere and become an empire builder. It would take time but what was time to me? I had an abundance of time. "I'll do it," I told myself resolutely.

Why not? Was I not a man of imagination? Was I not young and did I not have a strong body?

As I washed the dried blood off my face, put on my Sunday suit and adjusted my tie I in fancy swept the field of commercial adventure with my somewhat damaged eyes. There were the great cities of Chicago and New York I had not yet seen, although I had read much about them and about men who had grown from poverty to riches and power in them. Like all young Americans I had read innumerable tales of men who had begun with nothing and had become great leaders, owners of railroads, governors of states, foreign ambassadors, generals of armies, presidents of great modern republics. Abraham Lincoln walking miles through a storm after a hard day's work to borrow his first book, Jay Gould the young Wall Street clerk, setting up a great dynasty of wealth, Daniel Drew the cattle dealer becoming a millionaire, Garfield the canal-boat boy and Vanderbilt the ferryman become President and millionaire, Grant the failure, hauling hides from his father's tannery at Galena, Illinois, to St. Louis—and, it was said, getting so well piped sometimes on the homeward journey that he fell off the wagon—he also became great, the winner of a mighty war, President of his country, a noted traveler, receiving the homage of kings. "And I can carry my liquor better than he could, by all reports," I said to myself.

Were these men any better than myself? At the moment and in spite of the gloom of an hour before, I thought not, and as for my having but ninety-eight dollars, what did that matter? As a matter of fact one gathered from having read American history that there was a sort of advantage to be gained from starting with nothing. One had something to talk and brag about in one's old age, and when one became a candidate for President one furnished one's campaign managers with materials for campaign slogans.

And now I was dressed and had tiptoed out of the house, tapped on Nora's door and was waiting for her outside. I had decided that when she came out I would not make an appeal for her woman's sympathy by telling of what had actually happened to me. "I do not want woman's sympathy," I thought proudly. What I wanted was woman's respect. I wanted to conquer them, to have them at my feet, to stand before them the conquering male.

When Nora came and when we had walked to where there was a street light and she had seen my damaged countenance I began at once to brag and to reconstruct the fight at the warehouse more to my own fancy. Not one but four men had attacked me and I had valiantly stood my ground. An inspiration came. I had got into the fight, I told Nora, because of a woman. A young woman, a working girl like Nora herself had passed the platform and the men at work there with me had begun making remarks that were not very nice. What was I to do? I was one who could never stand quietly by and hear an innocent woman, particularly one who had to work for her living and had perhaps no men of her own to stand up for

214

her, hear such a woman subjected to insult. I had, I
told Nora, at once pitched into the four men and there
had been a terrible fight.

As I described the fancied affair to Nora the feint
and the cross on which I had so depended had worked
wonderfully. I had received many hard blows, it was
true, and Nora could see by looking at my face how
I had suffered, but I had given better than I had received. Like a tornado I had swept up and down the
warehouse platform making feints with my right and
whipping my powerful left to the jaws of my opponents until at last they were all laid out like dead men
before me. And then I had come home, a little fearful that I might have killed one or two of the men but
not waiting to see. "I did not care," I said. "If my
opponents have suffered a terrible beating at my hands
and if one or two of them die of their injuries it was
their own fault. They should have known better
than to have insulted a woman in my presence."

I had told Nora my story and we had walked in
silence until we had come to a street lamp when she
suddenly stopped and, taking my left hand, turned it
up to the light. As I had not succeeded in the actual
fight in striking a blow with it, the hand was unmarked
by a bruise. "Huh!" said Nora and we went on in
silence.

The silence, which was one of the hardest I have
ever had to bear, continued until we had finished our
walk—which on that evening did not last very long,—
and had got back to the house.

On the steps in front we stopped and Nora stood
for a time looking at me. It was a look I did not
much fancy, but what was I to do? Two or three

times during our walk I had tried to begin talking a little and had attempted to patch up the structure of my yarn so that it would not be quite so full of holes and leaky but could think of no way to explain the unbruised surface and uninjured knuckles of my left, so I had taken refuge in a kind of sullen silence.

I had even begun to feel a little injured and angry and was asking myself what right Nora had to question my story—was feeling, to tell the truth, much as I was later to feel when some editor or critic rejected, as not sound, one of my written tales—that is to say, resentful and intolerant of the editor or critic and inclined to call him a fool and to attribute to him all kinds of secret and degrading motives. I was feeling much in this mood, I say, when we had got back to the steps and were standing in the darkness in front.

And then Nora suddenly put her strong arm about my neck and pulled my head down upon her shoulder and I began to cry like a child.

That in an odd way made me more resentful than ever. It faced me with a problem I have all my life been trying to face and have never quite succeeded. One does so hate to admit that the average woman is kinder, finer, more quick of sympathy and on the whole so much more first class than the average man. It is a fact perhaps but a fact that I have always thought we men should deny with all the strength of our more powerful wills. We men should conquer women. We should not stand in the darkness with our heads on their shoulders, blubbering as I was doing at that moment.

However, I continued crying and being ashamed of myself and Nora did not press her advantage. When, now and then, I lifted my face from her shoulder and looked at her face, dimly seen in the darkness, it seemed to me just kindly and filled with sympathy for my position.

I felt, I presume, most of all the story-teller's shame at the failure of his yarn and there was something else too. There was a suspicion that Nora, the woman who had been for weeks listening to my talk and whom I had somewhat looked down upon as not being my equal, had suddenly become my superior. I had prided myself on my mind and on the superiority of my imaginative flights. Could it be that this woman, this maker of beds in a cheap laborers' rooming house, had a better mind than my own?

The thought was unbearable and so, as soon as I could conveniently manage it, I got my head off Nora's shoulder and made my escape.

In my room I sat again on the edge of the bed and I had again bolted the door. The notion of using Nora to plant and sow fields for me while I rode about on a magnificent black stallion was now quite gone and I had to construct another and at once. That I realized. I had to construct a new dramatization of myself and leave Nora out of it. I was not ready for the Noras. Perhaps I would never be ready for them. Few American men I have ever known have ever shown any signs of being ready for the Noras of the world or of being able really to understand or face them.

My mind turned again to the field of business and affairs. I had already known a good many men and, while such fellows as the baseball player at the warehouse had the better of me because I had been fool enough to let the struggle between us get on a physical plane, I had not met many men who had caused me to tremble because of any special spiritual or intellectual strength in themselves.

To be sure the world of affairs was one of which I knew nothing and yet I thought I might tackle it. "It cannot be worse than the world of labor," I thought as I sat in the darkness, trying not to think of Nora—thoughts of whom I was convinced might weaken the resolution I had taken and might even cause me to begin blubbering again—and keeping my mind fixed on the laborers I had known, even as the laborers who lived in the house with me tramped heavily, one by one, up the stairs and went off to their rooms and to sleep.

"I will become a man of action, in the mood of the American of my day. I will build railroads, conquer empires, become rich and powerful. Why should I not do something of the sort as well as all the other men who have done it so brilliantly? America is the land of opportunity. I must keep that thought ever in my mind," I told myself as I tiptoed out of the house at two o'clock in the morning, having left a note of good-by to Nora and the amount of my room rent in an envelope on my bed. I was being very careful not to make any noise as I went along the hallway and past Nora's door. "I had better not wake up the woman," I was wise enough to say to myself as I went away, hugging my new impulse in life.

NOTE VIII

I HAD come to that period of a young man's life where all is uncertainty. In America there seemed at that time but one direction, one channel, into which all such young fellows as myself could pour their energies. All must give themselves wholeheartedly to material and industrial progress. Could I do that? Was I fitted for such a life? It was a kind of moral duty to try and then, as now, men at the heads of the great industrial enterprises filled or had filled all the newspapers and magazines with sermons on industry, thrift, virtue, loyalty and patriotism, meaning I am afraid by the use of all these high-sounding terms only devotion to the interests in which they had money invested. But the terms were good terms, the words used were magnificent words. And I was by my nature a word fellow, one who could at most any time be hypnotized by high-sounding words. It was confusing to me as it must be confusing to many young men now. During the World War did we not see how even the very government went into the advertising business, selling the war to the young men of the country by the use of the same noble words advertising men used to forward the sale of soap or automobile tires? To the young man a kind of worship of some power outside himself is essential. One has strength and enthusiasm and wants gods to worship.

There were only these gods of material success. Chivalry was gone. The Virgin had died. In America there were no churches. What were called churches were merely clubs, ruled over by the same forces that ruled over the factories and great mercantile houses. Often the men I heard speaking in churches spoke in the same words, used the same terms to define the meaning of life that were used by the real-estate boomer, the politician, or the enterprising business man talking to his employees of the necessity of steadfastness and devotion to the interests of his firm.

The Virgin was dead and her son had taken as prophets such men as Ralph Waldo Emerson and Benjamin Franklin, the one with his little books in which he set down and saved his acts and impulses, striving to make them all serve definite ends as he saved his pennies and the other preaching the intellectual doctrine of Self-reliance, Up and Onward. The land was filled with gods but they were new gods and their images, standing on every street of every town and city, were cast in iron and steel. The factory had become America's church and duplicates of it stood everywhere, on almost every street of every city belching black incense into the sky.

A passion for reading books had taken possession of me and I did not work when I had any money at all but often for weeks spent my time reading any book I could get my hands on. In every city there were public libraries and I could get books without spending money.

The past took a strong hold on my imagination and I went eagerly down through the ages, reading of the lives of the great men of antiquity; of the Romans and their conquest of the world; of the early Christians and their struggles before the great organizer Paul came to "put Christianity across"; of the Cæsars, Charlemagnes and Napoleons, marching and counter-marching across Europe at the head of their troops; of the cruel but powerful Peters and Ivans of Russia; of the great and elegant dukes of Italy—the poisoners and schemers listening to the words of their Machia-vellis; of the magnificent painters and craftsmen of the Middle Ages; of English and French kings; round-heads; Spanish kings of the days of conquest and of gold ships bringing riches from the Spanish Main; the Grand Inquisitor; the coming of Erasmus, the cool scholarly questioner whose questions brought to the front Luther, the conscientious barbarian—all, all spread out before me, the young American coming into manhood, all in the books.

It was a feast. Could I digest it? I had saved a little money and knew how to live very cheaply. After working for some weeks, and when I did not spend money for drinking bouts to ease the confusion of my mind I had a few dollars put aside and dollars meant leisure. That is perhaps all dollars have ever meant to me.

Since I was always making the acquaintance of some fellow who lived by gambling I went now and then into a gambling place and sometimes had luck. I had five dollars when I went in at a certain door and came out with a hundred dollars in my pocket. Oh, glori-ous day! On such an amount I could live among books for weeks and so, renting a small room on a poor street, I went every day to a public library and got a new book. The book some man had spent years in composing was often waded through in a day and then thrown aside. What a jumble of things in my head! At times the life directly about me ceased to have any existence. The actuality of life became a kind of vapor, a thing outside of myself. My body was a house in which I lived and there were many such houses all about me but I did not live in them. Perhaps I was but trying to make solid the walls of my own house, to roof it properly, to cut windows, becoming accustomed to living in the house so that I could have leisure to look out at the windows and into other houses. Of that I do not know. To make such a claim for myself and my purpose seems giving my life a more intelligent direction than I can convince myself it has had.

I walked in and out of the little rooms in which I lived, often in what was called the tough part of a city, hearing all about me the oaths of drunken men, the crying of children, the weeping of some poor girl of the streets who has just been beaten by her pimp, the quarreling of laborers and their wives, walked hearing and seeing nothing, walked gripping a book in my hand.

In fancy I was at the moment with the great Florentine Leonardo da Vinci on a day when he sat on a little hill above his country house in Italy studying the flight of birds or was making the mathematical and geometrical calculations he so loved. Or I was sitting in a carriage beside the scholar Erasmus as he drove across Europe going from the court of one great duke or king to the court of another. The lives of the dead men and women had become more real to me than the lives of the living people about me.

How bad an American I had become, how utterly out of touch with the spirit of my age! Sometimes for weeks I did not read a newspaper—a fault in me that would have been considered almost in the light of a crime had it been generally known to my fellows. A new railroad might have been built, a new trust formed or some great national excitement like the free silver affair—that did fall in at about that time—might have shaken the whole country while I knew nothing about it.

There was indeed a kind of intimate acquaintance with an unknown and unheralded kind of people I was unconsciously getting. In Chicago, where I had now gone I for a time lived in a room in a huge cheaply constructed building that had been erected about a little court. The building was not old, had in fact been built but a few years before—during the Chicago World's Fair—but already it was a half-tumbledown unsafe place with great sags in the floors in the hallways and cracks in the walls. The building surrounded the little brick-paved court and was divided into single rooms for bachelor lodgers and into small two- and three-room apartments. Since it was near the end of several street-car lines and a branch of the Chicago elevated railroad it was occupied for the most part by street-car conductors and motormen with their wives and children. Many of my fellow-lodgers were young fellows having wives but no children and not intending to have children if the accidents of life could be avoided. They went off to work and came home from work at all sorts of odd hours.

I hadn't very much money but did not mind. My

room was small and cost little and I lived on fruit and on stacks of wheatcakes that could be had at ten cents the stack at a near-by workingmen's eating place. When I was broke I told myself I could always go again to some place where laborers were wanted. I was young and my body was strong. "If I cannot get work in the city I can get on a freight train at night and go away to the country and work on a farm," I thought. Sometimes I had qualms of conscience because I had not already started on the great career as an industrial magnate I had half-heartedly mapped out for myself but I managed to put my sins of omission aside. There was plenty of time I told myself and in any event I planned eventually to do the thing with a grand rush.

In the meantime I lay for long hours on the little bed in my room reading the last book I had got from the library or walked in a near-by park under the trees. Time ceased to exist and the days became night while the nights became days. Often I came back to my room at two in the morning, washed my shirt, underwear and socks at a washbowl in a corner, hung them out at my window facing the court to dry and lying down naked on my bed read by a gaslight until daylight had come.

Marvelous days! Now I was marching with the conqueror Julius Cæsar over the vast domains of the mighty Roman Empire. What a life and how proud Julius and I were of his conquests and how often we spoke together of the doings of Cicero, Pompey, Cato and the others in Rome. Indeed Cæsar and I had become for the nonce the most intimate of friends and often enough we discussed the unworthiness of some of the other Romans, particularly of that Cicero. The man was no better than a dog, a literary hack, when all was said and done, and such fellows are never to be trusted. Often enough Cicero had talked with Cæsar and pretended to be Cæsar's friend but, as Julius often pointed out to me, such fellows were wont to veer about with every wind that blew, "Writers are the greatest cowards in the world and my own greatest weakness is that I have a kind of hankering that way myself. Let a man but get into power and he will always find such scribbling fellows willing and anxious to sing his praises. They are the greatest cur dogs in the world," he declared vehemently.

And so I had become in fancy the friend of Cæsar and all day I marched beside him and at evening went with him and his men into their camp.

The days and weeks passed. I sat by the window looking into the little brick-paved court and there were many other windows. As it was summer they were all open. Evening came, after a day of walking in dreams, and I had come into my room and taking off my coat had thrown myself down on my bed. When darkness came I did not light a light but lay quietly listening.

I had stepped now out of the past and into the present and all about me were the voices of living people. The men and women in the rooms along the court did not laugh or sing often and indeed in the many times, during my life, I have lived, as I did then, lying like a little worm in the middle of the apple of modern life, I have never found that American men and women, except only the Negroes, laugh or sing much in their homes or at their work.

It was evening and a street-car conductor had come home to his wife. They were silent in each other's presence for a time, then they began to quarrel. Sometimes they fought and after that they made love. The love-making of the couples along the court aroused my own passions and I had bad dreams at night.

What a strange thing love-making had become among modern factory hands, street-car conductors and all such fellows! Almost always it was preceded by a quarrel, often blows were struck, there were tears, repentance and then embraces. Did the tired nerves of the men and women need the stimulation of the fights and quarrels?

A red-faced man who stumbled as he walked along the hallways to his small apartment had secured a small flat stick which he kept behind a door. His wife was young and fat. When he had come home from work and had in silence eaten his evening meal he sat by the window facing the court and read a newspaper while his wife washed the dishes. Suddenly, when the dishes were washed, he jumped to his feet and ran to get the stick. "Don't, John, don't," his wife pleaded half-heartedly, as he began to pursue her about the narrow room. Chairs were knocked over and tables upset. He kept hittting her with the flat stick upon the nether cheeks and she kept laughing and protesting. Sometimes he struck her too hard and she grew angry and, turning upon him, scratched his face with her finger nails. Then he swore and wrestled with her. Their period of more intense love-making had now come and silence reigned over the little home for the rest of the night.

I lay on my bed in the darkness and closed my eyes. Once more I was in the camp of Cæsar and we were in Gaul. The great captain had been writing at a small table near the door of his tent but now a man had come to speak with him. I lay in silence upon a kind of thick warm cloth spread on the ground beside the tent.

The man who talked with Cæsar was a bridge-builder and had come to speak with him regarding the building of a bridge that the legions might cross a river beside which they now lay encamped. A certain number of men would be needed with boats and others were at daylight to go hew great timbers in a near-by forest and roll them into the stream.

How very quiet and peaceful it was where I lay! Cæsar's tent was pitched on a hillside. In person he was like . . . there was an Italian fruit dealer who had a small store on a street near the park where I went every day to sit, a tall gaunt man who had lost one eye and whose black hair was turning gray. The fruit dealer had evidently lost his eye in a fight as there was a long scar on his cheek. It was this man I had metamorphosed into a Cæsar.

Below, at the foot of the hill on which the tent stood and on the banks of a river the legions were camped. They had built fires and some of the men were bathing in the river but when they came out they dressed quickly because of little biting flies that swarmed about their heads. I was glad Cæsar's tent was pitched on a hill where there was a little breeze and there were no biting flies or insects. Below, the fires in the valley glowed and cast yellow and red lights over the tawny bodies and faces of the soldiers.

The man who had come to Cæsar was a craftsman and had a maimed hand. Two of the fingers of his left hand had been cut sharply off as by a blow with an ax. He went away into the darkness and Cæsar went within his tent.

I lay on my bed in the room in the building in Chicago not daring to open my eyes. Had I been asleep? Now there was no quarreling in the other places along the court but there were still lights at some of the windows. The workers had not yet all come home. Two women were talking together across the space between their windows. Street-car conductors and motormen, who had been all day working their cars slowly through crowded streets, propitiating quarrelsome passengers, cursing and being cursed at by teamsters and crossing policemen, were now asleep. Of what were they dreaming? They had come from the car barns, had read a newspaper, telling perhaps of a fight between English troops and the natives of Thibet, had read also a speech by the German emperor demanding a place in the sun for Germany, had noted who had beaten the Chicago White Sox or who had been beaten by them. Then they had quarreled with their wives, blows had been struck, there had been lovemaking and then sleep.

I arose and went to walk in the silent streets and twice during that summer I was stopped by holdup men who took a few dollars from me. The World's Fair had been followed by a time of industrial depression. How many miles I have walked in the streets of American cities at night! In Chicago and the other industrial cities long streets of houses—how many houses almost universally ugly and cheaply constructed, like the building in which I then lived! I passed through sections where all the people were Negroes and heard laughter in the houses. Then came the sections entirely inhabited by Jews, by Greeks, Armenians, Italians, Germans, or Poles. How many elements not yet combined in the cities! The American writers, whose books I read, went on assuming that the typical American was a transplanted Englishman, an Englishman who had served his term in the stony purgatory of New England and had then escaped out into the happy land, this Heaven, the Middle West. Here they were all to grow rich and live forever, a happy blissful existence. Was not all the world supposed to be watching the great democratic experiment in government and human happiness they were to conduct so bravely?

I wandered on into factory districts, long silent streets of grim black walls. Had men but escaped out of the prisons of the Old World into the more horrid prisons of the New? Dread took hold of me as on a dark street I was approached by a man who put a gun to my face. He wanted money and I tried to be facetious with him, telling him I hadn't enough money to buy drinks for the two of us but would match him pennies for what I had but he only growled at me and taking my few pieces of silver hurried away. Perhaps he did not even understand my words. America, once a place that prided itself on its sense of humor, was now, since the coming of the factories, a place where the very robbers were all too serious about life.

Periods of lust kept coming and going. In the

building where I lived there was a woman, very young yet, a high-school graduate from an Illinois town who had married a young man of the place. They had come to live in Chicago, to make their way in the great world, and as he could get no other work he had taken a place as street-car conductor. Oh, it was but a temporary arrangement. He was one who intended, as for that matter I did myself, to rise in the world.

The man I never saw but all afternoon the woman sat by a window in one of the two rooms of her apartment or went for short walks in the park. We began presently to smile shyly at each other but did not speak, both being embarrassed. Like myself she read books and that was a kind of bond between us. I got into the habit of sitting by my window with my book in my hand while she sat by her window also holding a book.

And here was a new confusion. The pages of the books no longer lived. The woman, sitting there, but a few feet away from me, across the little court, I did not want. Of that I was quite sure. She was another man's wife. What thoughts had she in her head, what feelings had she? Her face was round and fair and she had blue eyes. What did she want? Children perhaps, I thought. She wanted to have a house like all the other houses lived in by the people of her home town who had made money and who held positions of some importance in the town's life. One day she sat on a bench in the park and I, walking past, saw the title of the book she read. It was a popular novel of the day but I have forgotten its name and the name of its author. Even at that time, although

I knew little enough, I did know that such books had always been written, would always be written, books that sold by the hundreds of thousands and were often proclaimed as great works of art and that after a year or two were utterly forgotten. In them was no sense of strangeness, no wonder about life. They lacked the touch of life. "Dead books for men and women who dare not live," I thought contemptuously. There was a kind of pretense of solving some problem of life but the problem was so childishly stated that later a childish solution seemed quite natural and right. A young man came to an American city from a country town and, although at bottom he was true and fine, the city for a time diverted him from his noble aims. He committed some near crime that made both himself and the girl he really loved suffer terribly, but she stood firmly by him and at the last, and with her help, he pulled himself up again, by the bootstraps as it were, and became a rich manufacturer who was kind to his employees.

The book she read expressed perhaps the high-school girl's dream, the dream she had when she married and came to Chicago. Was her dream the same now? I had already, as far as I reacted to the life about me at all, started upon another road, was becoming, a little, the eternal questioner of myself and others. Not for me the standardized little pellets of opinion, the little neatly wrapped packages of sentiment the magazine writers had learned to do up, I told myself. In modern factories food was packed in convenient standard-sized packages and I half suspected that behind the high-sounding labels the food was often enough sawdust or something of the sort.

It was apparent publishers also had learned to do up neat packages containing sawdust and put bright-colored labels on them.

Oh, glorious contempt! Seeing the book the woman was reading, knowing she was the wife of another and that never by any chance could we come close to each other, give to each other anything of value, I enjoyed my contempt for an hour and then it faded. I sat as before by my window and held an open book but could not follow the thoughts and ideas of the writer of the book. I sat by my window and she with her book sat by her window.

Was something about to happen that neither of us wanted, of which we were both afraid, that would be without value to either of us?

One evening when I met her in the hallway of the building I stopped before her and we stood thus for a minute facing each other. We both blushed, both felt guilty, and then I tried to say something to her but did not succeed. I stammered out a few words about the weather, saying how hot it was, and hurried away but a week later, when we again met in the same place it was dark and we kissed.

We began then to walk in silence together in the park in the early evenings and sometimes we sat together on a park bench. How careful we were not to be seen by others who lived in our building. Her husband left the house at three in the afternoon and did not return until midnight and when he came home he was tired and discouraged. He scolded at his wife. "He is always scolding," she said. Well, one wanted to save money, get into business for oneself. And now he had a wife to support and the wages of street-car conductors were not large. The young man who wanted to rise in the world had begun to resent his wife and she felt it vaguely, uneasily. She also was filled with resentment. Did she want revenge? She had no words to express what she felt and I had no way of understanding. Was I not also confused, wanting something very much, that at the same time I did not want? I sat in my room until darkness came holding the book I now could not read and when the darkness had come threw it with a loud bang on a table. The sound had become a signal to her and when I went into the park she came to join me. One evening when we had kissed in the darkness of the park I went home ahead of her but did not close the door of my room. I stood in the darkness by the door waiting. She had to pass along the hallway to reach her own place and I put out my hand and drew her inside.

"I'm afraid," she kept saying, "I don't want to. I'm afraid." What a queer silent frightened love-making it was—no love-making at all. She was afraid and I was afraid, not of her husband but of myself. Later she went away crying silently along the hallway and after that she and I did not sit at our two windows or walk in the park and I returned to my books. Once, on a night two or three weeks later as I lay in my own bedroom, I heard the husband and wife talking together. Something had happened that had pleased and excited her. She had been able to offer something she thought would help her husband and was urging him to give up being a street-car conductor and to go back to the town from which they had come. Her father owned a store there, I gathered, and had objected to her marriage but she had secretly written, perhaps been very humble, and had persuaded her father to take the younger man into partnership in his business. "Don't be proud now, Jim. I'm not proud any more. Something has happened to me Jim. I'm not proud any more," I heard her saying as I lay in my own room in the darkness, and I leave the reader to judge whether, under the circumstances, I could be proud. But perhaps after all the woman and I have done something for each other, I thought.

ON a certain Sunday morning of that summer I found myself sitting in a little garden under apple trees back of a red brick house that had green window blinds and that stood on the side of a hill near the edge of an Illinois town of some five or six thousand people. Sitting by a small table near me was a dark slender man with pale cheeks, a man I had never seen until late on the evening before and who I had half thought would die but a few hours earlier. Now, although the morning was warm, he had a blanket wrapped around him and his thin hands, lying on the table, trembled. Together we were drinking our morning coffee, containing a touch of brandy. A robin hopped on the grass near by and the sunlight falling through the branches of the trees made yellow patches at our feet.

I sat in silence filled with wonder at the strangeness of the circumstances that had brought me to the spot and of my own mood. The garden in which we sat had a gravel path running down through the centre and on one side vegetables grew, with narrow beds of flowers about the vegetable plots. Along the further side against a fence were tall berry bushes and on our side there was grass under the trees and near by a tall hedge of elders. Looking toward the foot of the garden one got a view of a river valley dotted with

235

farmhouses and beyond the elders there was a road that led along a hillside down into town.

The town itself was old, for that Illinois country, and had already had two lives. First, it had been a river town on the banks of a stream that led down into the Mississippi, and now it was a merchandising centre. Later perhaps it would become a factory town. The river life had died, when the railroads came but there still were some remnants of the older place, one or two streets of small log stores and houses standing on a bluff above the river and now used as residences by farm laborers. The old town, left thus off by itself half forgotten by the new town, was picturesque. In the company of my strange new acquaintance and once with his father, an old man who had lived in the river town in the days of its prosperity, I later spent several hours among the old houses. Dogs and pigs wandered through the deep dust of the principal street facing the river or slept in the shade of the old buildings and the old man told me that even in its better days it was a quite terrible place. In the winter, in the early days, the roads were hub deep to the wagons with mud, the houses were small and near each house was an outhouse that smelled horribly in summer and invited millions of flies. Pigs, cows and horses were kept in little sheds near the houses and often diseases, encouraged by the utter lack of sanitation, swept through the town and sometimes carried off whole families.

The older of the two men, named Jim Berners, was a merchant, owning with his son a large store on the principal street of the newer town and had been brought to the Illinois town when he was a child. His father, an Englishman, had come to America as a young man and for several years had been a merchant in the city of Philadelphia. Having married there and wanting to establish himself as the head of a landed family in the new country he had come to Illinois when land could be had at a low price and had bought five hundred acres of river bottom land.

With his young wife and his three children he lived in the river town and had cleared and got ready for planting most of his land when misfortune came down upon him. In the crude little towns of that day doctors were for the most part half educated, the houses were stuffy and full of drafts in winter and epidemics of smallpox, followed by scarlet fever, diphtheria and typhus came and could not be checked. Within two years the merchant's rather delicate wife died and her death was followed by his own and by the death of two of his three children. There was only the babe left alive and he had been put in charge of an old judge with whom the father had formed a friendship.

The young Berners had grown into manhood in the household of the judge, whose great boast it was that he was a personal friend of Abraham Lincoln. He told me he had never been ill a day in his life. Upon reaching manhood he sold three hundred acres of his land and like his father became a merchant.

Father and son still owned the Berners merchandising establishment although they seemed to give it little attention.

What a place it was! Some ten years before I made his acquaintance the younger Berners, named Alonzo, had gone to Chicago where he had got quite hopelessly drunk. During his whole life the man had been a sufferer from some obscure nervous disease and was never without pain. The sprees he sometimes went on were but a kind of desperate attempt to free himself for a short time from the presence of pain. After the drunken time he was dreadfully ill and seemed about to die and then there came a time of weakness and a kind of physical peace. The tense nerves of his slender body relaxed, he slept at night and spent the days talking with a few friends, reading books or riding about town in a buggy.

On the sprees, of ten years before, sprees indulged in twice a year at regular intervals outside his own town, when he had stolen away without warning to his father or to an older sister of the household, young Alonzo had been picked up in the city of Chicago by an English deep-sea sailor. The sailor had been working for a time on a lake steamer but had tired of the place and had left his ship at Chicago and had also gone on a drunk. He rescued Alonzo Berners from the men into whose hands he had fallen and brought him home and later became attached to the Berners establishment, staying in the Illinois town at first as clerk in the store and later as the store's manager. He was a heavily built man of fifty-five when I saw him and had a white scar, evidently from an old knife wound, on his brown cheek and a peculiar waddling gait. As he hustled about the store one thought of a fat duck trying to make its way rapidly along on land.

In the Berners establishment were sold hardware, agricultural implements, house and barn paints, jack-knives and a thousand other things and there was also a harness shop in the main building facing the town's principal street. Back of the main building there was an alleyway and across the alleyway half a dozen large frame buildings in which were kept hides bought from the farmers, coal, lumber, bins of corn, wheat and oats in bags and hay in bales.

The whole establishment, an infinitely busy place, was run by the sailor who could neither read or write but who was helped by a stern-looking woman book-keeper. The sailor was shrewd wise and jolly and had always some tale of life on the deep sea to tell to his farmer customers. He was the most popular man in town and there was another feature that added tre-mendously to the popularity of the store. In the spring, just before planting time, and in the fall after the crops were harvested, the Berners gave a great feast in one of the sheds. The hay corn and lumber were taken out and long wooden tables erected, while invitations were sent far and wide to the town and country people. Women of the town and country wives came to help prepare the feast, the old sailor waddled about shouting, pigs, turkeys, calves and lambs were killed, bushels of potatoes baked, pies and cakes, baked in advance by the women, were brought and there was a feast lasting sometimes all afternoon and far into the night. Alonzo Berners had provided many barrels of beer and the sailor and his pals among the farmers got half drunk and sang songs and made speeches while the professional men of the town, the lawyers, judges and doctors, all came and made speeches. What a storm of talk! Even the preach-ers and the rival merchants were there and a prayer was said as each new group sat down to the feast, the ministers shaking their heads over the beer drinking but falling to with a will at the food. The two annual affairs must often have cost the Berners a good part of the profits made during the year but they did not mind. "It doesn't matter," said the elder Berners. "I'm old and nearly ready to die, it isn't likely Alonzo will live very long and as for Hallie," meaning the daughter, "I have already given her one of my two farms. The Berners are going to peter out anyway and why should they care about leaving money behind them?"

The elder Berners, a man of seventy, rarely went into town but spent most of his days in his little garden and during my own visit at the house he came every day to sit with me, smoking his pipe and talking until he fell asleep in his chair. When he had been a younger man and before his wife died he had owned several trotting horses of which he loved to talk. One of the horses, named "Peter Point," had been the pride and joy of his life and he spoke of the horse as of a beloved son.

Oh, what a great magnificent beast the stallion Peter Point had been and how he could trot! Sometimes when he spoke of him the old man jumped to his feet and climbing on the chair seat touched the limb of an apple tree with his fingers. "Looket here now. He was taller than that. Yes, siree! He was taller than that when he threw up his head," he declared, jumping down from the chair and hopping about like an excited boy and walking up and down before me rubbing his hands together. He told me a long tale of a trip he had once taken with his stallion and two trotting mares as far east as Pennsylvania and of how Peter Point won every race in which he started, always the trotting free-for-all, and spoke fervently of the moment when he came out with the others and paraded before the grandstand before the first heat of a race. Jim Berners, then young and strong, sat in the sulky and what a moment it was for him. The memory of it filled him with excitement. "My father used to talk of the English aristocracy to his friend the judge, with whom I was left when all my family died, and the judge told me tales of what he had to say. Sometimes on days like that, when we came out for the first heat and were scoring down for the start or going slowly back for another try after a false start, I used to think of his words. There was me, sitting in the sulky, and there was the man, old Charlie Whaley, who took care of Peter Point, standing over near the grandstand with a blanket over his shoulder. Charlie winked and nodded at me and I winked at him. How swelled up with pride I was. I usually had two or three hundred dollars bet on Peter's chances and he never once went back on me. I thought we were pretty aristocratic ourselves, Peter and me.

"Well, and so there we were jogging slowly up to the starting place and the people in the grandstand were shouting and down in the betting ring there was a hubbub and I used to look at the people and think about them and about myself and the horse too. 'Lordy,' I used to say to myself, 'what a lot we do think of ourselves and what God-awful things we are, we humans, come right down to it.' I was raised in the old Judge Willard's house, right here in this town, you know, and in the old days a lot of what we called our big men used to come to talk their affairs over with the judge. Abe Lincoln used to come and once the editor of the *Chicago Tribune* and young Logan

241

who afterward got to be governor, and a lot of others, congressmen, and other such truck. They came and planned and schemed and then they used to make speeches up in front of the town hall that was down by the river in the old town but that later burned to the ground. They talked and talked, and I used to listen.

"And such talk! 'All men are created free and equal,' 'Nature's noblemen,' 'Noble pioneers' and all that kind of stuff about men just like me. Lordy, what a lot of big sounding words I had listened to when I was a kid. It used to make me sick to think of it sometimes later, when I was sitting up there behind Peter and to think that I had sometimes believed such bunk myself, I who had seen and known a lot of them same pioneers pretty intimately and should have known better than to listen.

"As I say, I used to think about it and a lot of other foolishness I'd heard, when I was up behind Peter, and he with his head up so high and looking—say, he could walk past one of them grandstands and past all of them people like God Almighty himself might have walked! What I mean is, not giving the people or the other horses in the race or the other drivers or the judges up in the stand or me or anyone anything but his darned contempt. It was lovely to see. Sometimes when he'd see a mare he'd throw up his head and snort and sometimes there was a little quiet noise he made just as though he was saying to us 'You worms, you worms,' to all of us, all of the people in the world including myself.

"Why, hell, no one ever knew how fast that Peter could trot. He got sick and died before he ever got to the grand circuit where horses of his own class usually raced," the old man declared proudly. Jim Berners had taken his horses over into Ohio and with Peter had won a race at a place called Fostoria and then that night the horse was taken violently ill and lying down in his stall quietly died.

His owner had been in at the death and after the stallion was dead had walked about the dark race course the rest of the night and had decided to give up racing. "I took a turn about the track," he said, "and stood a long time at the head of the stretch thinking of the times I had made the turn up there, with Peter leading all the other horses, and not half extending himself at that, and of how proud I had been so many times, sitting behind him and pretending to myself I was doing the job. I wasn't doing a darned thing but sitting still and riding home in front. It was only after Peter died I ever told myself the truth.

"I stood up at the head of the stretch, as I said, and the moon came out and Peter was dead now and I decided to go home. And I had some thoughts that night about most human beings, including myself, that I haven't ever forgot. I thought a lot of us were swine and the rest a kind of half-baked lot, put us against a horse like Peter had been. 'And so,' I said to myself, 'I'll quit racing and go home and try to keep my mouth shut a good deal of the time.' And I haven't been too much stuck on myself or anyone else ever since."

243

BERNERS, the merchant and horseman, had for a
good many years been disappointed and hurt by the
thought that his family was not to carry on after his
death but in his old age had grown cheerful about the
matter. "We aren't so much. It doesn't matter.
I dare say the sun will come up mornings and the
moon at night when there are no more Berners in
Illinois, or anywhere else, for that matter." As a
child the boy Alonzo was always sickly. "We've always been thinking he'd die, about twice every year,
but you see he hasn't quite done it yet," the old man
said softly.

Hallie, the daughter of the house, was five years
older than her brother and was devoted to him.
After seeing them together one understood that she
could never have married. It was just a thing that
couldn't have happened. One thought of her as saying to herself: "Marriage is too intimate. I am not
made for intimate relations." The idea of Hallie
Berners held in a man's arms was for some obscure
reason monstrous and yet how affectionate she was!
There was a sense in which her brother and father
were babes in her charge, babes never touched by her
hands or her lips but constantly caressed by her
thoughts. She was a tall rather stern-looking woman
with graying hair, large strong hands and quiet gray

eyes and she was very shy. Her shyness expressed itself in severity and when she was much touched she grew silent and almost haughty in her bearing. It was as though she were saying to herself: "Look out now! If you are not careful you will let something precious escape you."

The son Alonzo was a man of thirty-five with a little black mustache, thin features, small delicate hands and thick black hair. As a young man he had gone away to an eastern college but a desperate illness had compelled him to come home almost at once and he had not again tried getting out from under his sister's care, only leaving the family roof when he crept away for the brief periods of drunkenness that gave him a temporary means of escape out of his house of pain. He stayed at home and on fair days sometimes rode about town and the surrounding country behind an old black horse that belonged to the family or sat in the garden under the apple trees talking with friends who came to see him. In a large room in the house where he stayed on dull or cold days there were a couch, a fireplace and many books on shelves built into the walls.

How many people came up along the hillside road to sit and talk with Alonzo Berners! Were they sorry for him? At first I thought they were and then I saw they came to receive rather than to give. It was Alonzo who did the giving to all. What did he give? Among those I saw at the house was a local judge, son of that judge with whom his father had lived when he was a boy, a man named Marvin Manno, who lived in Chicago but who often came to the town and spent two or three days for the sake of talking with the invalid and who paid him a visit during my time there, two or three doctors who came, not in a professional way but for something unprofessional they wanted, a cripple of the town who made his living by taking people's photographs, a man who bought and sold horses, and a tall silent boy who wore glasses and who had large protruding teeth so that he looked something like a horse when on rare occasions he smiled.

Life in the Berners household—in reality presided over by the sick man, in a queer way absolutely controlled by him—was a revelation to me. Like that Judge Turner I had known a few years before, and for that matter like myself too, the man had read a great many books and was still constantly reading— he spent more than half his time with a book in his hands and told me once that but for books he thought he should have gone mad from the gnawing pains that were always eating at him—but in the single fact that we were all readers the similarity between Judge Turner, Alonzo and myself ceased.

In this new man whose path I had unexpectedly crossed was a quiet kind of sanity unknown in any other I had seen. He was a giver. What did he give? The question amazed and startled me. He was loved by all who knew him and during the week I spent in his house, seeing him with other men and riding with him about town and out into the country, I was startled by the feeling of love and well-being that came into the eyes of people when he appeared among them. My own mind, always given to asking questions, unable to take anything for granted, raced like the stallion Peter Point carrying old Jim Berners to one of his victories. Was there a kind of power in pain to remake a man? My own conception of life was profoundly disturbed. The man before me had spent his entire life sitting in the dark house of pain. He sat there now looking out through the windows and into other houses that were alive and cheerful with health. Why had he health and sanity within himself while, almost without exception, the others including myself had not?

As I looked at him and at the men who came to visit him a kind of wonder grew within me. The man Marvin Manno, a slender man, rather elegantly clad and with gold-rimmed glasses on his large nose, was talking. He was connected, in an official capacity, with some large commercial establishment of the city, an establishment that sold goods to the Berners store, but he did not come to the town on business. Why had he come? He spoke continually of his own schemes and hopes and balanced oddly back and forth between devotion to the business interests he served and a kind of penchant he had for writing poetry. An odd effect was produced. The man was sincerely devoted to two interests in life that could not by any chance be combined and as one listened to his talk one became more and more puzzled. Only Alonzo Berners was not puzzled. He entered into the man's thoughts, understood him, gave him what he apparently wanted, sympathetic understanding without sentimentality. We sat in the garden back of the Berners house, the man Manno talked, a doctor came and spoke of his patients, and in particular of an old woman lying in a cabin down by the river, who for two years had been on the point of death but who could not

247

die. Then the judge spoke of his father and of political affairs in the state, the elder Berners boasted of the speed of the stallion Peter Point and the boy with the large teeth smiled shyly but remained silent.

Then when evening came and they had all gone away I looked at Alonzo Berners and wondered. In all the talk no mention was ever made of himself or his own affairs. Even the pain always present in his body had been forgotten by the others. Any mention of his suffering would have seemed out of place.

My own mind was groping about in a new medium for the expression of a life. I was very young then, had not yet come to the age of citizenship, but for a long time I had been building within myself my own consciousness of men. Well, they were a kind of thing, selfish and self-centred, and they were right in being so. One played the game, won if he could and tried not to be a bellyacher if he lost. In me was a kind of contempt for men including myself that Alonzo Berners did not have. Where had I got my contempt and how had he escaped getting it? Was he right and I wrong or was he a sentimentalist? My mind had run into a thicket of new ideas and I could not find my way out. "Tread softly," I said to myself.

I sat aside, near the boy with the teeth, looking at my new acquaintance and trying to straighten all these things out in my mind. Hundreds of men, famous and infamous, I had met in the books I had read, went as in a procession across the field of my fancy. How many books I had read and how many stories of the lives of men, so-called great men and rascals, lovely women with gold and jewels in their hands, great killers of men, lawgivers, daring breakers of the law, devout men, starving in deserts for the glory of God; what men and women, what vast resounding names!

Was there something in the books I had missed? A vagrant thought came. Across the pages of some of the books there had wandered a different kind of man or woman. The writers of books had little to say about such people. There was little enough to be said. In the stories told of the great they appeared always as minor characters. The great strutted. The others walked softly. Clement VII had sent an ambassador to Charles of Spain. What the ambassador, one of the mysterious quiet fellows, said to Charles "Emperor of the Romans and Lord of the whole world" (*Romanorum Imperitor semper augustus, mundi totius Dominus, universus dominis, Universis Principibus et Populis semper verandus*) one did not know, but a peculiar thing happened. The ambassador served faithfully both Charles and the Pope, endeared himself to the two mortal enemies. They were both happier with him about. A thousand conflicting interests swirled about him but he kept himself quite clear. Could it have been that such a one loved men, as men, and that men loved him? There was so little for the writers of books to say of such fellows. They had not sought exalted office and seemed content to play the minor rôle in life. What were they up to? Was there a power greater than obvious power, a power not having in it the disease of obvious power?

I looked about me and wondered. Before me, sitting among men in an Illinois village, was a pale man with delicate hands who, two or three times a year, be-

249

came hopelessly drunk and who then had to be brought back helpless to his home, as I had brought him a few days before. Men gathered about and talked of their own affairs and he sat for the most part in silence, saying only now and then a few words, always in their interests. His mind seemed always to follow the minds of the others. Did he have no life of his own?

I began to resent the man but as I sat with him the cynicism of Judge Turner I had so much admired lost some of its force in me and the elder Berners, condemning men as less worthy of life than race horses became a half-amusing figure. I was mystified and amazed. Did most men and women remain children and was Alonzo Berners grown up? Was it grown up to come to the realization that oneself did not matter, that nothing mattered but a kind of consciousness of the wonder of life outside oneself?

I sat under the apple trees smiling to myself and wondering why I smiled. Was there possible such a thing as goodness in men, a goodness that was not stuffy and hateful? Like most young men I had a contempt of goodness. Had I been making a mistake? The man before me now did not, like Judge Turner, say wise and witty things that remained fixed in the mind and that could afterward be passed off in conversations as one's own. Later in New York and in other American cities I was to see a good many men of a sort not unlike Judge Turner but few like Alonzo Berners. The smart fellows of the American Intelligentsia sat about in restaurants in New York and wrote articles for the political and semi-literary weeklies. A smart saying they had heard at dinner or at lunch the day before was passed off as their own in the next article they wrote. The usual plan was to write of politics or politicians or to slaughter some second-rate artist—in short, to pick out easy game and kill it with their straw shafts and they gained great reputations by pointing out the asininity of men everyone already knew for asses. For a great many years I was filled with admiration of such fellows and vaguely dreamed of becoming such another myself. I wanted then, as a young man, I think, to sit with Alonzo Berners and his friends and suddenly say something to upset them all. Alonzo's life of physical suffering was forgotten by me as by the others but unlike them there was in me a kind of unpleasant dislike of him, a dislike he saw and understood but let pass as being boyish vanity. The smart-seeming things I thought of to say sounded flat enough when I said them over to myself and I remained silent. Occasionally Alonzo turned to me and smiled. I had done him a kindness, had risked something for him, and I was his guest. Perhaps he thought me not mature enough to understand him and his kind of men. Would I ever become mature?

DID I in reality also love the man?

I had found him, on a Saturday evening, very drunk in a saloon in Chicago. It was about nine o'clock and some time after I had fled from Nora. I was nearly broke and thought I had better be thinking of doing something that would bring me in a little money. What should I do? The devil! It was apparent I would soon have to go to work again with my hands. After some weeks of idleness my hands had become soft and velvety to the touch and I liked them so. Now they were hands to hold a pen or a paint brush. Why was I not a writer or a painter? Well, I fancied one had to be a fellow of the schools before one dared approach the arts. Often I went about cursing the fate that had not permitted me to be born in the fifteenth century instead of the twentieth with its all-pervading smell of burning coal, oil and gasoline, and with its noises and dirt. Mark Twain might declare the twentieth the most glorious of all the centuries but it did not seem so to me. I thought often of the fifteenth century in Italy when the great Borgia was just coming into power, was at that time full of the subject. What glorious children! Why could not I be a glorious child? Aha! the Lord Rodrigo de Lancol y Borgia, Cardinal-Bishop of Porto and Santa Rufina, Dean of the Sacred College, Vice-Chancellor

of the Holy Roman Church, etc., had just been made
Pope. Did I not myself have an Italian grandmother?
What a place and a time that might have been for
me! It was the day of the coronation of the new
Pope and all Rome was excited. On the day before
four mules, laden with silver, had gone from Cardinal
Rodrigo's house to the house of Cardinal Sforza-
Visconti. It was the gentle privilege of the Romans
in those fine days to pillage the house of a cardinal
when he had been made pope. Was it not said, in
the sacred laws, that the vicar of Christ should give
his substance to the poor? Fearing he might not do
it the poor went and took. Armed bands of desperate
fellows, with feathers in their hats, roamed the streets
of the old city at such times and a turn of the wheel
of fortune might at any moment make any one of
them rich and powerful, a patron of the arts, a rich
and powerful grandee of Church or State. How I
longed to be a richly gowned, soft-handed cunning but
scholarly grandee and patron of the arts!

How much better times those than my own for such
haphazard fellows as myself, I thought, and cursed the
twentieth century and the fate that had thrown me
into it. At that time in Chicago I knew a young Jew
named Ben Hecht, not yet a well-known writer, and
sometimes he and I went forth to do our cursing together. Outwardly he was a more adept curser than
myself but inwardly I felt I could outdo him and often
we had walked together, he cursing aloud our common
fate and declaring dramatically that life was for us
an empty cup, a vessel turned upside down, a golden
goblet with cracks in the bowl, the largest crack being
the fact that we both unfortunately had our livings to

make, and I striving to cap his every curse with a more violent one. We went together into a street and stood under the moon. Before us were many huge ugly warehouses. "I hope they burn," I said feebly, but he only laughed at the weakness of my fancy. "I hope the builders die slowly of a painful inflammation of the membranes of the bowels," he said, while I envied.

I had been walking alone on the streets of Chicago on that Saturday evening when I found the younger Berners and had crossed the river to the west side. I was gloomy and distraught and on a side street, off West Madison Street and near the Chicago River, went into a small, dark saloon. Several men sat at a small table at the back, among whom was Alonzo Berners and there was a red-faced bartender leaning over the bar and watching the group at the table. To all these I at the moment paid no attention.

I was absorbed in the contemplation of my own difficult position in life and was thinking only of myself. Sitting at a table I called for a glass of brandy and when it was paid for realized that I had but two dollars left in my pocket. I took the two dollars in my hand and looked at them and putting them away continued looking at my empty hands. They had, at the moment, as I have said, grown soft and velvety and I wanted them to remain so. Wild dreams floated through my mind. Why had I not more physical courage? It was all very well to talk with Ben Hecht of the many advantages to be gained by being an Italian desperado of the fifteenth century, but why had I not the courage to be a desperado of the twentieth? Surely Rome or Naples or Florence, in the days of their glory, never offered any better pickings than the Chicago of my own day. In the older day a man slipped a slender knife delicately between his victim's neck and spine and made off with a few ducats at the risk of his life but in Chicago men habitually got thousands of dollars by robbery apparently without any risk at all. I looked at my own hands and wondered. Could they hold a pistol steadily to the head of a timid bank clerk or a mail-wagon driver? I decided they could not and was ashamed of myself. Then I decided they might some day be induced to hold a pen or a painter's brush but reflected that the great patrons of the arts were all long since dead and that my own brother, a painter, had been compelled to make magazine covers for commercial "gents" in order to get the slender amount necessary to educate himself in his craft. "Huh!" I said to myself, not wanting I'm afraid, to work for any commercial "gent" at all. Drinking my brandy I looked about the room into which I had wandered.

It was a desperately dark little hole, lighted by two gaslights and with two beer-stained tables in the semi-darkness at the rear. I looked at the bartender, who had a large flat nose and bloodshot eyes and decided it was just as well I had but two dollars. "I may be robbed before I leave this hole," I told myself and ordered another glass of brandy, thinking I might as well drink up the little money I had rather than have it taken from me.

And now the men at the other table in the room caught and held my attention. With the exception of Alonzo Berners, whom the others had picked up on the street, they were a hard-looking lot. One did not think of them as desperate fellows. They were of the sort one saw hanging about the places of Hinky Dink, Bathhouse John or of Conners, the gray wolf, men famous in Chicago at that time, sullen fellows without money, by no means desperate but hangers-on of the desperate, fellows who robbed full of fright at their own temerity but the more dangerous sometimes because of their fears.

I looked at them and at the man who had fallen into their clutches and who was now spending his money upon them and at the same moment they seemed to have become aware of my presence. Sullen eyes looked at me sullenly. I was not of their world. Was I a fly cop? Their eyes threatened. "If you are a fly cop or are in any way connected with the man we have so fortunately picked up, a man quite apparently helplessly drunk and having money, you had better be minding your business. As a matter of fact it would be well for you to get out of here."

I returned the stare directed at me and hesitated a moment. The sick drunken man sitting among the others had a large roll of bills held in his left hand that hung at his side, and his right elbow was on the table.

What a look of suffering in his face! From time to time the others ordered drinks brought from the bar and the sick man took a bill from the roll and threw it on the table. When the change was brought by the bartender one of his companions put it in his pocket. They were taking turns, it was apparent, in robbing the man and as I looked an idea came to me. Was it true that the bartender, a more out-and-out fellow than the others, was disgusted at this slow and comparatively painless method of committing robbery?

Did I see in his eyes a kind of sympathy for the man being robbed?

It was a ticklish moment for me. Having been thinking so grandiloquently of Cæsar Borgia, Lorenzo the Magnificent and other grand and courageous personages of my world of books, having just been gazing at my own hands and wondering why they would not or could not do some act of personal courage that would make me think better of myself, having these thoughts, I of a sudden wanted to rescue the man with the roll of bills but I did not want to make a fool of myself. I have always wanted not to be a fool and have been a fool so often!

I had decided to perform a certain act and at the same time began laughing at myself, not thinking I would be foolish enough to attempt it. One of these conflicts between myself, as I live in my fancy, and myself as I exist in fact, that have been going on in me since I was a child had now started. It is the sort of thing that makes autobiography, even of the half-playful sort I am now attempting, so difficult to manage. One wants to treat oneself as a person of more dignity and worth than one has the courage to attempt. Among advertising men with whom I later associated we managed things better. We took turns doing what we called "staging" each other. I was to speak highly of Smith who in turn did the same of me. The trick is not unknown to literary men, but it is difficult to manage in autobiography. The self of the fancy persists in laughing at the self of fact and does it sometimes at unfortunate moments. Also the fancy is a great liar. How often later, when I became a man of business, I did in fancy some shrewd or notable act

257

that was never done in fact at all, but that seemed so real that it was difficult not to believe in it as a fact. I had been talking with a certain man and later thought of a number of brilliant things I might have said. Then I met a friend and told him of the conversation, putting the brilliant things in. The story several times repeated became a part of the history of my life and nothing would have later so amazed me as to have been compelled to face the facts of the conversation and the figure I had cut in it.

Was the thing I now thought myself about to do in the saloon a fact or was it but another of the fanciful acts, created in my own imagination, I might and no doubt would later relate as a fact? Would it not be better not to attempt to rescue the man in the room and later just to say I had and in the end make myself believe I had?

There was little doubt I could do the thing more gaudily in fancy. The place in which I sat was in a part of the city little frequented at night. Near it were only vacant lots and rows of dark and now empty factory buildings. It was unlikely there were any policemen in the neighborhood and in case of need and if a policeman did appear what sort of fellow was he likely to be—a fellow really appointed to the district to knock aside such interfering fools as myself? As for the men seated at the table, if they were cowards it was unlikely the bartender was one.

I kept smiling to myself, at my own thoughts, at my trick of always threshing my acts out in advance and in the end doing nothing except to create later the fiction of an act performed. "My book reading and my conversations with such fellows as Judge Turner are making a bigger fool of me than I need be," I told myself, still looking at the empty hands lying on the table before me. What really empty things they were, 'those same hands of mine. They had never grasped anything, never fulfilled any purpose for me. So many fingers, so many pads of flesh in the palms, so many little muscles to grasp things, to lay hold of some situation, to drive a knife into an enemy, to lift a friend, to make love to a woman, hands to become servants of the brain and to make their owner something other than a meaningless thing of words and fancies drifting through life with millions of other meaningless men. I really thought at that time I had a brain. It is an illusion that I believe almost everyone has.

In disgust of myself my eyes stopped looking at my empty hands ·and looked instead about the room. What seemed to me a stream of deliciously romantic notions now came. There was no doubt the man sitting with the crew from the city's underworld was very ill. One might have said he was about to die. A chalky pallor had spread over his face and except for his eyes everything about his face and figure expressed utter weariness. It was so people looked when they were about to die, when they were through with life, done for, glad to throw life aside.

The face and figure of the man were like that but the eyes were not. They were alive and only seemed curious and puzzled. As they looked at me from out the pale face I had the curious illusion of a voice speaking, speaking as though out of a coffin or a cavern.

Now the man's eyes were looking from my eyes to the eyes of the bartender. Was there something commanding in them? Had the sick man, in his help-less position, the power to command the two men in the room who might conceivably be of use to him? The man had been drunk for several days, and now he was not drinking but the poison from the vile stuff he had taken had permeated his system. The same eyes had looked at the men among whom he sat and his brain had come to a decision concerning them. Men's eyes could be impersonal sometimes. The other men at the table were of no value, had been thrown aside as useless. One fancied a thin sick body going on for days, eyes not looking about, eyes alive in a corner of the head of a man waiting for a moment of sanity.

And now they command. The sick man was not afraid, as in his place I would have been. There was no fear in the eyes that now looked at me so steadily. It might be the man did not mind the fact that he was about to be robbed and perhaps his body had known so much pain that the additional pain of a beating would not too much matter.

As for myself I was thinking beyond my own depths, thinking of certain things as possible in another that could never have been possible in myself. I was a coward trying to think the thoughts of a brave man. From the very moment when I first became aware of the actuality of the man Alonzo Berners I began do-ing something I had never done before, I began to live in another, suffer in another, love another perhaps.

If the man's eyes were issuing a command what did he want? I grew resentful. What right had he to command me? Did he think me a fool? Unconsciously I had begun to resist a command. "I won't. You got yourself into this pickle, now get yourself out."

What a plague to have an imagination! It seemed to me a kind of wordless conversation, something after the following manner, now began between myself, the bartender and the man at the table.

From the bloodshot eyes of the bartender leaning over his bar words were now coming. I leaned forward to listen.

"Ah! Bah! I do not like this affair. You have fallen into the hands of these cheap thugs and from the looks of you I should say you are a rather decent sort. To me, situated as I am in life, that would not make any difference if the men robbing you were fellows I could respect. If any one of a dozen men I know chose to hit you over the head and throw your body into the river I would not lift a hand to prevent it. As the matter stands I think I will. I do not fancy these dogs you are with eating so fat a calf. As for myself you are not fair game. Poor chap, you are sick. I cannot leave my job here but the fellow over there at the table will take you away. Speak to him. He will do as you wish."

What a chattering of unheard voices my imagination had created in the room!

Words from the living eyes of the sick man.

"It does not matter about being robbed. If these men beat or kill me it does not matter. The point is I am tired now." The eyes smiled.

And now the man at the table was looking directly at me and his words, created, you understand in my

261

fancy, were directed at me. "Well, come on lad. Lift me up in your arms and carry me home. It is only because you are young and inexperienced you are afraid."

"AFRAID?" It was only because I was so thoroughly afraid I now arose from my seat and went toward the sick man. As for the imagined voices I did not believe in them. Did I not know the tricks of my own fancy and did the man think I was going to be fool enough to risk my hide for a stranger? It is true, had I been a man of physical courage, I might, without too great risk, have gone over to the table and snatched the roll of bills out of the sick man's hands. When it came right down to it I could at the moment use such a roll of bills very handily. Had I been a man of courage I might have gone blustering and swaggering to the table and bluffed everyone in the place but being, as I knew I was, a coward did the man sitting there think I was going to risk my hide for him?

I moved slowly toward the table, all the time laughing at myself and telling myself I was not going to do what I was at the same time obviously doing and the bartender coming from behind the bar with a hammer in his hand fell in behind me. I could see the hammer from a corner of my eye. Well, he was going to hit me with it. In a moment more my head would be crushed and, as would be quite plain to any man of sense, I would only be getting what I deserved. What a confounded fool! I was terribly frightened and at the same time there was a smile on my lips. My appearance at the moment must have been disconcerting to the men at the table.

They were apparently as great fools as myself. As I approached, the sick man, perhaps to free himself from the others, threw the roll of bills carelessly on the table and one of his companions put a large hairy hand over it. Was he also afraid? All of the men were looking intently at me and at the bartender behind me. Were they but waiting to see my head crushed? One of them got rather hesitatingly to his feet and doubling his fist raised it as though to strike me in the face—I had now got within a foot of the sick man—but the blow did not descend.

Reaching down I put my arms about the sick man's shoulder and half raised him to his feet, the foolish smile still on my face but as I saw he could not stand I prepared to take him in my arms. That would make me quite helpless but I was helpless enough as it was. What did it matter? "If I am going to be slugged I might as well be slugged doing something," I thought.

I lifted the man as gently as I could, placing the slender body over my shoulder and waiting for the blows that were to descend upon me but at that very moment the hand of the bartender reached over and snatching the roll of bills from under the hand on the table put it in my pocket.

All was done in silence and in silence, with Alonzo Berners slung over my shoulder, I walked to the door and to West Madison Street where there were lights and people passing up and down. At the corner I put him down and looking back saw the bartender standing at the door of his establishment watching. Was he laughing? I fancied he was. And one might also fancy he was keeping the others bluffed in the room until I had got safely away. I stood at the corner beside the sick man, who leaned helplessly against my legs, and waited for a cab that would take me to a railroad station. Already I had taken letters from his pocket and knew where he lived. He seemed unable to speak. "He will probably die on the way and then I'll be in a hell of a mess," I kept saying to myself after I had got with him into the day coach of a train.

My adventure with Alonzo Berners came to an end after I had been at his house for a week and during the week nothing I can set down as notable happened at all and later I was told he was dead, that he had again got drunk in the city of Chicago and had fallen or had been knocked off a bridge into the Chicago River where he drowned. There was the house on the hillside and the garden. During my visit to the house the elder Berners worked in the garden or sat with me boasting of the horse Peter Point and found in me a sympathetic audience. I have always understood horses better than men. It's easier.

I sat in the garden listening to the talk of the men who came to see Alonzo Berners, rode with him once in his buggy or went into town to walk by myself or to listen to some tale told by the sailor who managed the store. The sister, who on the night of my arrival had treated me coldly—no doubt strange characters had come to the Berners house on the same mission that had brought me and also no doubt she was in terrible fear when Alonzo was away on one of his helpless debauches—the sister later treated me with the silent kindliness characteristic of her.

Nothing happened at all during my visit and Alonzo Berners did not during the whole time say a notable

thing that I could later remember and that I can now
quote to explain my feeling for him.

Nothing happened but that I was puzzled as I had
never been before. There was something in the very
walls of the Berners house that excited and when I
had gone to bed at night I did not sleep. Notions
came. Odd exciting fancies kept me awake. As I
have explained I was then young and had quite made
up my mind about men and life. Men and women
were divided into two classes containing a few shrewd
wise people and many fools. I was trying very hard
to place myself among the wise and shrewd ones. The
Berners family I could not place in either of these
classifications and in particular Alonzo Berners puzzled and disconcerted me.

Was there a force in life of which I knew nothing
at all and was this force exemplified in the person of
the man I had picked up in a Chicago saloon?

At night as I lay in my bed new ideas, new impulses,
came flocking. There was a man in the house with
me, a man fairly worshiped by others and for no
reason I could understand but wanted to understand.
His very living in the house had done something to it,
to the very wall of the house, so that anyone coming
into the place, sleeping between the walls, was affected. Could it be that the man Alonzo Berners
simply loved the people about him and the places in
which they lived and had that love become a force in
itself affecting the very air people breathed? Sometimes in the afternoons when there was no one about
I went through the rooms of the house looking curi-
ously about. There was a chair here and a table
there. On the table lay a book. Was there also in

the house a kind of fragrance? Why did the sunlight fall with such a pronounced golden glory on the faded carpet on the floor of Alonzo Berner's room?

Questions invaded my mind and I was young and skeptical, wanting to believe in the power of the mind, wanting to believe in the power of intellectual force, terribly afraid of sentimentality in myself and in others.

Was I afraid also of people who had the power of loving, of giving themselves? Was I afraid of the power of unasking love in myself and in others?

That I should be afraid of anything in the realm of the spirit, that there should perhaps be a force in the world I did not understand, could not understand, irritated me profoundly.

As the week advanced my irritation grew and I have never had any doubt at all that Alonzo Berners knew of it. He said nothing and when I went away he had nothing to say. I spent the days of that week in his presence, saw the men who came to visit him and whom I thought I understood well enough and then at night went to my bed and did not sleep. I was like one tortured by a desire for conversion to something like the love of God, by a desire to love and be loved and sometimes in the night I lay in my bed like a very lovelorn maiden and sometimes I grew angry and walked up and down in the moonlight in my room swearing and shaking my fist at the shadows that flitted across the walls in the moonlight.

It was two o'clock of the morning of one of the last nights I spent in the house and I let myself out at the kitchen door and went for a walk, going down along the hillside to the town and through the newer town to the older place by the river. The moon was shining and all was hushed and silent. What a quiet night! "I will give myself over to these new impulses," I thought, and so went along thinking thoughts that had never before come into my head.

Could it be that force, all power was disease, that man on his way up from savagery and having discovered the mind and its uses had gone a little off his head in using his new toy? I had always been drawn toward horses dogs and other animals and among people had cared most for simple folk who made no pretense of having an intellect, workmen who in spite of the handicaps put in their way by modern life still loved the materials in which they worked, who loved the play of hands over materials, who followed instinctively a force outside themselves—they felt to be greater and more worthy than themselves—women who gave themselves to physical experiences with grave and fine abandon, all people in fact who lived for something outside themselves, for materials in which they worked, for people other than themselves, things over which they made no claim of ownership.

Was I, who thought of myself as a young man having no morality now face to face with a new morality? In the fifteenth century man had discovered man. Had man later been lost to man? Was Alonzo Berners simply one who loved his fellows and was he by that token stronger in his weakness, more notable in his obscure Illinois village life than all these great and powerful ones I had been following with my own mind across the pages of history?

There was no doubt I was in a magnificent mood and that I enjoyed it and when I got to the old town

I went and stood by a small brick building that had once been a residence but was now a cowshed. In a near-by house a child cried and a man and a woman awoke from sleep and talked for a time in low hushed voices. Two dogs came and discovered me where I stood in the silence. As I remained unmoved they did not know what to make of their discovery. At first they barked and then they wagged their tails, and then, as I continued to ignore them, they went away looking offended. "You are not treating us fairly," they seemed to be saying.

"And they are something like myself," I thought, looking at the dusty road on which the soft moonlight was falling and smiling at nothingness.

I had suddenly an odd, and to my own seeming a ridiculous desire to abase myself before something not human and so stepping into the moonlit road I knelt in the dust. Having no God, the gods having been taken from me by the life about me, as a personal God has been taken from all modern men by a force within that man himself does not understand but that is called the intellect, I kept smiling at the figure I cut in my own eyes as I knelt in the road and as I had smiled at the figure I had cut in the Chicago saloon when I went with such an outward show of indifference to the rescue of Alonzo Berners.

There was no God in the sky, no God in myself, no conviction in myself that I had the power to believe in a God, and so I merely knelt in the dust in the silence and no words came to my lips.

Did I worship merely the dust under my knees? There was the coincidence as there is always the co-incidence. The symbol flashed into my mind. A child cried again in a near-by house and I presume some traditional feeling come down from old tellers of tales took possession of me. My fancy played with the figure of myself in the ridiculous position into which I had got and I thought of the wise men of old times who were reputed to have come to worship at the feet of another crying babe in an obscure place. How grand! The wise men of an older time had followed a star to a cowshed. Was I becoming wise? Smiling at myself and with also a kind of contempt of myself and my own sentimentality I half decided I would try to devote myself to something, give my life a purpose. "Why not to another effort at the rediscovery of man by man?" I thought rather grandly, getting up and beating the dust off my knees, the while I continued the trick I had learned of pointing the laughing finger of scorn at myself. I laughed at myself but all the time kept thinking of the occasional flashes of laughter that came from the drawn lips of Alonzo Berners. Why was his laughter freer and more filled with joy than my own?

NOTE XIV

WAR, leisure and the South!

The leisure was not too much cut across by the hours spent in drills and manœuvres and the other duties of a soldier. Here was a life in which everything was physical, the mind on a vacation and the imagination having leisure to play while the body worked. One's individuality became lost and one became part of something wholly physical, vast, strong, capable of being fine and heroic, capable of being brutal and cruel.

One's body was a house in which had lived two, three, perhaps ten or twelve personalities. The fancy became the head of the house and swept the body away into some absurd adventure or the mind took charge and laid down laws. These then were in turn driven out of the house by physical desire, by the lustful self. Dumb nights of walking city streets, wanting women, wanting to touch with the hands lovely things.

"Dust and ashes!" So you creak it and I want the heart to scold.
Dear dead women, with such hair, too.—What's become of all the gold
Used to hang and brush their bosoms?

All gone now, that kind of imaginings, for the time anyway. In the distance, beckoning, the women of

272

the southern island, the dark Cuban women. Would they like us when we came, we American lads, in our brown clothes? Would they take us as lovers, we the land's deliverers?

Long days of marching. We were in a forest of the South where once our fathers had fought a great battle. Everywhere camps among the trees and the ground worn hard as bricks by the constant tramping of feet. In the morning one awoke with five other men in a tent. There was morning roll call standing shoulder to shoulder. "Corporal Smith!" "Here!" "Corporal Anderson!" "Here!" Then breakfast out of flat tin dishes and the falling into line for hours of drill.

Out from under the trees into a wide field we went, the southern sun pouring down on us and presently the back tired, the legs tired. One sank into a half-dead state. This did not signify battles, killing other men. The men with whom one marched were comrades, feeling the same weariness, obeying the same commands, being molded with oneself into something apart from oneself. We were being hardened, whipped into shape. For what? Well, never mind. Take what is before you! You have come out from under the shadow of the factory, the sun shines. The tall boys marching with you were raised in the same town with yourself. Now they are all silent, marching, marching. Times of adventure ahead. You and they will see strange people, hear strange tongues spoken.

The Spaniards, eh! You know of them from books? Stout Cortez, silent upon his peak in Darien. Dark cruel eyes, dark swaggering men—in one's fancy. In the fancy picture ships coming suddenly

273

up out of the western seas, bearing gold, bearing dark, adventurous men.

Is one going to fight such men, with one's comrades, some thousands of such men? Tall boys from an Ohio town, baseball players, clerks in stores, Eddie Sanger over there who got Nell Brinker into trouble and was made to marry her at the point of a shotgun; Tom Means, who was once sent to the state reform farm; Harry Bacon, who got religion when the evangelist came to preach in the Methodist Church but got over it afterward—are these men to become killers, to try to kill Spaniards, who will try to kill them?

Now, never mind! There is before you now but the marching for long hours with all these men. Here is something your mind has always been groping about trying to understand, the physical relation of man to man, of man to woman, of woman to woman. The mind is ugly when the flesh does not come in too. The flesh is ugly when the mind is put out of the house that is the body. Is the flesh ugly now? No, this is something special. This is something felt.

Suppose a man spend certain months, not thinking consciously, letting himself be swept along by other men, with other men, feeling the weariness of a thousand other men's legs in his own legs, desiring with others, fearing with the others, being brave sometimes with the others. By such an experience can one gain knowledge of the others and of oneself too?

Comrades loved! Never mind now the thoughts of the hour of killing. One gets little enough. Take what is offered. And the killing may not come. Let the Roosevelts and others of that sort, the men of action, talk and think now of the hour of action, of the

274

drawn sword, the pointed gun, victory, defeat, glory, bloody fields. You are not a general or a statesman. Take the thing before you, the physical marching fact of an army of which you are a part.

There is just the possibility that you are yourself a disease and that you may be cured here. This tremendous physical experience may cure you of the disease of yourself. Can one lose oneself utterly, become as nothing, become but a part of something, the state, the army? The army is something physical and actual while the state is nothing. The state exists but in men's minds and imaginations and you have let your own imagination rule in your house too long. Let this young body of yours, so straight, so fair, so strong, let it have full possession of the house now. The imagination may play now over fields, over mountain tops if it please. "We are coming, Father Abraham, a hundred thousand strong!" You have forced your fancy to grovel in factory dust too long. Let it go now. You are nothing, so many little pounds of flesh and bone, a small unit in a vast thing that is marching, marching—the army. Blossoms on apple trees, sap in the branches of trees, a single head of wheat in a vast wheat field, eh?

All day long the march goes on and dust gathers in little circles about the eyes of weary men. A thin sharp voice is heard, an impersonal voice. It is speaking, not to you, not to one man only, but to a thousand men. "Fours right into line."

"Fours right into line!" You have so wanted that, have so hungered for it. Has not your whole life been filled with a vague indefinite desire to wheel into some vast line with all the others you have known and seen?

It is enough! The legs respond. Tears sometimes gather in the eyes at the thought of being able, without question, to do some one thing with thousands of others, with comrades.

NOTE XV

I HAD enlisted for a soldier shortly after my visit
to Alonzo Berners and because I was broke and could
see no other way to avoid going back into a factory.
The voices crying out for war with Spain, for the free-
ing of Cuba, I had heard not at all but there had been
a voice within myself that was plain and clear enough
and I did not believe there was danger of many battles
being fought. The glory of Spain, read about in the
books, was dead. We had old Spain at a disadvan-
tage, poor old woman. The situation was unique.
America, the young and swaggering giant of the West
had been fortunate. She had not been compelled to
face, on the field of battle, the giant of the Old World
in the days of her Old World strength. Now the
young western giant was going to assert himself and
it would be like taking pennies from a child, like robbing an old gypsy woman in a vacant lot at night after
a fair. The newspapers might call into service Stephen
Crane, Richard Harding Davis, all the writers of
battle tales trying to work up the illusion of a great
war about to be fought, but no one believed, no one
was afraid. In the camps the soldiers laughed. Songs
were being sung. To the soldiers the Spaniards were
something like performers in a circus to which the
American boys had been invited. It was said they had
bells on their hats, wore swords and played guitars

277

under the windows of ladies' bedrooms at night.

America wanted heroes and I thought I would enjoy being a hero and so I did not enlist for a soldier in Chicago, where I was unknown and my rushing to my country's aid might have passed unnoticed, but sent off a wire to the captain of militia of my home town in Ohio and got on a train to go there. Alonzo Berners had pressed upon me a loan of a hundred dollars but I did not want to spend any of it for railroad fare so beat my way homeward on a freight train and even the hoboes with whom I sat in an empty freight car treated me with respect as though I were already the hero of a hundred hard-fought battles. At a station twenty miles from home I bought a new suit of clothes, a new hat, neckties and even a walking stick. My home town would want to think I had given up a lucrative position in the city to answer my country's call, they would want a Cincinnatus dropping his plow handles, and why should I not give them the best imitation I could manage? What I achieved was something between a bank clerk and an actor out of work.

I was received with acclaim. Never before that time or since have I had a personal triumph and I liked it. When, with the others of my company, I marched away to the railroad station to entrain for war the entire town turned out and cheered. Girls ran out of houses to kiss us and old veterans of the Civil War—they had known that of battles we would never know—stood with tears in their eyes.

To the young factory hand of the cities—that was myself, as I now remember myself at that moment—it was grand and glorious. There has always been a kind of shrewdness and foxiness in me and I could not

278

convince myself that Spain, clinging to its old traditions, old guns, old ships, could offer much resistance
to the strong young nation now about to attack and I
could not get over the feeling that I was going off
with many others on a kind of glorious national picnic.
Very well, if I was to be given credit for being a hero
I could not see why I should object.

And then the camp at the edge of a southern city
under forest trees, the physical hardening process that
I instinctively liked. I have always enjoyed with a
kind of intoxicating gusto any physical use of my body
out in the sun and wind. In the army it brought me
untroubled sleep at night, physical delight in my own
body, the drunkenness of physical well-being and often
in my tent at night, after a long day of drilling and
when the others slept, I rolled quietly out under the
tent flap and lay on my back on the ground, looking at
the stars seen through the branches of trees. About
me many thousands of men were sleeping and along a
guard line, somewhere over there in the darkness,
guards were walking up and down. Was it a kind of
vast child's play? The guards were pretending the
army was in danger, why should not my own imagination play for a time?

How strong my body felt! I stretched and threw
my arms above my head. For a time my fancy
played with the notion of becoming a great general.
Why might not Napoleon in his boyhood have been
just such a fellow as myself? I had read somewhere
that he had had an inclination to be a scribbler. I
fancied the army, of which I was a part, hemmed in
on all sides by untold thousands of fierce Spaniards.
No one could think what to do and so I (Corporal

Anderson) was sent for. The Americans were in the same position the French revolutionists had been in when young Napoleon appeared and with "a whiff of grapeshot" took the destinies of a nation in his hands. Oh, I had read my Carlyle and knew something also of Machiavelli and his Prince. Aha! In fancy also I could be a great and cruel conqueror. The American army was surrounded by untold thousands of fierce Spaniards but in the American army was myself. This was my hour. I sat up on the ground outside the tent where my comrades were sleeping and in the darkness gave quick and accurate orders. Certain ones of my soldiers were to make a sortie. I did not quite know what a sortie was but anyway why not have one made? It would create a diversion, give my marvelous mind time to work. And now it was done and I began to fling bunches of troops here and there. My courier sprang upon a swift horse and rode away in the darkness. In his tent the Spanish commander was feasting—and here I, being a true Anglo-Saxon, must needs make out that the imaginary Spaniard was something of a monster. He was half drunk in his tent and was surrounded by concubines. Ah! he is sure to have concubines about and is proud and sure of victory but little does he know of me, the sleepless one. Grand phrases, grand ideas, flocking like birds! Now the Spanish commander has shown his true nature. A young boy comes to bring him wine and trips, spilling a little of the wine on the commander's uniform. He arises and unsheathing his sword plunges it into the little boy's breast. All are aghast. The Spaniards all stand aghast, and at that very moment I, like an avenging angel, and followed by thousands of pure clean-living Americans (Anglo-Saxon Americans, let it be understood), I swoop down upon him.

. . . .

At the time of which I am writing America had not learned as it did during the World War that in order to stamp out brutal militarism it is best to adopt brutal militarism, teach it to our sons, do everything possible to brutalize our own people. During the World War I am told boys and young men in the training camps were made to attack with the bayonet dummy figures of men and were even told to grunt as they plunged the bayonet into the figure. Everything possible was done to brutalize the imaginations of the young men, but in our war—"my war" I find myself calling it at times—we had not yet carried our education that far. There was as yet a childish belief in democracy. Men even supposed that the purpose of democracy was to raise free men who could think for themselves, act for themselves in an emergency. The modern idea of the standardization of men had not taken hold and was even thought to be inimical to the very notion of democracy. And we had not learned yet, as we did later, that when an army is to be organized you must split your men up, so that no man knows his fellows, that you must not have officers coming from the same towns as their soldiers, that everything must be made as machine-like and impersonal as possible.

And so there we were, just boys from an Ohio country town with officers from the same town in a wood in the South being made into soldiers and I am much afraid not taking the whole affair too seriously. We were heroes and we accepted the fact. It was enough.

In the southern cities ladies invited us to dine at their houses on our days off in town. The captain of our company had been a janitor of a public building back in Ohio, the first lieutenant was a celery raiser on a small farm near our town and the second lieutenant had been a knife grinder in a cutlery factory.

. . . .

In the camp I marched with the others for several hours each day and in the evening went with some other young soldier for a walk in the wood or in the streets of a southern city. There was a kind of drunkenness of comradeship. So many men so like oneself, doing the same thing with oneself. As for the officers— well, it was to be admitted that in military affairs they knew more than ourselves but there their superiority ended. It would be just as well for none of them to attempt to put on too much side when we were not drilling or were not on actual military duty. The war would soon be over and after a time we would all be going back home. An officer might conceivably "get away" with some sort of injustice for the moment— but a year from now, when we were all at home again. . . . Did the fool want to take the chance of four or five huskies giving him a beating some night in an alleyway?

The constant marching and manœuvring was a kind of music in the legs and bodies of men. No man is a single thing, physical or mental. The marching went on and on. The physical ruled. There was a vast slow rhythm, out of the bodies of many thousands of men, always going on and on. It got into one's body. There was a kind of physical drunkenness produced. He who weakened was laughed at by his

282

comrades and the weakness went away or he disappeared. One was afloat on a vast sea of men. There was a kind of music on the surface of the sea. The music was a part of oneself. One was oneself a part of the music. One's body, moving in rhythm with all these other bodies, made the music. What was an officer? What was a man? An officer was but one out of whose throat came a voice.

The army moved across a great open field. One's body was tired but happy with an odd new kind of happiness. The mind did not torture the body, asking questions. The body was moved by a power outside itself and as for the fancy, it played freely, far, freely and widely, over oceans, over mountain tops too.

> Beyond him not the ghost of shores,
> Beyond him only shoreless seas.

And now the voice and the words, caught up and repeated by other voices, harsh voices, tired voices, thin high pitched voices.

> Fours right into line—
> Fours right into line

. . . . . .

Three young men having run the guard line together are walking along a dark road toward a southern city. In the city and later when they have stood on street corners and walked through the section of the city where only Negroes live—being Ohio boys and fascinated by the strangeness of the notion of a race thus set aside—they go into a saloon where they sit drinking beer. They discuss their officers, the position of the officer in relation to his men. "I think it's all right," says a doctor's son. "Ed and Dug are all right. They have to live off by themselves and act as though they were something special, kind of grand and wise and gaudy. It's a kind of bluff, I guess, that has to be kept up, only I should think it would be kind of tough on them. I should think they might get to feeling they were something special and get themselves into a mess."

And now Ed, the raiser of celery, comes into the saloon. He is saving all he can of his officer's pay hoping to buy a few additional acres of land when he gets back home and he doesn't much like spending money. He sees the three sitting there and wants to join them but hesitates. Then he calls to me and he and I go off together along a street and into another saloon.

The celery raiser is a devout Catholic and he and I get into a discussion. I have some money and am buying the beer and so it goes on for a long time. I speak of the feeling I have when I have marched for a long time in rhythm with many other men and Ed nods his head. "It's the same way I feel about the Church," he says. "That's just the way we Catholics get to feeling about the Church."

At the camp Ed, being an officer, can walk boldly in but I, being but a corporal and having gone off to town without leave, must creep along the guard line to where a fellow from my own town is stationed. "Who goes there?" he demands sternly; and "Ah, cut it Will, you big boob. Don't make such a racket," I answer as I go past him and creep away in the darkness to my tent.

And now I am in the tent, awake beside five

sleeping men and I am filled with drinks and thinking of war. What a strange idea that men should need a war to throw many of them for a time into a common mood. Is there unison only in hatred? I do not believe it but the idea fascinates me. Men form a democracy but in the end must throw the democracy aside in order to make the army that shall protect and preserve democracy. The guard and myself creeping past him to my tent are as soldiers a little absurd. Is all feeling of comradeship, of brotherhood between many men, a little absurd?

BOOK THREE

NOTE I

"There is no lighter burden, nor more agreeable, than a pen. Other pleasures fail us, or wound us while they charm; but the pen we take up with rejoicing and lay down with satisfaction, for it has the power to advantage not only its lord and master, but many others as well, even though they be far away—sometimes, indeed, though they be not born for thousands of years to come. I believe I speak but the strict truth when I claim that as there is none among earthly delights more noble than literature, so there is none so lasting, none gentler, or more faithful; there is none which accompanies its possessor through the vicissitudes of life at so small cost of effort or anxiety."

—Petrarch's letter to Boccaccio.

I ONCE knew a devout smoker who went to spend the winter in Havana and when he had got there and was unpacking his trunk he began to laugh, realizing suddenly that he had packed the trunk half full of boxes of cigars, and I have myself on more than one occasion when going from one city to another on some affair of business carried with me thousands of sheets of paper, fearing, I presume, that all the stationers in the new place had died. The fear of finding myself without paper, ink or pencils is a kind of disease with me and it is with a good deal of effort only that I restrain myself from stealing such articles whenever I am left unobserved in a store or in someone's house. In houses where I live for some time I cache small stores of paper as a squirrel stores nuts and at one time in my life I had forcibly to be separated, by a considerate friend, from something like half a bushel of lead pencils I had for a long time carted about with me in a bag. There were enough pencils in the bag to have rewritten the history of mankind.

To the writer of prose, who loves his craft, there is nothing in the world so satisfying as being in the presence of great stacks of clean white sheets. The feeling is indescribably sweet and cannot be compared with any reaction to be got from sheets on which one has already scribbled. The written sheets are already covered with one's faults and oh, it is seldom indeed these sentences, scrawled across these sheets, can compare with what was intended! One has been walking in a street and has been much alive. What stories the faces in the streets tell! How significant the faces of the houses! The walls of the houses are brushed away by the force of the imagination and one sees and feels all of the life within. What a universal giving away of secrets! Everything is felt, everything known. Physical life within one's own body comes to an end of consciousness. The life outside oneself is all, everything.

Now for the pen or the pencil and paper and I shall make you feel this thing I now feel—ah, just that boy there and what is in his soul as he runs to look in at the window of the neighboring house in the early evening light; just what that woman is thinking as she sits on the porch of that other house holding the babe in her arms; just the dark, brooding thing in the soul of that laborer going homeward under those trees.

He is getting old and was born an American. Why did he not rise in the world and become the owner or at least the superintendent of a factory and own an automobile?

Aha! You do not know, but I do. You wait now, I shall tell you. I have felt all, everything. In myself I have no existence. Now I exist only in these others.

I have run home to my room and have lighted a light. Words flow. What has happened? Bah! Such tame, unutterably dull stuff! There was something within me, truth, facility, the color and smell of things. Why, I might have done something here. Words are everything. I swear to you I have not lost my faith in words.

Do I not know? While I walked in the street there were such words came, in ordered array! I tell you what—words have color, smell; one may sometimes feel them with the fingers as one touches the cheek of a child.

There is no reason at all why I should not have been able, by the instrumentality of these little words, why I should not have been able to give you the very smell of the little street wherein I just walked, made you feel just the way the evening light fell over the faces of the houses and the people—the half moon through the branches of that old cherry tree that was all but dead but that had the one branch alive, the branch that touched the window where the boy stood with his foot up, lacing his shoe. And there was the dog sleeping in the dust of the road and making a little whining sound out of his dreams and the girl on a nearby street who was learning to ride a bicycle. She could not be seen but her two young brothers laughed loudly every time she fell to the pavement.

These the materials of the story-writer's craft, these and the little words that must be made to run into sentences and paragraphs; now slow and haltingly, now quickly, swiftly, now singing like a woman's voice in a dark house in a dark street at midnight, now viciously, threateningly, like wolves running in a winter forest of the North.

Oh! This unutterable rot spoken sometimes about writing. "One is to consider the morals of the people who read, one is to please or amuse the people with these words and sentences. One lives in an age when there is much talk of service—to automobile owners, to riders on trains, to buyers of packages of food in stores. Is no one to do service to the little words, the words with which we make love, defend ourselves with lies after we have killed the friend who stole the woman we wanted—the words with which we bury our dead, comfort our friend, with which we are in the end to tell each other, if we may, all the secrets of our dreams and hopes?

I am servant to the words. Are you to tell me what words I shall put aside and not write? Are you to be the master of my mood, caught from yourself perhaps as you walked in the street and I saw you when you did not see me and when you were more sweet and true in all your bearing than you have ever been before, or when alas you were more vicious and cruel. Bah! The words I have put here on this paper!

But there are the clean sheets, the unwritten sheets.

On them I shall write daringly, boldly and truly—to-morrow.

. . . .

The writer has just come from the stationer's, where he has got him a fresh supply of sheets. He had money with him and bought five thousand. Ah, the weight of them on the arm as he walked off along a street to his own house. Four thousand nine hundred and ninety-nine times he may destroy the sheet on which he has been writing and there, lying before him, will be again the fresh white surface.

Makers of paper, I exclude you from all the curses I have heaped upon manufacturers when I have walked in the street breathing coal dust and smoke. I have heard your industry kills fish in rivers. Let them be killed. Fishermen are, in any event, noisy lying brutes. Last night I dreamed I had been made Pope and that I had issued a bull, excommunicating all owners of factories, consigning them to burn everlastingly in hell, but ah, I left you out of my curses, you busy makers of paper. Those who made paper at a low price and in vast quantities somewhere up in the forests of Canada, I sainted. There was one man—I invented him—named Saint John P. Belger, who furnished paper to indigent writers of prose free of charge. For virtue I put him, in my dream, almost on a level with Saint Francis of Assisi.

And now the writer has got to his room and has stacked the bundles of paper on the desk where he sits to write. He goes to a window and throws it open and there is a man passing. Who is the man?

The writer does not know but is tempted to throw a dish or a chair at his head, merely to show his contempt of the world. "Take that mankind! Go to Hades! Have I not five thousand sheets?"

It is without doubt a moment! In my boyhood I knew an old woodworker who on Sundays went to walk alone in a forest. Once I was lying on my back by a clump of bushes and saw his actions when he thought there was no one about.

What has mankind, in America, not missed because men do not know, or are forgetting, what the old workman knew? There was Sandro Botticelli who knew. He was in danger once of becoming married to a woman but at the critical moment he fled. All night he ran in the streets of Florence wrestling with himself and in the end won the victory. The woman was not to come between him and his surfaces, those cathedral walls, those dumb strips of canvas on which he was to paint—not all his dreams —what he could of his dreams. Nothing was to come between him and his materials.

The old woodworker in the forest approached a living tree and then walked away. He went close again and let his eye travel up along the tree's trunk. Then, hesitatingly, lovingly he touched the tree with his fingers. That was all. It was enough.

It was the workman en rapport with his materials. Oh, there is a feeling in the breasts of men that will not die. Ages come and go, but always the feeling is alive, haltingly, in the breasts of the few. To the workman his materials are as the face of his God seen over the rim of the world. His materials are the promise of the coming of God to the workman.

Ford factories cannot kill the love of materials in the workmen and always and in the end the love of materials and tools in the workmen will kill the Fords. Standardization is a phase. It will pass. The tools and materials of the workmen cannot always remain cheap and foul. Some day the workmen will come back to their materials, out of the sterile land of standardization. If the machine is to survive it will come again under the dominance of the hands of workmen, as it already no doubt is doing, in a hundred, perhaps a thousand unknown places. The day of re-discovery of man by man may not be so far off as we fancy. Has there not been, in our own time, a slackening of the impulse toward purely material ends? Has not the cry for success and material growth become already a bore to the average American?

These the thoughts of a man. To the boy lying in the silent place on the Sunday afternoon long ago and seeing the old workman touching so tenderly the tree that he dreamed might some day become the materials of his craft no such thoughts.

What happened? Just a tightening of the cords of the boy's body. There was an inclination to be at the same time sad and full of joy. A door had been jerked open by the hand of the workman but the boy could not see within the house. He was, I remember, known as something of a "nut" in our town—a silent old chap—and once he went away to work in a city factory but later came back to his own little shop. He was a wagon-maker and the making of wagons by individual workmen lasted out his time. But he had no young workman to whom he taught the love of his trade. That died with him.

Not quite, perhaps. The picture of the old workman and just the way his fingers touched the trunk of a tree on a certain Sunday afternoon and of how, as he walked away along a path, he kept stopping to turn back and take another look at his materials, stayed in a boy's mind through long years of being smart, of trying mightily to be shrewd and capable in a world where materials did not matter, in the company of workmen vulgarized by the fact that the old workman's love of materials was unknown to them.

. . . .

The writer with his sheets in a room. Will he accomplish his purpose? It is sure he will not. And that too is a part of the joy of his fate. Do not pity the workman, you who have succeeded in life. He wants no pity. Before him always there is the unsolved problem, the clean white unwritten sheets, and the workman also knows his moments of surrender, of happiness. There will always be the moments when he is lost in wonder before the possibilities of the materials before him.

As for myself I had been, at the time in my life of which I am now writing a man of business for many years, had been buying and selling, but had all the time been secretly scribbling in my room at night.

During the day I for years wrote advertisements —of soaps, of plows, house paints, incubators for the hatching of chickens.

Was there something hatching in me? With all my scribbling had I something to say? Were there tales I had picked up I might in the end tell truly and well? I had seen and known men and women, going from their homes to their work, going from their work to their homes, had worked with them in offices and shops. On all sides the untold tales looked out at me like living things.

I had bought and sold but had no real interest in buying and selling. All day I wrote advertisements and perhaps the advertisements helped sell So-and-so many dollars' worth of goods. As I walked homeward through streets, across bridges, I could not remember what I had been writing about.

At times too there was a sharp sense of uncleanliness. In my room the white sheets looked up at me. I remembered the workman seen in the forest in the presence of the tree when I was a boy. "I will launch out upon new adventures," I said to myself.

NOTE II

On an evening of the late summer I got off a train
at a growing Ohio industrial town where I had once
lived. I was rapidly becoming a middle-aged man.
Two years before I had left the place in disgrace.
There I had tried to be a manufacturer, a money-
maker, and had failed, and I had been trying and failing ever since. In the town some thousands of
dollars had been lost for others. An effort to conform to the standard dreams of the men of my times
had failed and in the midst of my disgrace and
generally hopeless outlook, as regards making a living,
I had been filled with joy at coming to the end of it
all. One morning I had left the place afoot, leaving
my poor little factory, like an illegitimate child, on
another man's doorstep. I had left, merely taking
what money was in my pocket, some eight or ten
dollars.

What a moment that leaving had been! To one of
the European artists I afterward came to know the
situation would have been unbelievably grotesque.
Such a man could not have believed in my earnestness
about it all and would have thought my feelings of the
moment a worked-up thing. I can in fancy hear one
of the Frenchmen, Italians or Russians I later knew
laughing at me. "Well, but why get so worked up?
A factory is a factory, is it not? Why may not one

298

break it like an empty bottle? You have lost some money for others? See the light on that field over there. These others, for whom you lost money, were they compelled to beg in the streets, were their children torn by wolves? What is it you Americans get so excited about when a little money is lost?"

A European artist may not understand but an American will understand. The devil! It is not a question of money. No men are so careless and free with money as the Americans. There is another matter involved.

It strikes rather deeply at the roots of our beings. Childish as it all may have seemed to an older and more sophisticated world, we Americans, from the beginning, have been up to something, or we have wanted to think we were up to something. We came here, or our fathers or grandfathers came here, from a hundred diverse places—and you may be sure it was not the artists who came. Artists do not want to cut down trees, root stumps out of the ground, build towns and railroads. The artist wants to sit with a strip of canvas before him, face an open space on a wall, carve a bit of wood, make combinations of words and sentences, as I am doing now—and try to express to others some thought or feeling of his own. He wants to dream of color, to lay hold of form, free the sensual in himself, live more fully and freely in his contact with the materials before him than he can possibly live in life. He seeks a kind of controlled ecstasy and is a man with a passion, a "nut," as we love to say in America. And very often, when he is not in actual contact with his materials, he is a much more vain and disagreeable ass than any man, not an artist, could possibly be. As a living man he is almost always a pest. It is only when dead he begins to have value.

The simple truth is that in a European country the artist is more freely accepted than he is among us, and only because he has been longer about. They know how harmless he really is—or rather do not know how subtly dangerous he can be—and accept him only as one might accept a hybrid cross between a dog and a cat that went growling mewing barking and spitting about the house. One might want to kill the first of such strange beasts one sees but after one has seen a dozen and has realized that, like the mule, they cannot breed their own kind one laughs and lets them live, paying no more attention to them than modern France for example pays to its artists.

But in America things are somewhat different. Here something went wrong in the beginning. We pretended to so much and were going to do such great things here. This vast land was to be a refuge for all the outlawed brave foolish folk of the world. The declaration of the rights of man was to have a new hearing in a new place. The devil! We did get ourselves into a bad hole. We were going to be superhuman and it turned out we were sons of men who were not such devilish fellows after all. You cannot blame us that we are somewhat reluctant about finding out the very human things concerning ourselves. One does so hate to come down off the perch.

We are now losing our former feeling of inherent virtue, are permitting ourselves occasionally to laugh at ourselves for our pretensions, but there was a time

here when we were sincerely in earnest about all this
American business, "the land of the free and the
home of the brave." We actually meant it and no
one will ever understand present-day America or
Americans who does not concede that we meant it and
that while we were building all of our big ugly
hurriedly—thrown-together towns, creating our great
industrial system, growing always more huge and
prosperous, we were as much in earnest about what we
thought we were up to as were the French of the
thirteenth century when they built the cathedral of
Chartres to the glory of God.

They built the cathedral of Chartres to the glory of
God and we really intended building here a land to
the glory of Man, and thought we were doing it too.
That was our intention and the affair only blew up in
the process, or got perverted, because Man, even the
brave and the free Man, is somewhat a less worthy
object of glorification than God. This we might have
found out long ago but that we did not know each
other. We came from too many different places to
know each other well, had been promised too much,
wanted too much. We were afraid to know each
other.

Oh, how Americans have wanted heroes, wanted
brave simple fine men! And how sincerely and
deeply we Americans have been afraid to understand
and love one another, fearing to find ourselves at the
end no more brave heroic and fine than the people of
almost any other part of the world.

I however digress. What I am trying to do is to
give the processes of my own mind at two distinct moments of my own life. First, the moment when after

301

many years of effort to conform to an unstated and but dimly understood American dream by making myself a successful man in the material world I threw all overboard and then at another moment when, having come back to the same spot where I passed through the first moment, I attempted to confront myself with myself with a somewhat changed point of view.

As for the first of these moments, it was melodramatic and even silly enough. The struggle centred itself at the last within the walls of a particular moment and within the walls of a particular room.

I sat in the room with a woman who was my secretary. For several years I had been sitting there, dictating to her regarding the goods I had made in my factory and that I was attempting to sell. The attempt to sell the goods had become a sort of madness in me. There were certain thousands or perhaps hundreds of thousands of men living in towns or on farms in many states of my country who might possibly buy the goods I had made rather than the goods made in another factory by another man. How I had wheedled! How I had schemed! In some years I gave myself quite fully to the matter in hand and the dollars trickled in. Well, I was about to become rich. It was a possibility. After a good day or week, when many dollars had come, I went to walk and when I had got into a quiet place where I was unobserved I threw back my shoulders and strutted. During the year I had made for myself so many dollars. Next year I would make so many more, and the next year so many more. But my thoughts of the matter did not express themselves in the dollars.

302

It never does to the American man. Who calls the American a dollar-lover is foolish. My factory was of a certain size—it was really a poor haphazardly enough run place—but after a time I would build a great factory and after that a greater and greater. Like a true American, I thought in size.

My fancy played with the matter of factories as a child would play with a toy. There would be a great factory with walls going up and up and a little open place for a lawn at the front, shower baths for the workers with perhaps a fountain playing on a lawn, and up before the door of this place I would drive in a large automobile.

Oh, how I would he respected by all, how I would be looked up to by all! I walked in a little dark street, throwing back my shoulders. How grand and glorious I felt!

The houses along the street in which I walked were small and ugly and dirty-faced children played in the yards. I wondered. Having walked, dreaming my dream for a long time I returned to the neighborhood of my factory and opening my office went in to sit at my desk smoking a cigarette. The night watchman came in. He was an old man who had once been a school-teacher but, as he said, his eyes had gone back on him.

When I had walked alone I had been able to make myself feel somewhat as I fancied a prince might have felt but when anyone came near me something exploded inside. I was a deflated balloon. Well, in fancy, I had a thousand workmen under me. They were children and I was their father and would look out for them. Perhaps I would build them model houses to live in, a town of model houses built about my great factory, eh? The workmen would be my children and I would look out for my children. "Land of the free—home of the brave."

But I was back in my factory now and the night watchman sat smoking with me. Sometimes we talked far into the night. The devil! He was a fellow like myself, having the same problems as myself. How could I be his father? The thought was absurd. Once, when he was a younger man, he had dreamed of being a scholar but his eyes had gone back on him. What had he wanted to do? He spoke of it for a time. He had wanted to be a scholar and I had myself spent those earlier years eagerly reading books. "I would really like to have been a learned monk, one of those fellows such as appeared in the Middle Ages, one of the fellows who went off and lived by himself and gave himself up wholly to learning, one who believed in learning, who spent his life humbly seeking new truths—but I got married and my wife had kids, and then, you see, my eyes went back on me." He spoke of the matter philosophically. One did not let oneself get too much excited. After a time one got over any feeling of bitterness. The night watchman had a boy, a lad of fifteen, who also loved books. "He is pretty lucky, can get all the books he wants at the public library. In the afternoon after school is out and before I come down here to my job he reads aloud to me."

.   .   .   .

Men and women, many men and many women! There were men and women working in my factory, men and women walking in streets with me, many men and women scattered far and wide over the country to whom I wanted to sell my goods. I sent men, salesmen, to see them—I wrote letters; how many thousands of letters, all to the same purpose! "Will you buy my goods?" And again, "Will you buy my goods?"

What were the other men thinking about? What was I myself thinking about? Suppose it were possible to know something of the men and women, to know something of oneself, too. The devil! These were not thoughts that would help me to sell my goods to all the others. What were all the others like? What was I myself like? Did I want a large factory with a little lawn and a fountain in front and with a model town built about it?

Days of endlessly writing letters to men, nights of walking in strange quiet streets. What had happened to me? "I shall go get drunk," I said to myself and I did go and get drunk. Taking a train to a near-by city I drank until a kind of joy came to me and with some man I had found and who had joined in my carousal I walked in streets, shouting at other men, singing songs, going sometimes into strange houses to laugh with people, to talk with people I found there.

Here was something I liked and something the others liked too. When I had come to people in strange houses, half drunk, released, they were not afraid of me. "Well, he wants to talk," they seemed to be saying to themselves. "That's fine!" There was something broken down between us, a wall broken down. We talked of outlandish things for Anglo-

Saxon trained people to speak of, of love between men and women, of what children's coming meant. Food was brought forth. Often in a single evening of this sort I got more from people than I could get from weeks of ordinary intercourse. The people were a little excited by the strangeness of two unknown men in their houses. With my companion I went boldly to the door and knocked. Laughter. "Hello, the house!" It might be the house of a laborer or that of a well-to-do merchant. I had hold of my new-found friend's arm and explained our presence as well as I could. "We are a little drunk and we are travelers. We just want to sit and visit with you a while."

There was a kind of terror in people's eyes, and a kind of gladness too. An old workman showed us a relic he had brought home with him from the Civil War while his wife ran into a bedroom and changed her dress. Then a child awoke in a near-by room and began to cry and was permitted to come in in her nightgown and lie in my arms or in the arms of the new-found friend who had got drunk with me. The talk swept over strange intimate subjects. What were men up to? What were women up to? There was a kind of deep taking of breath, as though we had all been holding something back from one another and had suddenly decided to let go. Once or twice we stayed all night in the house to which we had gone. And then back to the writing of letters—to sell my goods. In the city to which I had gone to carouse I had seen many women of the streets, standing at corners, looking furtively about. My thoughts got fixed upon prostitution. Was I a prostitute? Was I prostituting my life?

What thoughts in the mind! There was a note due and payable at the bank. "Now here, you man, attend to your affairs. You have induced others to put money into your enterprises. If you are to build a great enterprise here you must be up and at it."

How often in after years I have laughed at myself for the thoughts and emotions of that time. There is a thought I have had that is very delicious. It is this, and I dare say it will be an unwelcome thought to many, "I am the American man. I think there is no doubt of it. I am just the mixture, the cold, moral man of the North into whose body has come the warm pagan blood of the South. I love and am afraid to love. Behold in me the American man striving to become an artist, to become conscious of himself, filled with wonder concerning himself and others, trying to have a good time and not fake a good time. I am not English Italian Jew German Frenchman Russian. What am I? I am tremendously serious about it all but at the same time I laugh constantly at myself for my own seriousness. Like all real American men of our day I wander constantly from place to place striving to put down roots into the American soil and not quite doing it. If you say the real American man is not yet born, you lie. I am the type of the fellow."

This is somewhat of a joke on me but it is a greater joke on the reader. As respectable and conventional a man as Calvin Coolidge has me in him—and I have him in myself? Do not doubt it.

I have him in me and Eugene Debs in me and the crazy political idealists of the Western States and Mr. Gary of the Steel Trust and the whole crew. I accept them all as part of myself. Would to God they would thus accept me!

. . . .

And being this thing I have tried to describe I return now to myself sitting between the walls of a certain room and between the walls of a certain moment too. Just why was that moment so pregnant? I will never quite know.

It came with a rush, the feeling that I must quit buying and selling, the overwhelming feeling of uncleanliness. I was in my whole nature a tale-teller. My father had been one and his not knowing had destroyed him. The tale-teller cannot bother with buying and selling. To do so will destroy him. No class of men I have ever known are so dull and cheerless as the writers of glad sentimental romances, the painters of glad pretty pictures. The corrupt unspeakable thing that had happened to tale-telling in America was all concerned with this matter of buying and selling. The horse cannot sing like a canary bird nor the canary bird pull a plow like a horse and either of them attempting it becomes something ridiculous.

NOTE III

THERE was a door leading out from my office to the street. How many steps to the door? I counted them, "five, six, seven." "Suppose," I asked myself, "I could take those five, six, seven steps to the door, pass out at the door, go along that railroad track out there, disappear into the far horizon beyond. Where was I to go? In the town where my factory was located I had still the reputation of being a bright young business man. In my first years there I had been filled with shrewd vast schemes. I had been admired, looked up to. Since that time I had gone down and down as a bright young man but no one yet knew how far I had gone. I was still respected in the town, my word was still good at the bank. I was a respectable man.

Did I want to do something not respectable, not decent? I am trying to give you the history of a moment and as a tale-teller I have come to think that the true history of life is but a history of moments. It is only at rare moments we live. I wanted to walk out at a door and go away into the distance. The American is still a wanderer, a migrating bird not yet ready to build a nest. All our cities are built temporarily as are the houses in which we live. We are on the way—toward what? There have been other times in the history of the world when many

309

strange peoples came together in a new strange land. To assume that we have made an America, even materially, seems to me now but telling ourselves fairy tales in the night. We have not even made it materially yet and the American man has only gone in for money-making on a large scale to quiet his own restlessness, as the monk of old days was given the Regula of Augustine to quiet him and still the lusts in himself. For the monk, kept occupied with the saying of prayers and the doing of many little sacred offices, there was no time for the lusts of the world to enter in and for the American to be perpetually busy with his affairs, with his automobiles, with his movies, there is no time for unquiet thoughts.

On that day in the office at my factory I looked at myself and laughed. The whole struggle I am trying to describe and that I am confident will be closer to the understanding of most Americans than anything else I have ever written was accompanied by a kind of mocking laughter at myself and my own seriousness about it all.

Very well, then, I wanted to go out of the door and never come back. How many Americans want to go —but where do they want to go? I wanted to accept for myself all the little restless thoughts of which myself and the others had been so afraid and you, who are Americans, will understand the necessity of my continually laughing at myself and at all things dear to me. I must laugh at the thing I love the more intensely because of my love. Any American will understand that.

It was a trying moment for me. There was the woman, my secretary, now looking at me. What did she represent? What did she not represent? Would I dare be honest with her? It was quite apparent to me I would not. I had got to my feet and we stood looking at each other. "It is now or never," I said to myself, and I remember that I kept smiling. I had stopped dictating to her in the midst of a sentence. "The goods about which you have inquired are the best of their kind made in the—"

I stood and she sat and we were looking at each other intently. "What's the matter?" she asked. She was an intelligent woman, more intelligent I am sure than myself, just because she was a woman and good, while I have never been good, do not know how to be good. Could I explain all to her? The words of a fancied explanation marched through my mind: "My dear young woman, it is all very silly but I have decided to no longer concern myself with this buying and selling. It may be all right for others but for me it is poison. There is this factory. You may have it if it please you. It is of little value I dare say. Perhaps it is money ahead and then again it may well be it is money behind. I am uncertain about it all and now I am going away. Now, at this moment, with the letter I have been dictating, with the very sentence you have been writing left unfinished, I am going out that door and never come back. What am I going to do? Well now, that I don't know. I am going to wander about. I am going to sit with people, listen to words, tell tales of people, what they are thinking, what they are feeling. The devil! It may even be I am going forth in search of myself."

The woman was looking into my eyes the while I looked into hers. Perhaps I had grown a little pale

311

and now she grew pale. "You're sick," she said and her words gave me an idea. There was wanted a justification of myself, not to myself but to the others. A crafty thought came. Was the thought crafty or was I, at the moment, a little insane, a "nut," as every American so loves to say of every man who does something a little out of the groove.

I had grown pale and it may be I was ill but nevertheless I was laughing—the American laugh. Had I suddenly become a little insane? What a comfort that thought would be, not to myself but to the others. My leaving the place I was then in would tear up roots that had gone down a little into the ground. The ground I did not think would support the tree that was myself and that I thought wanted to grow.

My mind dwelt on the matter of roots and I looked at my feet. The whole question with which I was at the moment concerned became a matter of feet. I had two feet that could take me out of the life I was then in and that, to do so, would need but take three or four steps to a door. When I had reached the door and had stepped out of my little factory office everything would be quite simplified, I was sure. I had to lift myself out. Others would have to tackle the job of getting me back, once I had stepped over that threshold.

Whether at the moment I merely became shrewd and crafty or whether I really became temporarily insane I shall never quite know. What I did was to step very close to the woman and looking directly into her eyes I laughed gayly. Others besides herself would, I knew, hear the words I was now speaking.

312

I looked at my feet. "I have been wading in a long river and my feet are wet," I said.

Again I laughed as I walked lightly toward the door and out of a long and tangled phase of my life, out of the door of buying and selling, out of the door of affairs.

"They want me to be a 'nut,' will love to think of me as a 'nut,' and why not? It may just be that's what I am," I thought gayly and at the same time turned and said a final confusing sentence to the woman who now stared at me in speechless amazement. "My feet are cold wet and heavy from long wading in a river. Now I shall go walk on dry land," I said, and as I passed out at the door a delicious thought came. "Oh, you little tricky words, you are my brothers. It is you, not myself, have lifted me over this threshold. It is you who have dared give me a hand. For the rest of my life I will be a servant to you," I whispered to myself as I went along a spur of railroad track, over a bridge, out of a town and out of that phase of my life.

NOTE IV

ON the evening when I returned to the town my mood was quite another one. I was on my way from Chicago to the city of New York. Why had I wanted to stop? The impulse had come suddenly, as I stood at the railroad ticket window in Chicago.

It rained when I got off the train and the night promised to be dark but half an hour later the rain ceased and the stars came out. At the station I escaped notice. Already in the town I and my struggles had been forgotten. At the moment when I had so dramatically walked away from my factory there had been some little local newspaper furore—"Well-known business man mysteriously disappears. Not known to have had any troubles," etc. I went into a baggage check room and left my bag and then to a ticket window where I bought a ticket to New York on a later train. Both the check room boy and the ticket-seller were strangers to me. It was evident the town had grown, suddenly and furiously, as industrial towns do grow. Had it become a centre for the manufacture of automobiles shoes rubber tires or chewing gum? I did not know. In the station waiting room ten or twelve people stood or sat about and several taxi drivers were shouting at the door.

I walked away in the drizzling rain and stood on a bridge until the night cleared. Now it was plain to me that I had wanted to spend an evening alone with myself in the midst of the shadows of a former life. Since I had left the town much had happened. All during the last years of my life as a manufacturer and later as a Chicago advertising man I had secretly been writing tales and now they were beginning to be published. In some places they had been praised, in others blamed. I had loved the praise. It had made me feel very much as I had felt as a manufacturer when I had made a little money and had begun to dream of building a great factory and being father to workmen—that is to say, rather grand and noble. When my tales displeased people and when some critic wrote condemning me and calling me a dull or an unclean man I got furiously angry but always tried quickly to conceal my anger. I was really so angry that I did not want, on any account, to let the other fellow know how angry and hurt I was. Often the critic seemed merely to want to hurt. I had had a moment of exaltation, of joy in thinking I had penetrated a little into the life story of some man or woman. The person about whom I had been writing had been swept by some passion, of the flesh or spirit and I had been swept along with him. At such times I, as an individual, had no existence. Sometimes I had been seated writing all night at my desk and could not have told whether I had been there two hours or ten. Then the morning light streamed in at my window and my hands trembled so that I could no longer hold the pen. What a sweet clean feeling! During those hours there had been no life of my own at all. I had lived but in the characters I was trying to bring to life in my story and in the

early morning light I felt as one shriven of all gross-
ness, of all vanity, of all cheapness in himself. The
process of writing had been for me purifying and fine.
It had been curative and later I was filled with unholy
wrath when someone said that, during that period of
work, I had been unclean or vile.

And most of all I was furiously angry when someone said that the people of whom I wrote, being only
such people as I myself had known, were of a lower,
more immoral, less healthy order of beings. They
were not respectable, were queer and did unaccountable things. I had myself been a respectable man and
at one time in my life all of my friends had been respectable men and women and had I not known what
was underneath the coats of many such, what they
were too? I was furious for the men and women
about whom I had written and furious for myself too
but actually, on the outside, in the face of scurrilous
criticism, had always assumed a sort of heavy bucolic
genial manner, something in the manner of a certain
type of benevolent old gentleman I had always de-
tested. "They may be right," I said aloud generously
when inside myself I thought the critics often enough
only dogs and fools.

I was thinking of myself and my critics as I walked
that evening in the rain and I presume that what I
had wanted in coming back thus to the Ohio town was
to try to arrive at some sort of basis for self-criticism.

It was going to be a somewhat difficult undertaking,
finding such a basis, of that I was sure. When I had
been doing my writing, unknown and unseen, there
was a sort of freedom. One worked, more or less in
secret, as one might indulge in some forbidden vice.

There were the bankers and others who had put money into my enterprises. They had expected I would be giving myself wholly to the matter in hand and I had been cheating and did not want them to know. One wrote tales, played with them. One did not think of publication, of a public that was to read. In the evening one came home to one's house and going upstairs closed the door to a room. There was before one the desk and paper.

In a neighboring garden a man was picking potato bugs off potato vines. His wife came to the kitchen door and began to scold. He had forgotten to bring home five pounds of sugar from the store and now she was angry about it. There came one of those strangely vital little domestic flare-ups, the man with a tin can in which were the captured bugs, looking ridiculous as he stood listening to his wife, and she in turn looking unnecessarily angry about the small matter of the sugar.

They were in their garden unconscious of me and I was unconscious of a dinner being put on a table downstairs in my house, unconscious of any need of food I would ever feel again, unconscious of the régime of my own household, of the affairs of my factory. A man and a woman in a garden had become the centre of a universe about which it seemed to me I might think and feel in joy and wonder forever. People had outer motives that seemed to control their lives. Under certain circumstances they said certain words. Stealthily I went to lock the door of my room. A domestic régime would be upset by my determination, the affairs of a certain factory might be ruined by my inattention but what did all that, at the moment, matter to me? I became cruelly impersonal and could not avoid becoming so. Had a god been in my way or intent on disturbing me just then I would have at least tried to brush him aside. "You Jove, sit in that chair over there and keep your mouth shut! You Minerva, get down that stairway, go into the front room of my house and sit in a rocking-chair with your hands folded until I have attended to the business before me! At the moment I am concerned with a man standing in a potato patch with a can of potato bugs held in his hand and with a certain perplexed baffled look in his eyes and in the eyes of the wife in a gingham apron who is unnecessarily angry about a trifling matter of sugar not brought home from a store. You must see that I am a swimmer and have stripped myself of the clothes which are my ordinary life. You, my dear Minerva, should not stay in the presence of a naked man. People will say things about you. Get down the stairway at once. I am a swimmer and am about to leap off into the sea of lives, into the sea of present-day American lives. Will I be able to swim there? Will I be able to keep my head above water? That is a matter for greater gods than yourself to decide. Get out of here!"

Utter obscurity, the joy of obscurity. Why could not one cling to that? Why the later vanity that made one want to be proclaimed? I remember an evening alone in my room. I was not always writing. Sometimes I read the work of other men. There was a scene being depicted by an old master of prose. Three men were in a little room talking. What was attempted was that there should be actual words said

318

while the reader should be given the sense of things felt for which there were no words. One of the men kept talking in the most affable and genial manner while at the same time there was murder in his heart. The three had been eating and now the man who wanted to kill was fingering the handle of a knife.

I remember that I sat in my room with tears streaming out of my own eyes. Oh, so delicately and well was the scene being handled! There was everything in just the way the man's hands played with that knife. That told the whole story. The writer had not said too much about it. He had just, by a stroke of his pen, centred your attention there, upon the fingers of a hand fiddling with the handle of a knife at the edge of the table.

How easy to say too much! How easy to say too little! I remember that I half read through the scene and then put the book down and ran nervously up and down in my room. "He can't do it! He can't do it! No man can do a thing so beautifully restrained and sure!" Do you think, dear reader, I cared a hang about the social standing of the three men in that room, what kind of morals they had, their influence for good or evil on the characters of others, what they were up to? Indeed I did not. It is a long time at least since I have been such a child as that. A master had started to do a scene and I was in mortal terror lest he fail to draw his line sharp and true. I had never yet drawn my own line sharp and true, was not man enough to do so, was too timid, too weak vain and fearful.

But ah, that master, that man who had written the scene I was reading! Faith came back and I ran to pick up the book and read on and on. Oh, the delicate wonder of it, the joy of it! At the moment I could have crawled across the floor of my room and bathed with my happy tears the feet of the man who in another room long before had held his pen firmly, had spread upon a sheet of white paper, with such true and vital an economy of ink, the complete sense of his scene.

Utter obscurity, the joy of obscurity. Why had I not been content with it? In the nights alone in my room I had realized fully the danger of coming out of my obscurity and yet never did I write a tale, at all approaching good handling, but that I must need run down out of my room and go eagerly from one person to another asking praise. Time and again I said to myself: "You are an ignorant man. Every artist who goes to pieces and takes the joy of complete abandonment from his task, and the joy from his own life too, does so because he lets some outside impulse, want of fame, want of money, want of praise, come between him and his materials. The white surfaces before him become muddy and dirty, the scene before his mind's eye fades or becomes dim and blurred."

These things I had a thousand times said to myself and had made a dream of a life I was to live. I was to keep in obscurity, work in obscurity. When I had left the life of a manufacturer I would get, in Chicago or some other city, a clerkship or some other minor job that would just provide me with a living and would give me as much leisure as possible. Well, I would live somewhere in a cheap room on a street of laborers' houses. Clothes would not matter to me. I would live wholly for something outside myself, for the white clean surfaces on which, if the gods were good, I might some day have the joy of writing at least one finely drawn and delicately wrought tale.

As I had walked away from my factory on a certain day these had been the thoughts in my mind and now, after two years and after a few of my tales had been printed and I had been a little praised I was going to New York for the obvious purpose of doing everything possible to make myself better known, to strut before the very people I was trying to understand so that I could write of them fully and truly. What a tangle!

It was a dramatic moment in my own life and if, on that particular evening as I walked alone in the streets of the Ohio town, I achieved a certain victory over myself, it was not to be a lasting one. The kind of workman I had wanted to be I could not be but I did not know it at the moment. It was not until long afterward I came to the conclusion that I, at least, could only give myself with complete abandonment to the surfaces and materials before me at rare moments, sandwiched in between long periods of failure. It was only at the rare moment I could give myself, my thoughts and emotions, to work and sometimes, at rarer moments, to the love of a friend or a woman.

I went from the railroad station along a street and onto a bridge where I stood leaning over and looking at the water below. How black the water in the dim light! From where I stood I could look along the river bottom to the factory district where my own factory had stood. The bridge led into a street that was in the fashionable residence district of the town and presently a fat gray-haired old man, accompanied by a friend, walked past. They were smoking expensive cigars and the fragrance hung heavy on the air so that I also wanted tobacco and lit a cigarette. The fat man had formerly been my banker and no doubt had he recognized me might have told me a tale of money lost through me, of promises unfulfilled. The deuce! I smiled at the thought of how glad I was he had not recognized me. Would he have been nasty about the matter or would he and I have laughed together over the thought of the foolish impulse in himself that had led him to conclude I was a man to be trusted and one likely to succeed in affairs— a good banker's risk?

"Hello," I said to myself, "I'd better get out of here." Some of the men of the town I had succeeded in getting worked up to the point of investing in the wild business scheme I had formerly had in my head might at any moment pass along the bridge and recognize me. That might bring on an embarrassing moment. They might want their money back and I had no money to give. In fancy I began to see myself as a desperado revisiting the scene of some former crime. What had I done? Had I robbed a bank, held up a train, or killed someone? It might well be that at some time in the future I would want to write a tale of some desperate fellow's having got into a tight hole. Now he had to pass, say in a park, the wife of a man he had murdered. I slunk away off the bridge, throwing my cigarette into the river and pulling my hat down over my eyes, becoming in fancy as I passed a man accompanied by a woman and a child the murderer my own fancy had created. When I had got to them my heart stopped beating and quite automatically I put my hand to my hip pocket as though there had been a pistol there. "Well, I was an enemy to society and if the worst came to the worst would sell my life as dearly as possible."

More absurdity in myself, endless absurdities. My own childishness sometimes amused me. Would it amuse others? Were others like myself, hopelessly childish? Many men and women seemed, in outward appearance at least, to comport themselves in life with a certain dignity. All history was filled with the stories of men who had managed to get through life with at least an outward dignity. Was all history a lie? There was a man who owned a bank or an automobile factory or who was a college professor or a judge. He rode about through the streets of a city in an automobile, was called a great man. How did that affect him inside, how did it make him feel? I began now wondering about myself. Suppose someone were suddenly to call me a great man. I imagined a tall serious-looking man with whiskers saying it. "He writes novels and tales. He is a great man."

And now as there was no one else to say the words set down above I said them myself and at first I liked the sound of them and then a desire to laugh took possession of me and I not only wanted to laugh at myself but I wanted everyone in America to laugh with me, at myself and at themselves too.

Oh, glorious moment! No more great men again ever, no more bad men or good men, everyone on to everyone else. Was there a sense of something, I at that moment felt, in all American people everywhere? In the old days we Americans had been proud of what we thought of as our distinctive American humor but lately our humor had pretty much settled itself down into the universal dullness of the newspaper funny strip. A really great humorist like Mr. Ring Lardner had come to that. Would it not be a joke on us all if we were all, already, and in reality, pretty far beyond any outward expression of ourselves we were getting?

And now I was stumbling about in the dark streets of an Ohio manufacturing town poking sharp sticks into the tender flesh of myself and others. There was no one to refute any smart thing I thought and so I had a good time. Like everyone else I would so love to go through life criticizing everyone else and withholding from others any right to criticize me. Oh, the joy of being a king a pope or an emperor!

"Suppose," I now thought, "everyone in America really hungers for a more direct and subtle expression of our common lives than we have ever yet had and that we are all only terribly afraid we won't get it."

The notion seemed good. It would explain so much. For one thing it would explain the common boredom with life and with work characteristic of so many so-called successful men I had met. Whether he was a successful railroad-builder or a successful writer of magazine short stories, the brighter man always seemed bored. Also it would explain beautifully our American fear of the highbrow. Suppose the brighter men were really having a good time—on the sly as it were—well, laughing up their sleeves. And suppose some fellow were to come along who was really on to the entire emptiness of the whole success theory of life, the whole absurd business of building bigger and bigger towns, bigger and bigger factories, bigger and bigger houses, but had decided not to be a reformer and scold about it. I fancied such a one going blandly about and really laughing, not fake laughing as in the newspaper funny strips, made by poor driven slaves who think they must be rich or silly to get fun out of life, getting the old American laugh back again, the laugh that came from far down inside, an American Falstaff kind of a laugh.

Well, now I had got myself into deep water. I had fancied into existence a man I had not nerve or brains enough to be myself and one never likes that. The figure my fancy had made annoyed me as I am sure he would everyone else.

I had gone in the darkness down along a spur of a railroad track to where my factory had formerly stood and there it was, much as I had left it except that my name had been taken off the front. There was a wall of the building that looked up toward the railroad station and there I had once put a big sign on which was my name in letters three feet high. How proud I had been when the sign was first put up. "Oh, glorious day! I a manufacturer!" To be sure I did not own the building but strangers would think I did.

And now my name was gone and another man's name, in letters as large as I had once used, was in its place. I went near the building trying to spell out the new name in the darkness, hating the name with instinctive jealousy, and a man came out at a door of the factory and walked toward me. Oh Lord, it was the former school-teacher, the man who had once been my night watchman and who was now evidently night watchman for my successor. Would he recognize me, lurking about the place of my former grandeur?

I started walking away along the tracks singing the words of an old ditty my father had been fond of singing in his liquor when I was a boy and that had at that moment popped into my head, and at the same time staggering about as though I were drunk. It was my purpose to make the night watchman think me a drunken workman homeward bound and I succeeded. As I went away from him, staggering along the track, singing and not answering when he demanded to know who I was and what I was doing there, he grew angry, ran quickly up behind and kicked at me. Fortunately he missed and fortunately I remembered that his eyes had gone back on him long since. He now grabbed at me but I eluded his grasp, singing my ditty as I half ran, half staggered away:

" 'Twas a summer's day and the sea was rippled
    By the softest, gentlest breeze,
When a ship set sail with her cargo laden
    For a land beyond the seas.

Did she never come back? No, she never came back,
    And her fate is yet unlearned.
Though for years and years sad hearts have been waiting
    Yet the ship she never returned."

NOTE V

I HAD become a writer, a word fellow. That was my craft. Flinging aside the fake devotion that must always be characteristic of all such jobs as the advertising writing I had been doing for several years I had accepted my passion for scribbling as one accepts the fact that the central interest of one's whole being lies in carving stone, spreading paint upon canvas, digging in the earth for gold, working the soil, working in wood or in iron. The arts are after all but the old crafts intensified, followed with religious fervor and determination by men who love them and deep down within him perhaps every man wants more than anything else to be a good craftsman. Surely nothing in the modern world has been more destructive than the idea that man can live without the joy of hands and mind combined in craftsmanship, that men can live by the accumulation of monies, by trickery. In the crafts only one may exercise all one's functions. The body comes in, the mind comes in, all the sensual faculties become alive. When one writes one deals with a thousand influences that motivate his own and other lives. There is, first of all, the respect for what has gone before, for the work of the older craftsmen. One who has written as much as I have written—and for every word printed there are hundreds I have scrawled experimentally that will

327

never be printed—has also read much and often with great joy.

In Russia England France Germany a writer sat writing. Oh, how well he did his job, and how close I feel to him as I read! What a sharp sense he gives of the life about him! With him one enters into that life, feels the hidden passions of peoples, their little household traits, their loves and hates. There are sentences written by all writers of note in all countries that have their roots deep down in the life about them. The sentences are like windows looking into houses. Something is suddenly torn aside, all lies, all trickery about life gone for the moment. It is what one wants, what one seeks constantly in one's own craftsmanship, and how seldom it comes. The little faky tricks are always so ready to help over the hard places and when one has used them there is the little flush of triumph followed by—bah! followed always by the sick awakening.

One need not go too far afield to find sentences and paragraphs that stir deeply. No doubt they were in the Indian language before white men came and the first whites on our shores brought the sense of them. There was that Fredis, sister of that Norseman Eric, who had come to America long before Columbus came and had built him a house in Vinland. The sister was a strong-willed woman who bullied her husband and was avaricious for wealth. Came sailing to Greenland the brothers, Helgi and Finnbogi, with a strong ship, and she induces them to go adventuring with her to Vinland but at the very beginning tricks them. She in her ship is to have thirty men and they are to have thirty but unknown to them she conceals an

328

extra five in her own vessel so that in the far land, where are no white men and white men's laws are unknown, she shall have the upper hand. They get to Vinland and she will not let them stay in the house, built there by her brother Eric, and they go patiently away and build a hut of their own.

Still she schemes. See now with what truth, what fidelity and clearness some old writer tells of what happened. Well, the brothers had the larger and better ship and she wanted that too.

One morning early Fredis arose from her bed and dressed herself, but did not put on her shoes and stockings. A heavy dew had fallen, and she took her husband's cloak, and wrapped it about her, and then walked to the brothers' house and up to the door, which had been only partly closed by one of the men, who had gone out but a short time before. She pushed the door open and stood silently in the doorway for a time. Finnbogi, who was lying on the innermost side of the room, awoke. "What dost thou wish here, Fredis?" She answers: "I wish thee to rise and go out with me, for I would speak with thee." He did so; and they walked to a tree, which lay close by the wall of the house, and seated themselves upon it. "How art thou pleased here?" says she. He answers "I am well pleased with the fruitfulness of the land, but I am ill content with the breach that has come between us, for methinks there has been no cause for it." "It is even as thou sayest," says she, "and so it seems to me; but my errand to thee is that I wish to exchange ships with you brothers, for ye have a larger ship than I, and I wish to depart from here." "To this I must accede," says he, "if it is thy pleasure." Therewith they parted, and she returned home and Finnbogi to his bed. She climbed up into the bed and awakened Thorvard (her husband) with her cold feet; and he asked her why she was so cold and wet. She answered with great passion. "I have been

329

to the brothers',", says she, "to try to buy their ship, for I wish to have a larger vessel; but they received my overtures so ill that they struck me and handled me very roughly; that time thou, poor wretch, will neither avenge my shame nor thy own; and I find, perforce, that I am no longer in Greenland. Moreover I shall part from thee unless thou makest vengeance for this." And now he could stand her taunts no longer, and ordered the men to rise at once and take their weapons; and they then proceeded directly to the house of the brothers, and entered it while the folk were asleep, and seized and bound them, and led each one out when he was bound; and, as they came out, Fredis caused each to be slain.

Since I had been a boy it had been such passages as the one above that had moved me most strangely. There was a man, perhaps one of Fredis' men, who had seen a part of what had happened on that dreadful morning in the far western world and had sensed the rest. For such a one there would perhaps have been no thought of interference. One can think of him, the unknown writer of the memorable passage above, as even helping in the dreadful slaying there in the field at the edge of the wood and near the sea, not because he wanted to but because he would have been afraid. He would have done that and later perhaps have gone off alone into the woods and cried a little and prayed a little, as I can imagine myself doing after such an affair. The woman Fredis, after she had got what she wanted, swore all her men to secrecy. "I will devise the means of your death if there is any word of this when we have returned to Greenland," she said, and after she had gone home with the two vessels loaded and had made up her own lie to tell her brother Eric of what had happened to the brothers and their men in the far place, she made all of her own men handsome presents.

But there was that scribbler. He would put it down. Fear might have made him take part in the murder but no fear could now keep his hand from the pen. Do I not know the wretch? Have I not got his own blood in me? He would have walked about for days, re-living all of that dreadful morning scene in Vinland and then when he was one day walking he would have thought of something. Well, he would have thought suddenly of just that bit about Fredis crawling back into her husband's bed, after the talk with Finnbogi, and how her cold wet feet awoke the man. He would have been alone in the wood, back there in Greenland, when that bit came to him, but at once he hurried to his own house. Perhaps his wife was getting dinner and wanted him to go to the store but he would have brushed her aside, and sitting down with ink and paper—perhaps in her angry presence—he wrote all out, just as it is put down above. Not only did he write, but he read his piece to others. "You will get yourself into trouble," said his wife, and he knew what she said was true but that could not stop him. Do I not know the soul of him? He would have gone about boasting a little, strutting a little. "I say now, Leif, that bit, where Fredis gets into the bed and with her cold feet awakens Thorvald—not bad, eh? I rather nailed her there, now didn't I old man?" "But you yourself helped to do the murder, you know." "Oh, the deuce now! Never mind that. But I say now, you'll have to admit it, I did rather put a spike into my scene. I nailed it down, now didn't I, Leify old chap?"

331

WELL, there was my father, there was myself. If people did not want their stories told, it would be better for them to keep away from me. I would tell if I could get at the heart of it—as the fellow who went off to Vinland with Fredis told—and for just the reasons that made him tell. And like that fellow, after he returned to Greenland, I would have to walk alone in the woods or in city streets thinking, trying to think, trying to get all in accord, seeking always just that illuminating touch the Norse storyteller had found when he thought up the bit about Fredis—that about her getting into bed and touching the back of her sleeping husband with the cold feet. The foxy devil! Do I not know what happened after that? First he thought of the two in the warm bed— the determined woman and the startled weak man— with a little jump of delight and then he went back over his story and put that in about her having got up in the first place without putting on shoes and stockings and the cold wet dew on the grass and the log against the wall of the house on which they sat. Now he had got going just right and he knew he had got going just right. What a splendid feeling! It was like a dance. How neatly everything fitted in! Words came—ah—just the right words.

How many times, in these modern days when I

have seen how story-tellers and painters have got themselves so often all balled-up with the question of style I have wondered whether the story-tellers among the old Norse and those most marvelous story-tellers of the older Testaments, whether they also did not have their periods of escaping out into words because they had grown weary of seeking after the heart of their stories.

I dare say they stole when they could without being detected as I have so often done. Well, there was the heart of the tale itself. That had first to be got at and then one had to find the words wherewith to clothe it. One got a bit feverish at times and used feverish words, made his telling too turgid or too wordy. One was like a runner who has a long race to run but who is feverishly forcing the pace. How many times I have sat writing, hoping I had got at the heart of the tale I was trying to put down on the paper when inside myself I knew I had not. I have tried to bluff myself. Often I have gone to others, hoping they would say words that would quiet the voices within. "You have not got it and you know you have not got it. Tear all up. Well, then, be a fool and go on trying to bluff yourself. Perhaps you can get some critic to say you have got what you know well enough you have not got, the very heart, the very music of your tale."

In Chicago I had ruined my chances of becoming a successful man of affairs because I could not take affairs seriously but that had not bothered me. Often enough, to be sure, I dodged the fact that, after having started on the scent of some tale I turned aside because I could not follow the scent and consoled myself by saying that the need of money had been the cause of my defeat or that the need of leisure had upset me but it was always a lie.

I was an advertising man in Chicago and sat in a room with some half a dozen others. We had met to discuss some matter of grave importance to say a maker of plows or automobile tires. The matter was really of no importance to me. The man had come to Chicago with three or four others and we were to discuss methods of increasing his sales. So many thousands of tires made, so many thousands of plows. There were other makers of tires, other makers of plows too. Could we be more persuasive than they, more bold and daring in statement, more foxy and clever perhaps?

We sat in a room to talk it over and near me sat a large man with a beard. Someone had told me that he was the treasurer of the plow company but that had meant little. Now, as he sat there smoking a cigarette and gazing out at a window I saw, just when his head was slightly turned, that he had a long scar on his cheek, that he had grown the beard to conceal the scar. The talk went on but I sat fascinated. "We must develop the trade in the southwest, that's what we must do," said a voice from some far-distant place. Pictures had begun to form in my fancy. Beside the voices in the room, other voices were making themselves heard. Old memories had begun to stir.

There was something, a story within me that had been there a long time but had never been told and that the scar under the beard had brought to life. What an unfortunate time for the story to begin asserting itself at just that moment. Now I was to think of the promotion of the sale of plows in the newly opened State of Oklahoma and in Texas.

I sat with some six or eight men by a large table in a room and some man was talking. He had been to Texas and knew things I would later have to know when I wrote advertisements for the plow company. I tried to appear attentive. There was a trick I had cultivated for just such occasions. I leaned a little forward and put my head in my hands, as though lost in deep thought. Some of the men in the room had heard that I wrote stories and had therefore concluded that I had a good brain. Americans have always a kind of tenderness for such cheats as I was being at the moment. Now they gave me credit for thinking deeply on the subject of plows, which was what I wanted. One of my employers—he was president of our company and his name was Barton—tried to cover up my obvious inattention. Already he had decided I would have to write the plow company's advertisements but later he would tell me of all that had been said in the room. He would take me into his office and scold me gently, like a mother speaking to a badly behaved child. "Of course you didn't hear a blamed word they said but here is the gist of it. I had to tell that big man with a beard that you were a genius. My God, what lies do I not tell on your account? When the little man with the glasses was speaking of agricultural conditions in Texas I was afraid that at any moment you might begin to whistle or sing."

Voices inside the room and voices inside myself too. Was something coming a bit clear at last?

Now my fancy had taken me quite out of the room where the others talked of plows. One night, years before, when I was a young laborer and was beating my way westward on a freight train, a brakeman had succeeded in throwing me off the train in an Indiana town. I had remembered the place long afterward because of my embarrassment—walking about among people in my dirty torn clothes and with my dirty hands and face. However, I had a little money and after I had walked through the town to a country road I found a creek and bathed. Then I went back to town to a restaurant and bought food.

It was a Saturday evening and the streets were filled with people. After it grew dark my torn clothes were not so much in evidence and by a street light near a church on a side street a girl smiled at me. Half undecided as to whether or not I had better try to follow and pick up an acquaintance, I stood for some moments by a tree staring after her. Then I bethought me that when she had seen me more closely

336

and had seen the condition of my clothes she would in any event have nothing to do with me.

As is natural to man, under such circumstances, I told myself I did not want her anyway and went off down another street.

I came to a bridge and stood for a time looking down into the water and then went on across the bridge along a road and into a field where long grass grew. It was a summer night and I was sleepy but after I had slept, perhaps for several hours, I was awakened by something going on in the field and within a few feet of me.

The field was small and two houses stood facing it, the one near where I lay in a fence corner and the other a few hundred yards away. When I had come into the field lights were lighted in both houses but now they were both dark and before me—some ten paces away—three men were struggling silently while near them stood a woman who held her hands over her face and who sobbed, not loudly but with a kind of low wailing cry. There was something, dimly seen, something white, lying on the ground near the woman and suddenly by a kind of flash of intuition I understood what had happened. The white thing on the ground was a woman's garment.

The three men were struggling desperately and even in the dim light it was evident that two of them were trying to overcome the third. He was the woman's lover and lived in the house at the end of the path that crossed the field and the two others were her brothers. They had gone into the town for the evening and had come home late and as they were walking silently across the grass in the field they had stumbled upon the love-makers and in a flash there was the impulse to kill their sister's lover. Perhaps they felt the honor of their house had been destroyed.

And now one of them had got a knife out of his pocket and had slashed at the lover, laying his cheek open, and they might have killed the man as the woman and I watched trembling but at that moment he got away and ran across the field toward his own house followed by the others.

I was left alone in the field with the woman—we were within a few feet of each other—and for a long time she did not move. "After all I am not a man of action. I am a recorder of things, a teller of tales." It was somewhat thus I excused myself for not coming to the lover's aid, as I lay perfectly still in the fence corner, looking and listening. The woman continued to sob and now, from across the dark field, there was a shout. The lover had not succeeded in getting into his own house, was really but a step ahead of his pursuers, and perhaps did not dare risk trying to open a door. He ran back across the field, dodging here and there, and passing near us crossed the bridge into the road that led to town. The woman in the field began calling, evidently to her two brothers, but they paid no attention. "John! Fred!" she called between her sobs. "Stop! Stop!"

And now again all was silent in the field and I could hear the rapid steps of the three running men in the dusty road in the distance.

Then lights appeared in both the houses facing the field and the woman went into the house near me, still sobbing bitterly, and presently there were voices to be heard. Then the woman—now fully clad—

338

came out and went across the field to the second house and presently came back with another woman. Their skirts almost brushed my face as they passed me.

The three sat on the steps of the house on my side of the field, all crying, and above the sound of their crying I could still hear, far off, the sound of running feet. The lover had got into the town, which was but half a mile away, and was evidently dodging through streets. Was the town aroused? Now and then shouts came from the distance. I had no watch and did not know how long I had slept in the field.

Now all became silent again and there were just the four people, myself lying trembling in the grass and the three women on the steps of the house near me, and all three crying softly. Time passed. What had happened? What would happen? In fancy I saw the running man caught and perhaps killed in some dark little side street of an Indiana farming town into which I had been thrown by the accident that a railroad brakeman had seen me standing on the bumpers between two cars of his train and had ordered me off. "Well, get off or give me a dollar," he had said, and I had not wanted to give him a dollar. I had only had three dollars in my pocket. Why should I give one to him? "There will be other freight trains," I had said to myself, "and perhaps I shall see something of interest here in this town."

Interest indeed! Now I lay in the grass trembling with fear. In fancy I had become the lover of the younger of the three women sitting on the steps of the house and my sweetheart's brothers with open knives in their hands were pursuing me in a dark street. I felt the knives slashing my body and knew

339

that what I felt the three women also felt. Every few minutes the younger of the three cried out. It was as though a knife had gone into her body. All four of us trembled with fear.

And then, as we waited and shook with dread, there was a stir in the silence. Feet, not running but walking steadily, were heard on the bridge that led into the road that passed the field and four men appeared. Somewhere in the town, in the dark night streets of the town, the two brothers had caught the lover but it was evident there had been an explanation. The three had gone together to a doctor, the cut cheek had been patched, they had got a marriage license and a preacher and were now coming home for a marriage.

The marriage took place at once, there before me on the steps of the house, and after the marriage, and after some sort of heavy joke on the part of the preacher, a joke at which no one laughed, the lover with his sweetheart, accompanied by the third woman, the one from the house across the field and who was evidently the lover's mother, went off across the field. Presently the field where I lay was all dark and silent again.

. . . .

And that had been the scene playing itself out in my fancy as I sat in the advertising office in Chicago, pretending to listen to the man who spoke of agricultural conditions in Texas and looking at the man with the scar on his cheek, the scar that had been partly hidden from the sight of others by growing the beard. I remembered that the plow company, now wanting to sell its plows in greater numbers in the southwest, was located in an Indiana town. How fine it would

340

be if I could speak to the man of the beard and ask him if by any chance he was the lover of the field. In fancy I saw all the men in the room suddenly talking with the greatest intimacy. Experiences in life were exchanged, everyone laughed. There had been something in the air of the room. The men who had come to us were from a small city in Indiana while we all lived in the great city. They were somewhat suspicious of us while we were compelled to try to allay their suspicions. After the conference there would be a dinner, perhaps at some club, and afterward drinks—but there would still be suspicion. I fancied a scene in which no man suspected another. What tales might then be told! How much we might find out of each other!

And now in fancy the bearded man and I were walking and talking together and I was telling him of the scene in the field and of what I had seen and he had told me of what I had not seen. He told me of how during the running he had become exhausted and had stopped in a dark little alleyway behind stores in the town and of how the brothers had found him there. One of them came toward him threateningly but he began to talk and an explanation followed. Then they had gone to arouse a doctor and a small official who gave them the marriage license.

"Do you know," he said, "neither her mother nor my own knew just what had happened and didn't dare ask. Her mother never asked her and my mother never asked me. We went along later as though nothing had happened at all except that with all of us, her brothers and myself, and even our two mothers, there was a kind of formality. They did not come to our house without being invited and we did not go freely to their house as we always had done before the brothers saw us together in the field that night.

"It was all a little strange and as soon as I could I grew the beard to hide the scar on my face that I thought embarrassed all the others.

"As for Molly and myself—well, you see it was somewhat strange to find ourselves suddenly man and wife but she has been a good wife to me. After the ceremony that night on the porch of the house and after the preacher went away we all stood for a little time together, saying nothing, then my mother started for our house across the field and I took my wife's arm and followed. When we got to our house I took my Molly into my bedroom and we sat on the edge of the bed. There was a window that looked over across the field to the house where she had always lived and after a while the lights went out over there. My own mother kept moving about in our house and, although she made no noise, I knew she was crying. Was she crying because she was glad or sad? Had Molly and I married in the regular way I suppose there would have been rejoicing in both houses and I think there is no doubt we would inevitably have married. Anyway, my mother did things about the house she had already done once that night, opened the door to let out the cat that was already out, tried to wind the clock that was already wound. Then she went off upstairs and our house was dark and silent too.

"We just sat like that, on the edge of the bed, Molly and me, I don't know for how long. Then she did something. The doctor in town had sewed up the wound in my cheek and had covered the place with a soft cloth held in place by pieces of tape. What she did was to reach up and touch the end of the wound, timidly, with the tips of her fingers. She did it several times, and each time a soft little moan came from her lips.

"She did that, as I say six or eight times and then we both lay down on the bed and took each other's hands. We didn't undress. What we did was to lie there, all night, just as I have described, with our clothes on and holding fast to each other's hands."

BOOK IV

NOTE I

I walked about the city of New York looking at people. I was not too young any more and could not make myself over to fit a new city. No doubt certain characteristics of my own nature had become fixed. I was a man of the mid-western towns who had gone from his town to the mid-western cities and there had gone through the adventures common to such fellows as myself. Was there some salt in me? To the end of my life I would talk with the half slovenly drawl of the middle-westerner, would walk like such a middle-westerner, have the air of something between a laborer, a man of business, a gambler, a race horse owner, an actor. If I was, as I then fully intended, to spend the rest of my life trying to tell such tales as I could think and feel my way through, I would have to tell the tales of my own people. Would I gain new power and insight for the telling by having come East, by consorting with other story-tellers? Would I understand better my own people and what had made the tragedies, the comedies and the wonders of their lives?

I was in New York as a guest, as an onlooker, wondering about the city and the men of the city and what they were thinking and feeling. There were certain men I wanted to see, who had written things I thought had given me new lights on my own people, the subjects of my tales.

I dare say there was a good deal of a certain half-rural timidity in me.

There was Mr. Van Wyck Brooks, whose book "America's Coming-of-Age," had moved me deeply. He with Mr. Waldo Frank, Paul Rosenfeld, James Oppenheim and others had just started a magazine, *The Seven Arts* (that after its death was to be replaced by *The Dial*, published by a quite different group), and the magazine had not only offered to publish some of my things but its editors had asked me to come to see them.

I wanted to go and was at the same time a little afraid. At that time there was a good deal of talk abroad as to a new artistic awakening in America. Mr. Waldo Frank's "Our America" must have been in preparation at just about that time and it could not have been much later that Mr. William Allen White wrote in *The New Republic,* an article the import of which was that "The King is dead! Long live the King!" If there were new kings in the land, I wanted to see and consort with them if I could.

As for *The Seven Arts* magazine, there had been rumors of its coming birth, even in Chicago. Miss Edna Kenton had come from New York to Chicago at about that time and a meeting was held. There was a large party in a large house and upstairs somewhere the new day was under discussion. We, downstairs, did not just know what was being discussed but there was a kind of tingling sensation in the air. Little groups of us gathered in the rooms below. "What's up?" It is to be remembered this was in Chicago and we were all young and no doubt naïve. "What they whispering about upstairs?" "Don't you

348

know?" Not to know was, we all felt, a kind of cultural blight. I had run from one group to another trying to find out and at just that moment a young doctor, who in his spare moments wrote poetry, came into the house and went hurriedly upstairs. A rather ribald fellow among the guests—Ben Hecht perhaps —who like the rest of us was angry that he had not been let into the secret, made an announcement. "I know what it is. Someone's having a baby;" he said.

What about the men of New York, the writers whose work I admired, the painters whose work I admired? I had always wanted to be a painter myself, was always having sensations and seeing forms that could perhaps have been expressed in paint and in no other way but the materials of the painter's craft seemed to me to lie far outside my way of life. One had to know drawing, to know what green did to yellow and yellow to brown. When one talked to painters they spoke of things that lay far outside one's pathway. There had been one painter I had known quite well. He had lived in a room near my own in Chicago and painted landscapes. Rather he painted one landscape over and over. There was an old stone building that looked like pictures one had seen of peasants' cottages. It was evening and two cows were coming home along a road, to a barn one fancied, but the barn could not be seen for the deep shadows that had gathered behind the house. Then there were some trees, the tops of which could be but faintly seen on the horizon. The last rays of the sun had splashed the sky with red. Often in the evening the painter, a large man with red hair, came into my room and spoke to me. He also had been touched with the new day and had read Paul Gauguin's notebook and a work by Mr. Clive Bell. "The new fellows have nothing on me," he declared and taking me into his room he showed me half a dozen of his canvases and how that in one the tops of the trees could just be seen above the roof of the house and in another that there were really no trees at all. "What you think is trees is only clouds," he declared, "and what you think is the sun going down is really the moon coming up."

Returning with me to my room he had talked so long and well of the effect of light on color, of form and its significance, of the new cubistic and post-impressionistic movements, the import and significance of which he declared scornfully he had measured and for the most part discarded, that I became frightened and did not for years afterwards try to paint. Once in Chicago I went into a store, intending to buy some colors with which to play at idle moments in my room but a certain air of the clerk had frightened me. My own father, when he was alive, had often received from manufacturers certain cards on which the house-painter's colors were shown and the trade name of each color printed below and I had thought I might find such a card lying on a counter in the art store but saw none and was ashamed to ask. Perhaps I wanted the clerk to think me a painter who knew his craft. How glibly the red-haired man had reeled off the names of colors. I was like one who has wandered into a church where people are kneeling in prayer. I began walking on tiptoes. "I only wanted to buy a pencil eraser," I said.

And so now there I was in the city of New York and there were certain men in the city to whom I would have liked to go, to talk with them of my craft, but when I thought of doing so I was afraid.

My own position was something like this: there were in my head certain tales I knew but could not yet tell and certain others I had told but felt I had told badly or haltingly. Was there a certain formula one could learn that might help one out of the difficulty? There was a sense in which I thought of myself as an ignorant man. The tales I had already put down on paper had been as a sort of growth in me. There was *The Little Review,* run by two Chicago women who had preceded me to New York. They had published tales of mine and might publish more. When I went to see them we had much fun together and Miss Anderson and myself had in common a fondness for rather striking clothes and for strutting a bit upon the stage of life that drew us closely together but being at bottom fellow Chicagoans we were bound not to take each other too seriously —at least not under the rose.

Did I want, above everything else, to be taken seriously? No doubt I did. That may have been the notion I had in coming to the city. And I suppose I wanted also to find superior craftsmen at whose feet I could sit. I already had my own notions concerning American story-tellers in general.

I was walking in the street or sitting in a train and overheard a remark dropped from the lips of some man or woman. Out of a thousand such remarks, heard almost every day, one stayed in my head. I

could not shake it out.   And then people constantly
told me tales and in the telling of them there was a
sentence used that intoxicated.   "I was lying on
my back on the porch and the street lamp shone on my
mother's face.   What was the use?   I could not say
to her what was in my mind.   She would not have
understood.   There was a man lived next door who
kept going past the house and smiling at me.   I got
it into my head that he knew all that I could not tell
mother."

A few such sentences in the midst of a conversation overheard or dropped into a tale someone told.   These were the seeds of stories.   How
could one make them grow?

In telling tales of themselves people constantly
spoiled the tale in telling.   They had some notion of
how a story should be told got from reading.   Little
lies crept in.   They had done something mean and
tried to justify some action that for the tale's sake
did not need justification.

There was a notion that ran through all story-
telling in America, that stories must be built about a
plot and that absurd Anglo-Saxon notion that they
must point a moral, uplift the people, make better
citizens, etc.   The magazines were filled with these
plot stories and most of the plays on our stage were
plot plays.   "The Poison Plot," I called it in conversation with my friends as the plot notion did seem to
me to poison all story-telling.   What was wanted I
thought was form, not plot, an altogether more elusive
and difficult thing to come at.

The plots were frameworks about which the stories
were to be constructed and editors were inordinately

fond of them. One got "an idea for a story." What was meant was that a new trick had been thought out. Nearly all the adventure stories and the well-known American western stories were so constructed. A man went into the redwood forests or into the deserts and took up land. He has been a rather mean, second-rate chap in civilization but in the new place a great change comes over him. Well, the writer had got him out where there was no one looking and could do as he pleased with the fellow. Never mind what he had been. The forests or the deserts had changed him completely. The writer could make a regular angel of him, have him rescue downtrodden women, catch horse thieves, exhibit any kind of bravery required to keep the reader excited and happy.

A word of good sense dropped in anywhere would have blown the whole thing to pieces but there was no danger. In all such writing all consideration for human beings was thrown aside. No one lived in such tales. Let such a writer begin to think of human beings, care a little for human beings, and his pasteboard world would melt before his eyes. The man in the desert or in the redwood forests was of course the same man he had been before he went there. He had the same problems to face. God knows we would all flee to the forests or the deserts at once if going there could so transform anyone. At least I know I should waste no time in getting there.

In the construction of these stories there was endless variation but in all of them human beings, the lives of human beings, were altogether disregarded. An Alabama Negro was given the shrewdness of a Connecticut Yankee, a trick that made some writer temporarily famous and brought him wealth. Having made his Negro think like a Yankee, having made him practice all the smart cute tricks of the Yankee, there was nothing to stop the writer producing a thousand tales with the hybrid Negro as the hero of them all. Only the giving out of the patience of the editors or of the public could stop him, and both seemed inexhaustible.

As to what the writer himself suffered under these circumstances, that was a different matter. One supposed that any man who attempted the writer's craft had, at the beginning, some real interest in the people about him but this was quickly lost. The imaginative life of the romancer must be lived entirely in a queer pasteboard world.

It was a peculiarity of the writer's craft that one must of necessity give oneself to the people about whom one wrote, must in a quite special way believe in the existence of these people, and a peculiar childlike credulousness must result to the writer who so completely separated himself from actual life. Having acquired sudden fame and wealth such a writer woke up some morning to find himself irrevocably dead. The actuality of life could not reach him. On all sides of him people suffered, were touched with moments of nameless joy, loved and died, and the manufacturer of society detectives, desert heroes and daring adventures by sea and land could no longer see life at all. With unseeing eyes, deaf ears and benumbed senses he must walk through life—a movie hero, a stage star or a rich and successful manufacturer of romances—no longer a human being at all. One had no notion of giving oneself to that kind of death in

354

life but to find out what one did not want to do was but half the battle.

After all the tales themselves came quickly. In certain moods one became impregnated with the seeds of a hundred new tales in one day. The telling of the tales, to get them into form, to clothe them, find just the words and the arrangement of words that would clothe them—that was a quite different matter. I wanted to find, if I could, the men who would help me toward the solution of that problem.

For even an unknown and unsuccessful scribbler in America the situation is difficult enough. Even the very sweetness of our people in their attitude toward our writers is destructive. You have seen how I myself was allowed to play like a reckless child among advertising men, constantly forgiven for my impudence, often paid an absurd figure for writing an unimportant advertisement—that any one of forty men, not authors, would have gladly written with more care at half my price—simply because I was an author.

Well, I had published certain tales over my own name and my fate was sealed. That the tales were not liked by many of the critics did not matter too much. To be sure, my books did not sell, but I was discussed in the newspapers and literary magazines and my picture was occasionally printed and finally a very secondrate English writer of romances, very popular in our country, spoke well of me and Mr. Frank Harris spoke ill of me.

Ye gods, I was lost and must flee. The very grocer at the corner, with whom I was wont to sit on the steps by the back door of the store on summer evenings while he talked of his life as a young sailor on a lake steamer looked at me with new eyes. He began speaking like a very movie hero. His tales, that had been so naturally and humanly told, became grotesques of tales. The fellow had some idea I might make him the hero of some improbable romance of our inland seas, one always holding the helm in some desperate storm or jumping overboard to rescue some broker's daughter, and tried heroically to supply me with materials. He had in his youth read some novel of the seas and now he began to lie valiantly, telling me all the desperate escapades of which he had heard or read as having happened to himself. Shades of Defoe and Melville, such a sea and such a sailor's life as he manufactured! I remembered almost with tears in my eyes the little homely real stories he had formerly been in the habit of telling of himself, and left him never to return. I was even vicious enough to rob him, for his defection, of my grocery trade.

How utterly all my life had been changed by a little public attention! Even some of my friends went the road of the grocer. I remember that I had, at just that time, done a deed affecting my personal life that had lost me the respect of some of my acquaintances. One of them saw my picture, printed I think in the *Literary Digest,* and immediately afterward wrote me a letter. "You are a great artist and may do anything you please. I forgive you everything," he wrote and as I read the letter my heart went sick within me. "At any rate why do they want to dehumanize us?" I asked myself. Violently then I cursed the romancers. They were in reality at the bottom of it all. Not satisfied with the cowboys the sailors and the detectives they had descended upon their brothers of the pen and the brush. A poet was a certain kind of man with long hair and no food who went about muttering to himself. There was no escape for him. That he was and his fate was fixed. To be sure I had myself known some American poets and had found them in their everyday life much like all the other people I knew except that they were a trifle more sensitive to life and its beauties and, before they became widely known as poets, sometimes wrote beautiful bits describing their inner reaction to some flash of beauty that had come to them. They were that before they became widely known as poets and then later they were usually goners.

That was how it was with the poet. The painter usually starved in a garret and went about his small room pale and emaciated, with a palette stuck on his thumb, and then one day a lovely lady came along the street, saw how that he was a genius and married him. I'll say this for us scribblers and the actors. We got off better. We usually, in the romances, sat on a park bench with the tramps and had a dirty newspaper blown to us by a cold wind. On the front page of the newspaper was a large picture of ourselves and an announcement that fame had come. Then we went and bought the tramps a breakfast with our last dollar before we went to live in a great house with servants. We scribblers and the actors got off the least shamefully in the romances but then, it is to be remembered, fellows of our own craft got up these yarns that had so stuck in the public mind and that they had for that reason perhaps a little pity for us.

All of this however concerned the materials for tales. One had to do one's own winnowing in any event. I was in New York and was after something other than stories. Would I find what I wanted? I was somewhat afraid of the writers, particularly of the ones whose work I most admired because I thought they must be a special kind of being, quite different from the men I had known. (No doubt I was myself the victim of the same romancers I have just been cursing.) There were certain men I thought had written of America and American writing with an understanding that had been a help to me. I was what I was, a rough and tumble participant in life. As yet there had been little time for study, for quiet thought.

As for these other men, the fellows of the East, what of them? I fancied in them an erudition the contemplation of which made me afraid. Now I understood how Mark Twain felt when he went up to Boston. Did he, like myself, want something without knowing just what he wanted?

For such men as myself you must understand there is always a great difficulty about telling the tale after the scent has been picked up. The tales that continually came to me in the way indicated above could of course not become tales until I had clothed them. Having, from a conversation overheard or in some other way, got the tone of a tale, I was like a woman who has just become impregnated. Something was growing inside me. At night when I lay in my bed I could feel the heels of the tale kicking against the walls of my body. Often as I lay thus every word of the tale came to me quite clearly but when I got out of bed to write it down the words would not come.

I had constantly to seek in roads new to me. Other men had felt what I had felt, had seen what I had seen

—how had they met the difficulties I faced? My father when he told his tales walked up and down the room before his audience. He pushed out little experimental sentences and watched his audience narrowly. There was a dull-eyed old farmer sitting in a corner of the room. Father had his eyes on the fellow. "I'll get him," he said to himself. He watched the farmer's eyes. When the experimental sentence he had tried did not get anywhere he tried another and kept trying. Beside words he had—to help the telling of his tales—the advantage of being able to act out those parts for which he could find no words. He could frown, shake his fists, smile, let a look of pain or annoyance drift over his face.

These were his advantages that I had to give up if I was to write my tales rather than tell them and how often I had cursed my fate.

How significant words had become to me! At about this time an American woman living in Paris, Miss Gertrude Stein, had published a book called "Tender Buttons" and it had come into my hands. How it had excited me! Here was something purely experimental and dealing in words separated from sense—in the ordinary meaning of the word sense— an approach I was sure the poets must often be compelled to make. Was it an approach that would help me? I decided to try it.

A year or two before the time of which I am now writing an American painter, Mr. Felix Russman, had taken me one day into his workshop to show me his colors. He laid them out on a table before me and then his wife called him out of the room and he stayed for half an hour. It had been one of the most exciting moments of my life. I shifted the little pans of color about, laid one color against another. I walked away and came near. Suddenly there had flashed into my consciousness, for perhaps the first time in my life, the secret inner world of the painters. Before that time I had wondered often enough why certain paintings, done by the old masters, and hung in our Chicago Art Institute, had so strange an effect upon me. Now I thought I knew. The true painter revealed all of himself in every stroke of his brush. Titian made one feel so utterly the splendor of himself; from Fra Angelico and Sandro Botticelli there came such a deep human tenderness that on some days it fairly brought tears to the eyes; in a most dreadful way and in spite of all his skill Bouguereau gave away his own inner nastiness while Leonardo made one feel all of the grandeur of his mind just as Balzac had made his readers feel the universality and wonder of his mind.

Very well then, the words used by the tale-teller were as the colors used by the painter. Form was another matter. It grew out of the materials of the tale and the teller's reaction to them. It was the tale trying to take form that kicked about inside the tale-teller at night when he wanted to sleep.

And words were something else. Words were the surfaces, the clothes of the tale. I thought I had begun to get something a little clearer now. I had smiled to myself a little at the sudden realization of how little native American words had been used by American story-writers. When most American writers wanted to be very American they went in for slang. Surely we American scribblers had paid long and hard for the English blood in our veins. The·English had

360

got their books into our schools, their ideas of correct forms of expression were firmly fixed in our minds. Words as commonly used in our writing were in reality an army that marched in a certain array and the generals in command of the army were still English. One saw the words as marching, always just so—in books—and came to think of them so—in books.

But when one told a tale to a group of advertising men sitting in a barroom in Chicago or to a group of laborers by a factory door in Indiana one instinctively disbanded the army. There were moments then for what have always been called by our correct writers "unprintable words." One got now and then a certain effect by a bit of profanity. One dropped instinctively into the vocabulary of the men about, was compelled to do so to get the full effect sought for the tale. Was the tale he was telling not just the tale of a man named Smoky Pete and how he caught his foot in the trap set for himself?—or perhaps one was giving them the Mama Geigans story. The devil. What had the words of such a tale to do with Thackeray or Fielding? Did the men to whom one told the tale not know a dozen Smoky Petes and Mama Geigans? Had one ventured into the classic English models for tale-telling at that moment there would have been a roar. "What the devil! Don't you go high-toning us!"

And it was sure one did not always seek a laugh from his audience. Sometimes one wanted to move the audience, make them squirm with sympathy. Perhaps one wanted to throw an altogether new light on a tale the audience already knew.

Would the common words of our daily speech in

shops and offices do the trick? Surely the Americans among whom one sat talking had felt everything the Greeks had felt, everything the English felt? Deaths came to them, the tricks of fate assailed their lives. I was certain none of them lived felt or talked as the average American novel made them live feel and talk and as for the plot short stories of the magazines— those bastard children of De Maupassant, Poe and O. Henry—it was certain there were no plot short stories ever lived in any life I had known anything about.

Did it come to this, that Americans worked, made love, settled new western states, arranged their personal affairs, drove their fords, using one language while they read books, wanted perhaps to read books, in quite another language?

I had come to Gertude Stein's book about which everyone laughed but about which I did not laugh. It excited me as one might grow excited in going into a new and wonderful country where everything is strange—a sort of Lewis and Clark expedition for me. Here were words laid before me as the painter had laid the color pans on the table in my presence. My mind did a kind of jerking flop and after Miss Stein's book had come into my hands I spent days going about with a tablet of paper in my pocket and making new and strange combinations of words. The result was I thought a new familiarity with the words of my own vocabulary. I became a little conscious where before I had been unconscious. Perhaps it was then I really fell in love with words, wanted to give each word I used every chance to show itself at its best.

It had then not occurred to me that the men I had

really come to New York hoping to see and know, fellows of the schools, men who knew their Europe, knew the history of the arts, who knew a thousand things I could not know, it had never occurred to me that in the end I would find them as frankly puzzled as myself. When I found that out there was a new adjustment to make. It was then only the trick men, the men who worked from the little patent formula they had learned, the critics who could never get English literature out of their heads, who thought they were sure of their grounds? That knowledge was a relief when I found it out but I was a long long time finding it out. It takes a long time to find out one's own limitations and perhaps a longer time to find out the limitations of one's critics.

Was there really something new in the air of America? I remember that at about this time someone told me that I was myself something new and how thankful I was to hear it. "Very well," I said to myself, "if there are certain men launching a new ship from the harbor of New York and if they are willing to take me aboard I'll sure go." I was just as willing to be a modern as anything else, was glad to be. It was very sure I was not going to be a successful author and well enough I knew that, not being successful, there would be a great deal of consolation to me in being at least a modern.

What I at the moment felt toward all the more deeply cultured men whose acquaintanceship I sought and still in a sense feel toward them was something like what a young mechanic might feel when his boss comes into the shop accompanied by his daughter.

The young mechanic is standing at his lathe and there is grease on his face and hands. The boss's daughter has never been shown over the shop before and is a little excited by the presence of so many strange men and as she and her father approach the lathe where the young workman stands he does not know whether to appear surly and uncommunicative or bold and a bit impudent. (In his place I, being an American, should probably have winked at the girl and been terribly embarrassed and ashamed later.)

There he stands fumbling about with his fingers and pretending to look out of the window and—the devil!—now the boss has stopped behind his lathe and is attempting to explain something to the daughter, "This is a sprocket post, is it not?" he says to the workman, who is compelled to turn around. "Yes, sir," he mutters, in embarrassment but his eyes, in just that fraction of a second, have taken a sweeping glance at the daughter.

And now she is gone and the workman is asking himself questions. "If I was a swell now I suppose maybe I'd be invited to their house." He imagines himself in a dress suit going up a long driveway to the front of a grand house. He is swinging a cane and there on the front steps is the boss's daughter waiting to receive him. What will he talk to her about? Dare a man speak in such company of the only things he knows? What does he know?

He knows that Jack Johnson could probably have whipped Jess Willard if he had really tried. There is a woman lives in his rooming house who is unfaithful to her husband. He knows who with. She is going to have a child but the chances are it is not her husband's child.   Often he has asked himself how she will feel on the night when the child is born and when her husband is so excited and proud.

After all, the young workman knows a good many things of his own sort, but of how many of them can he, dare he, speak with the boss's daughter whose voice was so soft and whose skin looked so delicate that day when she came into the shop with her father? "Dare I ask her what she thinks the unfaithful wife will be thinking and feeling when the child is born?"

Young workmen have a kind of fear of the thing called culture.   Most middle-westerners think of it— in spite of their protestations to the contrary—as in some vague way to be breathed in the air of New York. New Yorkers seem to think of it as to be found in London or Paris.   Bankers and manufacturers of the Middle-West hope to get it for their sons by sending them to Yale or Harvard and as there are a good many bankers and manufacturers Yale and Harvard are inclined to be crowded.   Mark Twain thought he would find it in Boston—a whole generation of Americans thought that.

To the young workman culture is somewhat like a new suit of clothes that does not fit too well.   It binds under the arms when one first puts it on.

NOTE II

WHEN I lived in Chicago and had first begun to write stories an American critic who had seen some of my work had been very kind about securing the publication of the stories but once, when he was annoyed with me for writing a story he did not like, he wrote me a scolding letter. "You are, after all, nothing but an advertising writer who would like to be something else and can't make it," he said and after I had got to New York and had walked about a little looking at the tall arrogant buildings and at the smart alert-looking people in the streets I thought I had better, for the time at least, stay away from the people whose work and whose minds I admired. "They might find out how really little I know," I said to myself shrewdly.

I was however not too lonely, having plenty of people at whom I could look, to whom I could listen. My brother, who lived in New York, took me to the Salmagundi Club where I saw any number of successful painters and my boyhood friend Mr. John Emerson took me to the Players and Lambs and also, with other men and women I knew, I penetrated into the life of Greenwich Village.

How many strings to grasp! How many things I wanted of the city that was, I had no doubt, the artistic and intellectual capital of the country! The city's wealth did not impress me too much, as I had been in other wealthy places. One could make money as fast in Chicago as in New York, although it could probably not be spent with quite as much style. What I wanted most was the men who would help me solve certain problems connected with the craft to which I was devoted. Could I find such fellows? Would they do it?

The bitter truth was that of the actors I saw and heard talk none seemed much interested in the craft of the actor and of the painters the same lack of interest in what seemed to me so essential was apparent, and surely we scribblers were no better. The successful men of the arts talked of the market and little else. Writers even went into bookstores to see what kind of books were selling well in order to know what kind of books to write, actors talked of salaries paid and of getting some part that would bring them into prominence and the painters followed the same bent.

Were the successful practitioners of the arts much less decent fellows than the laborers and business men of the Middle West among whom my life had been spent? I was forced to ask myself that question too.

I SAT in a restaurant in New York thinking of my friends George and Marco in Chicago. We had been lads together and I remembered an evening of our young manhood when we all went out to walk together. We had stopped at a bridge and stood leaning over and I remembered that Marco had said something, expressive at the moment of what we had all felt. "The time'll come, I'll bet you what you please the time'll come when I'll be making my hundred and twenty-five every month," he had said.

Well, Marco's remark had expressed something more than a desire to make money. Later all of us had made money and then when youth was gone we had all tried something else. Marco wrote poetry and George and I wrote stories. None of us knew much of our crafts but we had struggled together with them and in the evenings had sat about talking. What we had all wanted was the leisure money might bring. We had all wanted to go to New York and live among men who knew more of the crafts we were trying to practice than we felt we would ever know.

And now I had come to New York and was sitting in a restaurant where the more successful of the practitioners of the arts congregated. What did I want? I wanted to hear men of my own craft, who loved the craft, speak of it. I remembered how as a boy in mid-western towns before the factories came in so thick the carpenters, wheelwrights, harness-makers and other craftsmen often gathered about to speak of their work and how I loved to be among them at such times. The factories had brushed such fellows aside. Had the same thing happened in the more delicate crafts? Were the great publishing houses of the city and the magazines but factories and were the writers and picture makers who worked for them but factory hands now?

If that had happened I thought I understood the men among whom I had now come. The older craftsmen had thought little on the subject of wages and had never talked on the subject when they gathered in groups in the evenings but the factory hands among whom I later worked had talked of little else. They had talked of how much money might be made and had boasted interminably of their potency in sex. Were the practitioners of the more delicate crafts becoming like them?

In the New York restaurant was a room filled with people, all in some way practitioners of the arts. Near me at a table sat three men and two women. They were talking in rather loud tones and seemed conscious that everything they said was of importance. One had a queer sense of their separateness from each other. Why, when one of them spoke, did he not look at his fellows? Instead he glanced about the room, as though saying to himself, "Is anyone looking at me?"

And now one of these men arose and walked across the room. There was something strange about his walk. I was puzzled and then the truth came to me. All the men and women in the room were obviously aware of what they thought of as their own importance. No man spoke naturally, walked naturally.

The man who had got up from the table to go speak to someone at another table did not want really to speak to him. He wanted to walk across the room for the same reason that I am told, nowadays, it is almost impossible to do anything with actors as they all want to get into one spot on the stage—upstage where the light is the clearest.

What a ghastly separation from life! I sat in the New York restaurant fully aware that what was true of the men and women about me was true also of myself. The people in the restaurant, the actors, painters and writers, had made themselves what the public thought it wanted from its artists, and had been well paid for doing so. What I felt in New York I might have felt with even more terrible certainty in Hollywood.

I fled from the restaurant and at a street corner stopped and laughed at myself. I remembered that at the moment I had on a pair of socks and a neckscarf, either of which might have been seen for a mile. "At any rate you're not such a blushing violet yourself," I said, grinning with myself at myself.

NOTE IV

It was time surely for me to review myself. I wanted to know just what I was doing in New York, what I was up to—if I could find out. I had time now to ask myself a lot of questions and I enjoyed doing so. Mornings to walk about, afternoons to go to the parks, sit with people or go to see paintings, evenings of my own. No advertisements to write, for a time anyway. "Crescent Soap Lightens the Day's Work. Tangletoes Catches the Flies," etc. For a man living as I lived a few hundred dollars would go far. For the American there are always plenty of books to be had without cost and one may see what the more successful painters are doing by simply walking in at the door of a museum or a gallery. The work of the more unsuccessful ones worth seeing Alfred Stieglitz will show you or tell you about. Cigarettes do not cost very much and there are happy hours to be spent sitting by the window of a room in a side street hearing what people have to say as they walk past. All the women of my street spent the time at the same thing. There was a fat old woman across the way who never left the window from morning till night. I wondered if she was planning to write a novel and was thinking about the characters, dreaming of them, making up scenes and situations in which they were to play a part.

If my life in the past had been split into two parts it need be that no longer. I have taken a resolution. In the future I would write no more advertisements. If I became broke I would become a beggar and sit with a beggar bowl in Fifth Avenue. Even the police are sentimental enough not to kick an author out. I would not sit swearing at the book publishers, the magazine editors or the public, that I was not rich. I had not tried to accommodate myself to them—why should they bother about me? I sat dreaming of what might be the takings of an author with a beggar bowl in his lap sitting in front of the Public Library on Fifth Avenue. The press of people would prevent the literarily inclined ladies from stopping to discuss books or to tell the author that his philosophy of life was all wrong. Also they could not accuse him of personal immorality. A beggar could not be immoral. He was at once above and below immorality. And the takings! There would be much good silver and I loved silver. If I should become blind my fortune would be made at last. A blind author sitting begging before the Public Library in the city of New York! Who dare say there was not glorious opportunity left in our country?

Had I less courage than my father? Perhaps I had. He also might have thought of so noble a plan but in my place he might also have put it into execution at once. Ladies often came to the Public Library to meet their lovers. Quarrels started there. One would learn much of life by sitting as I have suggested. No man or woman would hesitate to speak boldly before a beggar. The stones would be cold but perhaps one could have a cushion.

NOTE V

WHEN I went on my pilgrimage to New York I was not a young man any more. The gray had begun to show in my hair. On the very day after my arrival I chanced to pick up a novel of Turgenev's, "A House of Gentlefolk," and saw how that he had made his hero Levretsky an old man, through with life, at forty-five.

Pretty rough on an American who had not dared think of trying to do what he wanted until he was approaching that age. No American dared think of doing anything he enjoyed until youth was gone. Youth must be given to money making among us and leisure was a sin. A short time after the period of which I am now writing I was given the *Dial* prize for literature, the intent of which was that it was to be given to encourage some young man just starting out on the hard road of literary effort. It had been offered to me and I wanted it but thought seriously of investing in hair dye before going to call on the editors.

So little work of any account done! Mornings coming, noons, nights! Many nights of lying awake in my bed in some rooming house in the city thinking!

I had a penchant for taking my own life rather seriously. Americans in general pretended their own lives did not matter. They were continually talking of devoting their lives to business, to some reform, to their children, to the public. I had been called a modern and perhaps only deserved the title inasmuch as I was a born questioner. I did not take such words people were always saying too seriously. Often enough I used to lie on my bed in my room and on moonlight nights I lit a cigarette and spent some time looking at myself. I lifted up my legs, one after the other, and rejoiced at the thought that they might yet take me into many strange places. Then I lifted my arms and looked long and earnestly at my hands. Why had they not served me better? Why would they not serve me better? It was easy enough to put a pen into the fingers. I myself was perfectly willing to be a great author. Why would not the pen slide more easily and gracefully over the paper? What sentences I wanted to write, what paragraphs, what pages! If reading Miss Stein had given me a new sense of my own limited vocabulary, had made me feel words as more living things, if seeing the work of many of the modern painters had given me a new feeling for form and color, why would my own hands not become better servants to me?

On some nights, as I lay thus, the noise of the great city to which I had come growing fainter as the night wore on, I had many strange thoughts, brought into my head by reading the works of such men as Mr. Van Wyck Brooks or by talking with such men as my friends Alfred Stieglitz and Paul Rosenfeld. My own hands had not served me very well. Nothing they had done with words had satisfied me. There was not finesse enough in my fingers. All sorts of thoughts and emotions came to me that would not creep down my arms and out through my fingers upon the paper. How much was I to blame for that? How much could fairly be blamed to the civilization in which I had lived? I presume I wanted very much to blame something other than myself if I could.

The thoughts that came were something like this: "Suppose," I suggested to myself, "that the giving of itself by an entire generation to mechanical things were really making all men impotent. There was a passion for size among almost all the men I had known. Almost every man I had known had wanted a bigger house, a bigger factory, a faster automobile than his fellows. I had myself run an automobile and doing so had given me a strange sense of vicarious power, mingled with a kind of shame too. I pressed my foot upon a little button on the floor of the car and it shot forward. There was a feeling that did not really belong to me, that I had in some way stolen. I was rushing along a road or through a street and carrying five or six other people with me and, in spite of myself, felt rather grand doing it. Was that because I was in reality so ineffectual in myself? Did so many of my fellow writers want great sales for their books because, feeling as I did then the ineffectuality of their own hands to do good work, they wanted to be convinced from the outside? Was the desire all modern peoples had for a greater navy, a greater army, taller public buildings, but a sign of growing impotence? Was there a growing race of people in the world who had no use for their hands and were the hands paying them back by becoming ineffectual? Was the Modern after all but the man who had begun faintly to realize what I was then realizing and were all his efforts but at bottom the attempt to get his hands back on the ends of his arms? 'It may be that all the men of our age can at best but act as fertilizer,' Paul Rosenfeld had said to me. Was what I was then thinking in reality what he had meant?"

I am trying to give as closely as I can a transcript of some of my own thoughts as I lay on my bed in a rooming house in the city of New York and after I had walked about and had talked a little with some of the men I admired. I was thinking of old workers in the time of the crafts and of the new workers I had personally known in the time of the factories. I was thinking of myself and my own ineffectualness. Perhaps I was but trying to make excuses for myself. Most artists spend a large part of their time doing that. In the factories so many of the workers spent so large a part of their time boasting of their sexual effectiveness. Was that because they felt themselves every year growing more and more ineffectual as men? Were modern women going more and more toward man's life and man's attitude toward life because they were becoming all the time less and less able to be women? For two or three hundred years the western peoples had been in the grip of a thing called Puritanism. Mr. Brooks and Mr. Waldo Frank, in two books published at about that time, had declared that industrialism was a natural outgrowth of Puritanism, that having renounced life for themselves the Puritans were determined to kill life in others.

I had definite reasons for asking myself many of the questions that came to me as I lay in my bed at night. I had already published several stories and, for some

376

reason I had not clearly understood, many people in reading my stories had been made angry by them. Many abusive letters had been written me. I had been called a pervert, a thoroughly nasty man.

Was I that? I thought if I was I had better find out. My own hands looked all right to me as I lay on my bed looking at them in the moonlight. Were they unclean hands? There had been a few times, for brief periods only, when they had seemed to me to serve my purpose. I had felt something deeply, been quite impersonally absorbed in something in the life about me and my hands had of a sudden come to life. They had arranged words on paper I thought very skillfully. How clean I had felt during just those moments! It was the feeling I had always been seeking. At last, in a crippled way to be sure but after a fashion, my whole being had become a quite impersonal thing, expressing itself on paper through written words. The life about me seemed to have become my life. I sang as I worked, as in my boyhood I had often seen old craftsmen sing and as I had never heard men sing in the factories.

And for what I had written at such times I had been called unclean by men and women who had never known me, could have had no personal reasons for thinking me unclean. Was I unclean? Were the hands that, for such brief periods of my life, had really served me, had they been unclean at such moments of service?

Other thoughts came. Even my friend Paul Rosenfeld had called me "the Phallic Chekhov." Had I a sex obsession? Was I a goner?

Another American, Mr. Henry Adams, had evidently been as puzzled as I was at that moment although I am sure he would never have been so undignified as to have written, as I am doing here, of himself as lying on a bed in a New York rooming house and putting his own hands up into the moonlight to stare at them.

However he had been equally puzzled. "Singularly enough," he had said in his book, "The Education of Henry Adams," "singularly enough, not one of Adams' many schools of education has ever drawn his attention to the opening lines of Lucretius, though they were perhaps the finest in all Latin literature, where the poet invoked Venus exactly as Dante invoked the Virgin:

'Quae, quoniam rerum naturam Sola gubernas.'

"The Venus of Epicurean philosophy survived in the Virgin of the Schools.

'Donna, sei tanto grande, e tanta vali,
Che qual vuol grazia, e a te non ricorre,
Sua Disianza vuol volar senz' ali.'

"All this was to American thought as though it had never existed. The true American knew something of the facts, but nothing of the feelings; he read the letter, but he never felt the law. Before this historic chasm, a mind like that of Adams felt itself helpless; he turned from the Virgin to the dynamo as though he were a Branly coherer. On one side, at the Louvre and at Chartres, as he knew by the record of work actually done and still before his eyes, was the highest energy ever known to men, the creator of four-fifths

378

of his noblest art, exercising vastly more attraction over the human mind than all the steam engines and dynamos ever dreamed of; and yet this energy was unknown to the American mind. An American Virgin would never dare command; an American Venus would never dare exist."

If Mr. Adams had not spent his time as I was doing, lying on a bed and looking at his own hands, he had at least spent his time looking about. "An American Virgin would never dare command; an American Venus would never dare exist," he had said and it was an accusation that an American could neither love nor worship.

At any rate I was a man of the Middle West. I was not a New Englander. For my own people, as I had known them, it was absurd to say they had neither love nor reverence. Never a boy or man I had known at all intimately but that had both in him. We had simply been cheated. Our Virgins and Venuses had to be worshiped under the bush. What nights I had spent mooning about with middle-western boys, with hungry girls too. Were we but trying to refute the older men of New England who had got such a grip on our American intellectual life, the Emersons, Hawthornes and Longfellows? It was perhaps true to say of the intellectual sons of these men that a Virgin would never dare command, that a Venus would never dare exist. I knew little of New England men in the flesh but it was not necessarily true of us, out in my country. Of that I was pretty sure.

As for my own hands I continued looking at them. Questions kept coming. I was myself no longer young. Having made a few bicycles in factories, having written some thousands of rather senseless advertisements, having rubbed affectionately the legs of a few race horses, having tried blunderingly to love a few women and having written a few novels that did not satisfy me or anyone else, having done these few things, could I begin now to think of myself as tired out and done for? Because my own hands had for the most part served me so badly could I let them lie beside me in idleness?

I did not dare make such a surrender, nor did I dare dodge the issue with myself by going off into that phase of New York life I had already come to dislike, that phase of life which allows a man to employ his hands merely in writing smart and self-satisfying words regarding the failures of other men. In reality I was not trying to look at other men's lives just then and as for other men's work—it meant something to me when it taught me something. I was a middle-westerner who had come East to school if I could find the school.

I wanted back the hands that had been taken from me if I could get them back. Mr. Stark Young had talked to me one day of what thinking might be and his words kept ringing in my ears. Such words as he had said to me always excited like music or painting. He was a man who had been a professor in colleges and knew what was conventionally called thinking and he had said that thinking meant nothing at all unless it was done with the whole body—not merely with the head. I remember that one night I got out of bed and went to my window. I had a room far over on Twenty-second Street, near the Hudson River, and often, late at night, sailors from the ships lying in the river came along my street. They had been drinking, seeing the girls, having a time, and were now going back to the ships to sail away over the world. One of them, a very drunken sailor who had to stop every few steps and lean against a building, sang in a hoarse throaty voice:

> "Lady Lou. Lady Lou.
> I love you.
> Lady Lou."

I looked at my own hands lying on the window sill in the moonlight and I dare say had anyone seen me at that moment he might have decided I had gone quite insane. I talked to my own hands, made them promises, pleaded with them, "I shall cover you with golden rings. You shall be bathed in perfumes."

Perhaps there was an effort to be made I had not the courage or strength to make. When it came to tale-telling there were certain tales that fairly told themselves, but there were others, more fascinating, that needed a great deal of understanding, of myself first and then of others.

AND so there I was, an American rapidly approaching middle life, sitting in my room over in west Twenty-second Street at night after a day spent listening to the talk of the new men and trying with all my might to be one of the new men myself. Below me in the street the common life of people went on but I tried to put it away from me for the time, was having too good a time thinking of myself to think much of ordinary people. It is a mood that has appeared and reappeared in me at various times and I am trying to clear it out of my system by writing this book. When I have done that I hope to shut up on the subject for keeps. In my book I have had something to say of my father, emphasizing the showman side of his nature. I have perhaps lied now and then regarding the facts of his life but have not lied about the essence of it.

He was a man who loved a parade, bands playing in streets and himself in a gaudy uniform somewhere up near the head of the procession and I have myself had a pretty hard time not making a parade out of my own life.

Some time after the period of which I am now writing, my friend Mr. Paul Rosenfeld was with me in London stopping at the same hotel and one day I got away from him and when he wasn't watching wandered into a gents' furnishing store. When he came into the hotel later I took him to my room and displayed before him the things I had bought. He almost wept but there was little he could do. "Don't," he said. "Come out of the room. Promise me you won't wear these things until you get out again to Chicago."

I was in New York and was the son of my father. The New Movement in the Arts was under way. If it was going to be a parade I wanted, ached, to be in it. Was I but trying to put myself over to the literary world as formerly I had been employed to put over automobile tires to the public?

It was a question I was compelled to keep asking myself as it had something to do with the ineffectualness of my own hands lying before me on the window sill. I kept thinking of middle-western men like Dreiser, Masters, Sandburg and the others. There was something sincere and fine about them. Perhaps they had not worried, as I seemed to be doing, about the whole question of whether they belonged to the New Movement or not. I thought of them as somewhere out in the Middle West quietly at work, trying to understand the life about them, trying to express it in their work as best they could. How many other men were there in towns and cities of that great middle-western empire—my own land—younger men coming along. I had been unable to make my own beginning until most of the stronger years of my own life had passed. Perhaps I could not have begun at all but for them and perhaps, because of them, other men could now begin ten years younger than myself.

"The eastern men, among whom I had now come, were perhaps right in demanding something more than courage from American artists," I began telling myself. It was apparent there were two steps necessary and it might well be that we middle-western men had taken but one step. One had first of all to face one's materials, accept fully the life about, quit running off in fancy to India, to England, to the South Seas. We Americans had to begin to stay, in spirit at least, at home. We had to accept our materials, face our materials.

There was one thing, but there was something else too. We had to begin to face the possibilities of the surfaces of our pages.

Ah, here was something very difficult and delicate indeed! Was I right after all in sitting in the darkness of my room and looking at my own hands, pleading with my own hands? Had I really come to New York—not to find out and digest abstract thoughts about American life but to find there the men who would direct me more truly to the training of my own hands for my task?

In the days of the old crafts men became apprenticed craftsmen at fifteen. Had the men of the new day to live nearly three times that long before they found out they need go looking for the masters?

NOTE VIII

I was living in a rooming house in a side street in
New York and had spent more years of my life than
I cared to think about in just such places. When I
first began writing I used to read a great deal, in
George Moore and others, of writers, painters, poets
and the like sitting in cafés. That however happened in Paris, not in New York or Chicago.
Everyone has read about it. You know how they do.
In the evening one by one they come in at the door of
the café. On the arm of the painter there may
chance to be a beautiful grisette. The writers
are less fortunate with the ladies and are glad
to sit in silence listening to the talk. And how
brilliant the talk! Such things are said! There
is always an old wit, someone in the manner of
Whistler or Degas. The old dog sits at a table keeping everything in order. I remember that two or
three men I knew in New York tried something of the
sort but did not quite pull it off. Let someone get a
little "hifalutin' "—some scribbler, let us say. Suppose he sighs and says "The beautiful must remain the
unattainable," or something like that. Or let some
other scribbler go off on a long solemn pronouncement
about government, "All government should be done
away with. It's nonsense." Bang! The Jimmy
Whistler or the Degas of the café has shot him right

386

between the eyes.   There was a sense in which Miss
Jane Heap of *The Little Review* supplied the need of
such a one in New York, but she and Miss Margaret
Anderson could not cover the whole field.   That was
impossible.

And, in any event, neither New York nor Chicago
has any cafés.   When I first went to New York drinking was still publicly going on but one stood up at a
bar with the foot on a rail and shot the drink into
oneself.   There might be a moment of conversation
with the bartender.   "What chance you think the
Giants got?" etc.   Nothing specially helpful in that
and anyway what one secretly hoped was that the
White Sox of Chicago would win.

Everyone lived in rooms, except those who had
rich parents and most young American artists
gathered in the city, ate at cafeterias.   In Chicago, before I left, they had begun taking the chairs out
of the restaurants and one fancied that, in a few years,
all Chicagoans would eat as they drank, standing.
It would save time.

We more solemn and serious American scribblers,
painters, etc., for the most part lived in rooms and I
have myself a memory of rooms in which I have lived,
that is like a desert trail.   I can no longer recall all of
them.   In a sense they haunt my whole life.   At a
little distance they become gray, little gray holes into
which I have crept.

And we Americans have enough of the blood of the
northern races in us that we must have our holes into
which to creep, to contemplate ourselves, to say our
prayers.   In Paris, during a summer when I loitered
there, I found myself able to sit all afternoon in a café,

387

watching the people pass up and down a little street. At another café across a small square a young student made love to a girl. He kept touching her body with his hands and laughing and occasionally he kissed her. That happened and carts passed. One side of my mind made little delightful mental notes. The French teamsters did not make geldings of their horses. Magnificent stallions passed drawing dust carts. Why did Americans unman stallions while the French did not? The teamster walked in the road with his hat cocked to the side of his head and a bit of color in the hat. The stallion threw back his head and trumpeted. The teamster made some sort of sarcastic comment to the student with the girl, who answered in kind but did not quit kissing her. There was a small church on the west side of the square and old women were going in and coming out. All these things happened and I was alive to them all and still I sat in a café writing a tale of life in my own Ohio towns. How natural it seemed, in Paris, to lead one's secret inner life quite openly in the streets and how unnatural the same sort of thing would have seemed in an American city.

In Chicago alone there had been enough rooms, in which I myself had lived, had hidden myself away, to have made a long street of houses. How much had my own outlook on life been made by the rooms? How much were the lives of all Americans made by the places in which they lived? When Americans grew tired of their houses—or rooms—and went into the street there was no place to sit unless one went into a movie or went to eat expensive and unnecessary food in a crowded restaurant.   In the movies signs were put up: "Best place in town to kill time."

Time then was a thing to be killed.   It would seem an odd notion, I fancy, to a Frenchman or an Italian.

NOTE IX

ONE goes from Chicago to New York on a modern train very quickly but in the short time while the train is tearing along, while one sleeps and awakens once, one cuts the distance between oneself and Europe immeasurably. To the American, and in spite of the later disillusionment brought by the World War Europe remained the old home of the crafts. Even as the train goes eastward in one's own country, there is an inner ferment of excitement. Turgenev, Gogol, Fielding, Cervantes, De Foe, Balzac—what mighty names marched through the mind with the click of the car wheels. To the man of the American West how much the East means. How deeply buried the great European craftsmen had been in the soil out of which they had come. How intimately they had known their own peoples and with what infinite delicacy and understanding they had spoken out of them. As one sat in the train one found oneself bitterly condemning many of our own older craftsmen for selling out their inheritances, for selling out the younger men, too. Why were they not more consciously aware of what they, as craftsmen, were at? What had they got—a few automobiles, suburban homes, a little cheap acclaim.

Moments of wrath and then a smile too. "My boy, my boy, keep your shirt on!"

In the next seat a Detroit man talking loudly. "Advertising pays. What you got to do is put it across in a hurry."

Only yesterday there was myself too, talking so, pounding tables in offices, crying the gospel of size, of hustle.

"Keep your shirt on! Listen! You are starting rather late to do much. Perhaps if you are patient, if you listen work and learn you shall yet tell delicately a few tales."

As one approaches the Atlantic Coast there is a feeling comes that one, not born, not having lived, through youth and young manhood in the Middle or Far West will never quite understand. Near my own room in the city, lying in the Hudson River, were vessels that to-morrow would set sail for Europe, other vessels that had arrived from Europe but the day before. As I lay on my cot in my room at night I could hear the steamboats crying in the river. At night when there was a fog they were like cows lost in a forest, somewhere out in the Middle West, lost and bawling for the warm barns.

One went down to walk in the street facing the river. People were arriving on boats, departing on boats. They took the whole matter calmly, as one living in Chicago would entrain for Indianapolis. Out in my own country, when I was a boy, going to Europe meant something tremendous, like going to war for example. It was of infinitely more importance than, let us say, getting married. One got married or even went to war without writing a book about it but no man went to Europe from Ohio at least, without later writing a book about his travels.

Men and women of the Middle West became famous by way of European trips. Such and such a one had been to Europe three times. He was consulted upon all occasions, was allowed to sit on the platform at political meetings, might even claim the privilege of carrying a cane. Even the men of the barrooms were impressed. The bartender settled a quarrel between two men by referring the matter to Ed Swarts, who had been home to Germany twice. "Well, he's traveled. He has an education. He knows what he's talking about," the bartender said.

Had I myself come to New York, half wanting to go on to Europe and not quite daring? At least there was not in me the naïve faith in Europe my father must have had. I found myself able to go into the presence of men who had spent years in Europe without trembling, visibly at least, but something pulled. It was so difficult to understand life and the impulses of life here. There was so much phrase-making to cover up the reality of feelings, of hungers. Would one learn something by going to the sources of all this vast river of mixed bloods, mixed traditions, mixed passions and impulses?

Perhaps I thought that in New York I should find men, Americans in spirit and in fact, who had digested what Europe had to give America and who would pass it on to me. I was middle-western enough to think it a bit presumptuous of me to strike out as a man of letters, set myself up as a man of letters. I wanted to, but didn't quite dare.

However I took a long breath and plunged. All about me were men talking and talking. There was, at just that time, a distinct effort to awaken in New

392

York something like the group life among artists and intellectuals for which Paris had long been famous. There was the extreme radical political and intellectual group, gathered about *The Masses;* the *Little Review* with its sledgehammer pronouncements and a kind of flaunting joy of life, of which the others were both scornful and afraid; *The Seven Arts* group, inclined to make itself small and exclusive; the liberals, always apparently trembling on the edge of a real feeling for the crafts and never quite making it, that gathered about *The New Republic* and *The Nation,* and besides these Mencken and Nathan, knights errant at large, with pistols always loaded, ready at any moment to shoot anyone if the shooting would make a bit of stir in the town.

Among these men I walked and after walking went back to my room to lie on my cot. I began checking off names. As for myself I had no serious intention of becoming a New Yorker. I was a middle-westerner born and bred. All the rest of my days I might drift here and there about America but at heart I would be, to the New Yorker, a man from beyond the mountains, an Ohio man to the end.

I was a middle-westerner trying to pick up cultural scraps in New York, trying to go to school there.

I made little lists of names on the walls of my mind. There was Van Wyck Brooks, the man who never wrote a line that did not give me joy, but his mind seemed altogether occupied with what had happened to Twain, Howells, Whitman, Poe and the New Englanders, men for the most part dead before I was born. I was sorry they had the rotten luck to be born in a new land but could not stay permanently sorry. I had to live myself in the moment, in America as it was, as it was becoming. Often I thought of Brooks. "He has a theme. It is that a man cannot be an artist in America. The theme absorbs all his time and energy. He has little or no time to give to such fellows as myself and our problems." I did not put Brooks aside. He put me aside.

There were however others. Alfred Stieglitz, Waldo Frank, Henry Canby, Paul Rosenfeld, Leo Ornstein, Ben Huebsch, Alfred Kreymborg, Mary and Padraic Colum, Julius Friend, Ferdinand Schevill, Stark Young when I came to him later, Lawrence Gilman, Gilbert Seldes, Jane Heap, Gertrude Stein. Not all of them New Yorkers, but none of them, except Miss Heap and Ferdinand Schevill middle-westerners like myself.

There were in New York and Chicago no end of people who were willing to talk to me, listen to my talk, cry out for any good thing I did, condemn with quick intelligence what I did that was cheap or second-rate. Not one among them but had thought further than myself, that could tell me a hundred things I did not know. What a debt of gratitude I owe to men like Paul Rosenfeld, Stark Young, Alfred Stieglitz, Waldo Frank and others, men who have willingly taken long hours out of their busy lives to walk and talk with me of my craft.

I used to lie in my room thinking of them, in relation to myself, in relation to other writers who were coming out of the Middle West and who would come. It was rather odd how many of them had Jewish blood in their veins. I did not believe I was too much prejudiced because the people I have named liked certain

work of my own. Often enough they did not like it
and I had opportunity to realize their reactions to
other men's work, had seen how Stieglitz had labored
for Marin, Hartley, O'Keefe, Dove and others, how
Waldo Frank had given Sandburg the intelligent
appreciation he must have so wanted, had watched
with glowing pleasure the subtle workings of the minds
of men like Rosenfeld and Young.

I tried to feel and think my way into the matter because it had I thought some relation to my own problem which as you will remember was to try to find
footing for myself, a basis of self-criticism.

I wanted, as all men do, to belong.

To what? To an America alive, an America that
was no longer a despised cultural foster child of
Europe, with unpleasant questions always being asked
about its parentage, to an America that had begun to
be conscious of itself as a living home-making folk, to
an America that had at last given up the notion that
anything worth while could ever be got by being in
a hurry, by being dollar rich, by being merely big and
able to lick some smaller nation with one hand tied
behind its broad national back.

As for the men of Jewish blood, so many of whom
I found quick and eager to meet me half way, my
heart went out to them in gratitude. They were
wanting love and understanding, had in their natures
many impulses that were destructive. Was there a
sense of being outlaws? They did not want their
own secret sense of separateness from the life about
them commented upon but it existed. They themselves kept it alive and I thought they were not un-
wise in doing so. I watched them eagerly. Did

395

they have, in their very race feeling, the bit of ground under their feet it was so hard for an Ohio man to get in Cleveland Cincinnati or Chicago or New York? The man of Jewish blood, in an American city, could at any rate feel no more separateness from the life about him than the advertising writer in a Chicago advertising agency who had within him a love of the craft of words. The Jewish race had made itself felt in the arts for ages and even our later middle-western anti-Jewish crusader Henry Ford had no doubt as a child been taught to read the Bible written by old Jewish word-fellows.

As far as I myself could understand, the feeling of separateness from the life about was common to all Americans. It explained the everlasting get-together movements always going on among business men and as for race prejudices, they also were common. There was the South with its concern about the Negroes, the Far West and its orientals, the whole country a little later with its sudden hatred of the Germans and in the Middle West all sorts of little cross-currents of race hatreds as the factory hands came into the towns from all over Europe. No American ever met another American without drawing a little back. There was a question in the soul. "What are your people? Where did they come from?" "What kind of blood flows in your veins?"

Could it not very well be that the men of Jewish blood who had given themselves to the crafts in America could look at life a bit more impersonally, go out more quickly and warmly to individuals, throw up out of the body of the race more individuals who could give themselves wholeheartedly to the cultural life because of the very fact of a race history behind them?

One had always to remember that we Americans were in the process of trying to make a race. The Jews had been a part of the life of almost every race that had come to us and were for perhaps that very reason in a better position than the rest of us to help make our own race.

NOTE X

A GRAY morning and myself, no longer young, sitting on a bench before the little open space that faces the cathedral of Chartres. Thoughts flitting across a background of years. Had I finally accepted myself, in part at least, as a tale-teller, had I come that far on the road toward manhood?

It was sure I had been traveling, wandering from place to place, trying to look and listen. At that moment I was very far away from that land, the background of my tales, the Middle West of America. I was perhaps even farther away spiritually than physically. In my day men covered huge physical distances in a short time. As I sat there nearly all the reality of me was still living in the Middle West of America, in mining towns, factory towns, in sweet stretches of Ohio and Illinois countryside, in great smoke-hung cities, in the midst of that strange, still-forming muddle of peoples that is America.

I had drawn myself out of that for the time, had been in New York among the other writer folk, among the painters, among the talkers too. That after the years of active participation in life, in modern American life, cheating some, lying a good deal, scheming, being hurt by others, hurting others.

The younger years of being a business schemer, trying to grow rich—I have said little enough of those

years in my book. However, the book is long
enough, perhaps far too long.

Had I ever really wanted to be rich? Perhaps
I had only wanted to live, in my craft, in the practice of my craft. It was certain I had not, for many
years of my life, known what I wanted. After years
of striving to get money, to get power, to be successful,
I had found in the end well-nigh perfect contentment
in looking and listening, in sitting lost in some little
corner, writing, trying to write all down. "A little
worm in the fair apple of progress," I had called myself laughing—the American laugh.

Now, for a few years, I had been looking abroad.
I think it was Joseph Conrad who said that a writer
only began to live after he began to write. It pleased
me to think I was, after all, but ten years old.

Plenty of time ahead for such a one. Time to
look about, plenty of time to look about.

Well, I had been looking about. I an American
middle-westerner, ten years old, had been looking at
old London, at strong arrogant young New York, at
old France too.

It was apparent that although in France, in the
eleventh twelfth and thirteenth centuries, there had
been many men alive who had cared greatly for the
work of their hands, present-day Frenchmen obviously
did not. The cathedral before me was faced on one
side by ugly sheds, such as some railroad company
might have put up on the shores of a lake facing a city
of mid-America. I had taken a second leap from
New York to Paris, had been brought there by a
friend who now sat on the bench beside me. The
man was a friend dear to my heart. We had been

sitting for days on just that bench, wandering about the cathedral. Visitors came and went, mostly Americans, middle-western Americans like myself no doubt. Some of them looked at the cathedral without stopping the motors of theirs cars. They were in a hurry, had got the hurry habit. One day a little drama played itself out in the open space before the cathedral door. An American came with two women, one French the other American, his wife or his sweetheart. He was flirting with the French woman and the American woman was pretending she did not see. My friend and I watched the drama flit back and forth for two or three hours. There before us was a woman losing her man, and she did not want to admit it to herself. Once when they had all three gone inside the cathedral, the American woman came out and stood for a moment by the massively beautiful door, the old eleventh-century door facing us. She did not see us and went to lean against the door itself, crying softly. Then she wiped her eyes and went inside again to join the others. They were all presumably getting culture there, in the presence of the work of the old workmen. The stooped figures of old Frenchwomen with shawls about their shoulders kept hurrying across the open space, going into the cathedral to worship. My friend and I were also worshiping at the cathedral, had been doing that for days.

Life went on then, ever in the same tragic comic sweet way. In the presence of the beautiful old church one was only more aware, all art could do no more than that—make people, like my friend and myself, more aware. An American girl put her face against

the beautiful door of Chartres Cathedral and wept for
her lost lover. What had been in the hearts of the
workmen who once leaned over the same door carving
it? They were fellows who had imaginations that
flamed up. "Always wood for carvers to carve, always little flashing things to stir the souls of painters,
always the tangle of human lives for the tale-tellers
to mull over, dream over," I told myself. I remembered what an excited young man had once said to me
in Chicago. We had stood together in Lake Street,
that most noisy and terrible of all Chicago's downtown streets. "There are as many tales to be found
here as in any street of any city in the world," he had
said a little defiantly. Then he looked at me and
smiled. "But they will be different tales than would
be found in any street of any of the old world cities,"
he added.

I wondered.

My own mind was in a ferment, thoughts scurry-
ing across a background of fancies as shadows play
across the walls of a room when night comes on.
My friend sat in silence. He had got hold of Huys-
mann's "Cathedral" and was reading. Now and then
he put the book down and sat for a long time in silence looking at the gray lovely old building in that
gray light. It was one of the best moments of my
own life. I felt free and glad. Did the friend who
was with me love me? It was sure I loved him.
How good his silent presence.

How good the presence of my own thoughts too!
There was my friend, the Cathedral, the presence of
the little drama in the lives of the three strange
people who would presently come out of the church

and go away, the packed storehouse of my own fancy too. The end of the story immediately before me I would never know but some day, when I was alone, in Chicago perhaps, my fancy would take it up and play with it. Too bad I was not a Turgenev or someone equally skillful. Were I such a one I might make of what I had seen some such a tale as, say Turgenev's "Smoke." There was just the material for a tale, a novel perhaps. One might fancy the man a young American who had come to Paris to study painting and before he came had engaged himself to an American girl at home. He had learned French, had made progress with his work. Then the American girl had set sail for Paris to join him and, at just that moment, while she was at sea, he had fallen desparately in love with a French woman. The deuce, the French woman was skillful with men and she imagined the young American to be rich. With what uncertain thoughts was the breast of the young American torn at that moment.

The three of them just suddenly came out of the church together and walked away together in silence. That was all. All tales presented themselves to the fancy in just that way. There was a suggestion, a hint given. In a crowd of faces in a crowded street one face suddenly jumped out. It had a tale to tell, was crying its tale to the streets but at best one got only a fragment of it. Once, long after the time of which I am now writing, I tried to paint in an American desert. There was something about the light. My eyes were not accustomed to it. There was a wide desert and beyond the desert hills floating away into the distance. I could lie on my back on the sands of the desert and watch the evening light fade away over the hills and such forms come! I thought all I had ever felt could be expressed in one painting of those hills but when later I took a brush into my hands I was only dumb and stupid. What appeared on the canvas was dull and meaningless. I walked about swearing at myself and then at the desert light and the very hills that so short a time before had so filled me with peace and happiness. I kept blaming the light. "Nothing stands still in this light," I said to myself.

As though anything ever stood still anywhere. It was the artist's business to make it stand still—well, just to fix the moment, in a painting, in a tale, in a poem.

Sitting there with my friend, facing the cathedral, I remembered something. On my desk, somewhere back in America, was a book in which I had once written certain lines. Well, I had made a poem and had called it, "One who would not grow old." Now it came sharply back:

I have wished that the wind would stop blowing, that birds would stop dead still in their flight, without falling into the sea, that waves would stand ready to break upon shores without breaking, that all time, all impulse, all movement, mood, hungers, everything would stop and stand hushed and still for a moment.

It would be wonderful to be sitting on a log in a forest when it happened.

When all was still and hushed, just as I have described, we would get off the log and walk a little way.

The insects would all lie still on the ground or float, fixed and silent in the air. An old frog, that lived under a stone and that had opened his mouth to snap at a fly, would sit gaping.

There would be no movement, in New York, in Detroit, in Chicago down by the stock exchange, in towns, in factories, on farms.

Out in Colorado, where a man was riding a horse furiously, striving to catch a steer to be sent to Chicago and butchered—

He would stop, too, and the steer would stop.

You and I would walk a little way, in the forest, or on a prairie, or on the streets of a town, and then we would stop. We would be the only moving things in the world and then one of us would start a thought rolling and rolling, down time, down space, down mind, down life too.

I am sure I would let you do it if later you would keep all of the voices of your mind hushed while I did it in my turn. I would wait ten lives while others did it for my turn.

. . . .

That impulse gone long since as I sat that day before the cathedral of Chartres! It was an impulse that had come time and again to every artist but my own moments had come often enough. I had no cause to quarrel with my own life.

Such moments as I had already had in it. "Life owes me nothing," I kept saying over and over to myself. It was true enough. For all one might say about American life it had been good to me. On that afternoon I thought that if I were suddenly to be confronted with death in the form of the old man with a sickle in his hand, I would be compelled to say, "Well, it's your turn now, old fellow. I've had my chance. If I had done little enough, it's my fault, not yours."

At any rate life in America had poured itself out richly enough. It was doing that still. As I sat on the bench before Chartres on that gray day I remembered such moments.

.   .   .   .

A hot afternoon at Saratoga.   I had gone to the races with two men from Kentucky, one a professional gambler and the other a business man who could never succeed because he was always running off to the horse races or some such place with such no-accounts as the little gambler and myself.   We were smoking big black cigars and all of us were clad in rather garish clothes.   All about us were men just like us but with big diamonds on their fingers or in their neckties.   On a stretch of green lawn beneath trees a horse was being saddled.   Such a beauty!   What a buzz of colorful words!   The professional gambler, a small man with crooked legs, had once been a jockey and later a trainer of race horses.   It was said he had done something crooked, had got himself into disgrace with other horsemen but of that I knew little.   At the sight of such a horse as we were now watching as the saddle was put on something strange happened to him. A soft light came into his eyes.   The devil!   I had once or twice seen just such a light in the eyes of painters at work, I had seen such a light in the eyes of Alfred Stieglitz in the presence of a painting. Well, it was such a light as might have come into the eyes of a Stark Young holding in his hands some piece of old Italian craftsmanship.

I remember that as the little old gambler and I stood near the horse I spoke to him of a painting I had once seen in New York, that painting of Albert

405

Ryder's of the ghostly white horse running beneath a mysteriously encircled moon on an old race track at night.

The gambler and I talked of the painting. "I know," he said, "I like to hang around race tracks at night myself."

That was all he said and we stood watching the horse. In a few minutes now that tense trembling body would be at ease, fallen into the ease of its long, swinging stride, out there on the track.

The gambler and I went away to stand by a fence. Were men less fortunate than horses? Did men also seek but to express themselves beautifully as in a few minutes now the horse would do? The gambler's body trembled as did my own. When the horse ran (he broke the record for the mile, that day) he and I did not speak to each other. We had together seen something we together loved. Was it enough? "At least," I told myself, "we men have a kind of consciousness that perhaps the horses haven't. We have this consciousness of one another. That is what love is, perhaps."

There was a child, a young boy of fourteen walking beside his mother in a park at Cleveland, Ohio. I sat on a bench there and saw him go by and after that one moment of his passing never saw him again but I'll never forget while I live. The moment was like the moment of the running of the horse. Could it be that it was the boy's most beautiful moment? Well, I had seen it. Why was I not made to be a painter? The boy's head was thrown a little back, he had black curly hair and carried his hat in his hand. In just that moment of his passing the bench on which I sat his young body was all alive, all of the senses fully alive. Whose son was he? Such a living thing as that, to be thrown into the life of Cleveland, Ohio or of Paris or Venice either for that matter.

I am always having those moments of checking up like a miser closing the shutters of his house at night to count his gold before he goes to bed and although there are many notes on which I might close this book on my own imaginative life in America, it seems to me good enough to close it just there as I sat that day before Chartres Cathedral beside a man I had come to love and in the presence of that cathedral that had made me more deeply happy than any other work of art I had ever seen.

My friend kept pretending to read his book but from time to time I saw how his eyes followed the old tower of the church and the gladness that came into him too.

We would both soon be going back to America to our separate places there. We wanted to go, wanted to take our chances of getting what we could out of our own lives in our own places. We did not want to spend our lives living in the past, dreaming over the dead past of a Europe from which we were separated by a wide ocean. Americans with cultural impulses had done too much of that sort of thing in the past. The game was worn out and even a ladies' literary society in an Iowa city was coming to know that a European artist of the present day was not necessarily of importance just because he was a European.

The future of the western world lay with America.

Everyone knew that. In Europe they knew it better than they did in America.

It was for me a morning of such thoughts, such memories—just there before Chartres with my friend.

Once, in one of my novels, "Poor White," I made my hero at the very end of the book go on a trip alone. He was feeling the futility of his own life pretty fully, as I myself have so often done, and so after his business was attended to he went to walk on a beach. That was in the town of Sandusky, in the state of Ohio, my own state.

He gathered up a little handful of shining stones like a child, and later carried them about with him. They were a comfort to him. Life, his own efforts at life, had seemed so futile and ineffectual but the little stones were something glistening and clear. To the child man, the American who was hero of my book and, I thought, to myself and to many other American men I had seen, they were something a little permanent. They were beautiful and strange at the moment and would be still beautiful and strange after a week, a month, a year.

I had ended my novel on that note and a good many of my friends had told me they did not know what I was talking about. Was it because, to most Americans, the desire for something, for even little colored stones to hold in the hand now and then to glisten and shine outside the muddle of life, was it because to most Americans that desire had not become as yet conscious?

Perhaps it had not but that was not my story. At least in me it had become conscious, if not as yet well directed or very intelligent. It had made me a restless man all my life, had set me wandering from place to place, had driven me from the towns to the cities and from one city to another.

In the end I had become a teller of tales. I liked my job. Sometimes I did it fairly well and sometimes I blundered horribly. I had found out that trying to do my job was fun and that doing it well and finely was a task for the most part beyond me.

Often enough I sat thinking of my wasted years, making excuses for myself, but in my happier moments and when I was not at work on my job I was happiest when I was in the mood into which I had fallen on the day when I sat before the cathedral—that is to say, when I sat rolling over and over the little colored stones I had managed to gather up. The man with the two women had just dropped another into my hands. How full my hands were! How many flashes of beauty had come to me out of American life.

It was up to me to carve the stones, to make them more beautiful if I could but often enough my hands trembled. I wasn't young any more, but I had sought teachers and had found a few. One of them was with me at that moment sitting on the bench before the cathedral and pretending to read a book about it. He grew tired of the pretense and taking out a package of cigarettes offered me one, but then found he hadn't any match. To such confirmed smokers as my friend and myself the French notion of making a government monopoly of matches is a pest. It is like so much that is European nowadays.

It is like the penuriousness of an old age of which at least there is none in America. "The devil!" said my friend. "Let's go for a walk."

We did walk, down through the lovely old town, the town made lovely not by the men who live there now but by men of another age, long since fast asleep. If we were neither of us so young in years any more, there was a way in which we were both young enough. We were young with that America of which we both at that moment felt ourselves very much a part, and of which, for many other reasons aside from the French monopoly in matches, we were glad in our hearts to be a part.

EPILOGUE

EPILOGUE

IT seems but yesterday although a year has passed since that afternoon when Edward and I sat talking in a restaurant. I was staying at a small hotel in a side street in the city of New York. It had been an uncertain day with us, such days as come in any relationship. One asks something of a friend and finds him empty-handed or something is asked and a vacant look comes into one's own eyes. Two men, or a man and woman, were but yesterday very close and now they are far apart.

Edward came to lunch with me and we went to a restaurant in the neighborhood. It was of the cheap hurried highly-sanitary sort, shiny and white. After eating we sat on and on, looking at each other, trying to say to each other something for which we could find no words. In a day or two I would be going away to the South. Each of us felt the need of something from the other, an expression of regard perhaps. We were both engaged in the practice of the same craft—story-tellers both of us. And what fumblers! Each man fumbling often and often in materials not well enough understood—that is to say in the lives and the drama in the lives of the people about whom the tales were told.

We sat looking at each other and as it was now nearly three o'clock in the afternoon we were the only people in the restaurant. Then a third man came in and sat as far away from us as possible. For some time the women waiters in the place had been looking at Edward and myself somewhat belligerently. It may have been they were employed only for the noon rush and now wanted to go home. A somewhat large woman with her arms crossed stood glaring at us.

As for the third man in the place, the fellow who had just come in, he had been in prison for some crime he had committed and had but recently been let out. I do not mean to suggest that he came to Edward and myself and told his story. Indeed he was afraid of us and when he saw us loitering there went to sit as far away as possible. He watched us furtively with frightened eyes. Then he ordered some food and after eating hurriedly went away leaving the flavor of himself behind. He had been trying to get a job but on all sides had been defeated by his own timidity. Now like ourselves he wanted some place to rest, to sit with a friend, to talk, and by an odd chance I, and Edward as well, knew the fellow's thoughts while he was in the room. The devil!—he was tired and discouraged and had thought he would go into the restaurant, eat slowly, gather himself together. Perhaps Edward and myself—and the waitress with her arms crossed who wanted to get our tip and cut out to some movie show—perhaps all of us had chilled the heart of the man from prison. "Well, things are so and so. One's own heart has been chilled. You are going away to the South, eh? Well, good-by; I must be getting along."

II

I was walking in the streets of the city that evening of November. There was snow on the roofs of buildings, but it had all been scraped off the roadways. There is a thing happens to American men. It is pitiful. One walks along, going slowly along in the streets, and when one looks sharply at one's fellows something dreadful comes into the mind. There is a thing happens to the backs of the necks of American men. There is this sense of something drying, getting old without having ripened. The skin does something. One becomes conscious of the back of one's own neck and is worried. "Might not all our lives ripen like fruit—drop at the end, full-skinned and rich with color, from the tree of life, eh?" When one is in the country one looks at a tree. "Can a tree be a dead dried-up thing while it is still young? Can a tree be a neurotic?" one asks.

I had worked myself into a state of mind, as so often happens with me, and so I went out of the streets, out of the presence of all the American people hurrying along; the warmly dressed, unnecessarily weary, hurrying, hustling, half-frightened city people.

In my room I sat reading a book of the tales of Balzac. Then I had got up to prepare for dinner when there came a knock at the door and in answer to my call a man entered.

He was a fellow of perhaps forty-five, a short strongly-built broad-shouldered man with graying hair. There was in his face something of the rugged simplicity of a European peasant. One felt he might live a long time, do hard work and keep to the end the vigor of that body of his.

For some time I had been expecting the man to come to see me and was curious concerning him. He was an American writer like Edward and myself and two or three weeks before he had gone to Edward pleading. . . . Well, he had wanted to see and talk with me. Another fellow with a soul, eh?

And now there the man stood, with his queer old boyish face. He stood in the doorway, smiling anxiously. "Were you going out? Will I be disturbing you?" I had been standing before a glass adjusting a necktie.

"Come on in," I said, perhaps a little pompously. Before sensitive people I am likely to become a bit bovine. I do not wag my tail like a dog. What I do is to moo like a cow. "Come into the warm stall and eat hay with me," I seem to myself to be saying at such times. I would really like to be a jolly friendly sort of a cuss . . . you will understand. . . . "It's always fair weather, when good fellows get together" . . . that is the sort of thing I mean.

That is what I want and I can't achieve it, nor can I achieve a kind of quiet dignity that I often envy in others.

I stood with my hands fingering my tie and looked at the man in the doorway. I had thrown the book I had been reading on a small table by the bed. "The devil!—he is one of our everlastingly distraught Americans. He is too much like myself." I was tired and wanted to talk of my craft to some man who was sure of himself. Queer disconnected ideas are always popping into one's mind. Perhaps they are not so disconnected. At that moment—as I stood looking at the man in the doorway—the figure of another man came sharply to my mind. The man was a carpenter who for a time lived next door to my father's house when I was a boy in an Ohio town. He was a workman of the old sort, one who would build a house out of timber just as it is cut into boards by a sawmill. He could make the door frames and the window frames, knew how to cut cunningly all the various joints necessary to building a house tightly in a wet cold country.

And on Summer evenings the carpenter used to come sometimes and stand by the door of our house and talk with mother as she was doing an ironing. He had a flair for mother, I fancy, and was always coming when father was not at home but he never came into the house. He stood at the door speaking of his work. He always talked of his work. If he had a flair for mother and she had one for him it was kept hidden away but one fancied that, when we children were not about, mother spoke to him of us. Our own father was not one with whom one spoke of children. Children existed but vaguely for him.

As for the carpenter, what I remembered of him on the evening in the hotel in the city of New York was just a kind of quiet assurance in his figure remembered from boyhood. The old workman had spoken to mother of young workmen in his employ. "They aren't learning their trade properly," he said. "Everything is cut in the factories now and the young fellows get no chance. They can stand looking at a tree and they do not know what can be done with it . . . while I . . . well, I hope it don't sound like bragging too much . . . I know my trade."

III

You see what a confusion! Something was happening to me that is always happening. Try as much as I may I cannot become a man of culture. At my door stood a man waiting to be admitted and there stood I—thinking of a carpenter in a town of my boyhood. I was making the man at the door feel embarrassed by my silent scrutiny of him and that I did not want. He was in a nervous distraught condition and I was making him every moment more distraught. His fingers played with his hat nervously.

And then he broke the silence by plunging into an apology. "I've been very anxious to see you. There are things I have been wanting to ask you about. There is something important to me perhaps you can tell me. Well, you see, I thought—sometime when you are not very busy, when you are unoccupied. . . . I dare say you are a very busy man. To tell the truth now I did not hope to find you unoccupied when I came in thus, at this hour. You may be going out to dine. You are fixing your tie. It's a nice tie. . . . I like it. What I thought was that I could perhaps be so fortunate as to make an appointment with you. Oh, I know well enough you must be a busy man."

The deuce! I did not like all this fussiness. I wanted to shout at the man standing at my door and say . . . "to the devil with you!" You see, I wanted to be more rude than I had already been—leaving him standing there in that way. He was nervous and distraught and already he had made me nervous and distraught.

"Do come in. Sit there on the edge of the bed. It's the most comfortable place. You see I have but one chair," I said, making a motion with my hand. As a matter of fact there were other chairs in the room but they were covered with clothing. I had taken off one suit and put on another.

We began at once to talk, or rather he talked, sitting on the edge of the bed and facing me. How nervous he was! His fingers twitched.

"Well now, I really did not expect I would find you unoccupied when I came in here at this hour. I am living, for the time being in this very hotel—on the floor below. What I thought was that I would try to make an appointment with you. 'We'll have a talk'—that's what I thought."

I stood looking at him and then, like a flash, the figure of the man seen that afternoon in the restaurant came into my mind—the furtive fellow who had been a thief, had been sent to prison and who, after he was freed, did not know what to do with himself.

What I mean is that my mind again did a thing it is always doing. It leaped away from the man sitting before me, confused him with the figures of other men. After I had left Edward I had walked about thinking my own thoughts. Shall I be able to explain what happened at that moment? In one instant I was thinking of the man now sitting before me and who had wanted to pay me this visit, of the ex-thief seen in the restaurant, of myself and my friend Edward, and of the old workman who used to come and stand at the kitchen door to talk with mother when I was a boy.

Thoughts went through my mind like voices talking.

"Something within a man is betrayed. There is but the shell of a man walking about. What a man wants is to be able to justify himself to himself.

419

What I as a man want is to be able, some time in my life, to do something well—to do some piece of work finely just for the sake of doing it—to know the feel of a thing growing into a life of its own under my fingers, eh?"

IV

What I am trying to convey to you, the reader, is a sense of the man in the bedroom, and myself looking at each other and thinking each his own thoughts and that these thoughts were a compound of our own and other people's thoughts too. In the restaurant Edward and myself, while wanting to do so very much, had yet been unable to come close to each other. The man from prison, wanting us also, had been frightened by our presence and now here was this new man, a writer like myself and Edward, trying to thrust himself into the circle of my consciousness.

We continued looking at each other. The man was a popular American short story writer. He wrote each year ten, twelve, fifteen magazine stories which sold for from five hundred to fifteen hundred dollars each.

Was he tired of writing his stories? What did he want of me? I began to grow more and more belligerent in my attitude toward him. It is, with me, a common effect of feeling my own limitations. When I feel inadequate I look about at once for someone with whom I may become irritated.

The book I had been reading a half hour before, the book of "The Tales of Balzac," lay on a table near where the man sat and his fingers now reached out and took hold of it. It was bound in soft brown leather.

420

One who loves me and who knew of my love for the book had taken it from my room in a house in Chicago and had carried it off to an old workman who had put it in this new suit of soft brown leather.

The fingers of the man on the bed were playing with the pages of the book. One got the notion that the fingers wanted to begin tearing pages from the book.

I had been trying to reassure him. "Do stay, I have nothing to do," I had said and he smiled at my words as a child might smile. "I am such an egotist," he explained. "You see, I want to talk of myself. I write stories, you see, but they aren't any good. Really they aren't any good at all but they do bring me in money. I'm in a tight hole, I tell you. I own an automobile and I live on a certain scale that is fixed—that's what I mean—that's what's the trouble with me. I am no longer young, as you'll see if you look at my hair. It's getting gray. I'm married and now I have a daughter in college. She goes to Vassar. Her name is Elsie. Things are fixed with me. I live on a certain scale—that's what I mean—that's what's the trouble with me."

It was apparent the man had something of importance to himself he wanted to say and that he did not know how to begin.

I tried to help. My friend Edward had told me a little of his story. (For the sake of convenience and really to better .conceal his identity we will call him Arthur Hobson—although that is not his name.) Although he was born in America he is of Italian descent and there is in his nature, no doubt, something of the Italian spirit of violence, strangely mingled, as it so often is in the Latins, with gentleness and subtlety.

However, he was like myself in one thing. He was an American and was trying to understand himself— not as an Italian but as an American.

And so there was this Hobson—born in America of an Italian father—a father who had changed his name after coming to America and had prospered here. He, the father, had come to America to make money and had been successful. Then he had sent his son to an American college, wanting to make a real American of him.

The son had been ambitious to become a well-known football player and to have, during his college days, the joy of seeing his name and picture in the newspapers. As it turned out however, he could not become one of the great players and to the end of his college career remained what is called a substitute— getting into but one or two comparatively unimportant games to win his college letter.

He did not have it in him to be a great football player and so, in a world created in his fancy, he did what he could not do in life. He wrote a story concerning a man who, like himself, was of Italian descent and who also remained through most of his college career a substitute on a football team—but in the story the man did have, just at the end of his days in college, an opportunity of which he took brilliant advantage.

There was this Hobson in his room writing on an afternoon of the late Fall. It was the birth of a story-teller. He moved restlessly about the room, sat a long time writing and then got up and moved about again.

In the story he wrote that day in his room long ago he did what he could not do in the flesh. The hero of his story was a rather small square-shouldered man like himself and there was an important game on, the most important of the year. All the other players were Anglo-Saxons and they could not win the game. They held their opponents even but could make no progress toward scoring.

And now came the last ten minutes of play and the team began to weaken a little and that heartened the other side. "Hold 'em! . . . hold 'em! . . . hold 'em!" shouted the crowd. At last, at the very last, the young Italian boy was given his chance. "Let the Wop go in! We are going to lose anyway. Let the Wop go in!"

Who has not read such stories? There are infinite variations of the theme. There he was, the little dark-skinned Italian-American and who ever thought he could do anything special! Such games as football are for the nations of the North. "Well, it will have to be done. One of the halfbacks has injured himself. Go in there, you Wop!"

So in he goes and the story football game, the most important one of the year for his school, is won. It is almost lost but he saves the day. Aha, the other side has the ball and fumbles, just as they are nearing the goal line. Forward springs the little alert dark figure. Now he has the ball and has darted away. He stumbles and almost falls but . . . see . . . he has made a little twisting movement with his body just as that big fellow, the fullback of the opposing team, is about to pounce upon him. "See him run!" When he stumbles something happens to his leg. His ankle is sprained but still he runs like a streak. Now every step brings pain but he runs on and on. The game is won for the old school. "The little Wop did it! Hurrah! Hurrah!"

The devil and all! These Italian fellows have a cruel streak in them, even in their dreams. The young Italian-American writer, writing his first story, had left his hero with a slight limp that went with him all through life and had justified it by the notion that the limp was in some way a badge of honor, a kind of proof of his thorough-going Americanism.

Anyway, he wrote the story and sent it to one of our American magazines and it was paid for and published. He did, after all, achieve a kind of distinction during his days in college. In an American college a football star is something but an author is something, too. "Look, there goes Hobson. He's an author! He had a story in the *National Whiz* and got three hundred and fifty dollars for it. A smart fellow, I tell you! He'll make his way in the world. All the fraternities are after the fellow."

And so there was Hobson and his father was proud of him and his college was proud of him and his future was assured. He wrote another football story and another and another. Things began to come his way and by the time he left college he was engaged to be married to one of the most popular girls of his class. She wasn't very enthusiastic about his people but one did not need to live in the same city with them. An author can live where he pleases. The young couple came from the Middle-West and went to live in New England, in a town facing the sea. It was a good place for him. In New England there are many colleges and Hobson could go to football games all Fall and get new ideas for stories without traveling too far.

The Italian-American has become what he is, an American artist. He has a daughter in college now and owns an automobile. He is a success. He writes football stories.

V

He sat in my room in the hotel in New York, fingering the book he had picked up from the table. The deuce! Did he want to tear the leaves? The fellow who came into the restaurant where Edward and I sat was in my mind perhaps—that is to say, the man who had been in prison. I kept thinking of the story writer as a man trying to tear away the bars of a prison. "Before he leaves this room my treasured book will be destroyed," a corner of my brain was whispering to me.

He wanted to talk about writing. That was his purpose. As with Edward and myself, there was now something between Hobson and myself that wanted saying. We were both story-tellers, fumbling about in materials we too often did not understand.

"You see now," he urged upon me, leaning forward and now actually tearing a page of my book, "You see now, I write of youth . . . youth out in the sun and wind, eh? I am supposed to represent young America, healthy young America. You wouldn't believe how many times people have spoken to me saying that my stories are always clean and healthy and the editors of magazines are always saying it too. 'Keep on the track,' they say. 'Don't fly off the handle! We want lots of just such clean healthy stuff.' "

He had grown too nervous to sit still and getting up began to walk back and forth in the narrow space before the bed, still clinging to my book. He tried to give me a picture of his life.

He lived he said, during most of the year, in a Connecticut village by the sea and for a large part of the year did not try to write at all. The writing of football stories was a special thing. One had always to get hold of the subject from a new angle and so, in the Fall, one went to many games and took notes. Little things happened on the field that could be built up and elaborated. Above all, one must get punch into the stories. There must be a little unexpected turn of events. "You understand. You are a writer yourself."

My visitor's mind slipped off into a new channel and he told me the story of his life in the New England town during the long months of the Spring Summer and early Fall when, as I understood the matter, he did no writing.

Well, he played golf, he went to swim in the sea, he ran his automobile. In the New England town he owned a large white frame house where he lived with his wife, with his daughter when she was at home from school, and with two or three servants. He told me of his life there, of his working through the Summer months in a garden, of his going sometimes in the afternoons for long walks about the town and out along the country roads. He grew quieter and putting my book back on the table sat down again on the edge of the bed.

"It's odd," he said. "You see, I have lived in that one town now for a good many years. There are people there I would like to know better. I would like really to know them, I mean. Men and women go along the road past my place. There is a man of about my own age whose wife has left him. He lives alone in a little house and cooks his own food. Sometimes he also goes for a walk and comes past my place and we are supposed to be friends. Something of the kind is in the wind. He stops sometimes by my garden and stands looking over and we talk but do not say much to each other. The devil, that's the way it goes you see—there he is by the fence and there am I with a hoe in my hand. I walk to where he stands and also lean on the fence. We speak of the vegetables growing in my garden. Would you believe it we never speak of anything but the vegetables or the flowers perhaps? It's a fact. There he stands. Did I tell you his wife has left him? He wants to speak of that—I'm sure of it. To tell the truth when he set out from his own house he was quite determined to come up to my place and tell me all about everything, how he feels, why his wife has left him and all about it. The man who went away with his wife was his best friend. It's quite a story, you see. Everyone in our town knows about it but they do not know how the man himself feels as he sits up there in his house all alone.

"That's what he has made up his mind to talk to me about but he can't do it, you see. All he does is

427

to stand by my fence and speak of growing vegetables. 'Your lettuce is doing very well. The weeds do grow like the deuce, don't they though? That's a nice bed of flowers you have over there near the house.'"

The writer of the football stories threw up his hands in disgust. It was evident he also felt something I had often felt. One learns to write a little and then comes this temptation to do tricks with words. The people who should catch us at our tricks are of no avail. Bill Hart, the two-gun man of the movies, who goes creeping through forests, riding pell-mell down hillsides, shooting his guns bang-bang, would be arrested and put out of the way if he did that at Billings, Montana, but do you suppose the people of Billings laugh at his pranks? Not at all. Eagerly they go to see him. Cowboys from distant towns ride to where they may see his pictures. For the cowboy also the past has become a flaming thing. Forgotten are the long dull days of following foolish cows across an empty desert place. Aha, the cowboy also wants to believe. Do you not suppose Bill Hart also wants to believe?

The deuce of it all is that, wanting to believe the lie, one shuts out the truth, too. The man by the fence, looking at the New England garden, could not become brother to the writer of football stories.

"They tell themselves so many little lies, my beloved."

VI

I was sliding across the room now, thinking of the man whose wife had run away with his friend. I

428

was thinking of him and of something else at the same
time. I wanted to save my Balzac if I could. Already the football-story man had torn a page of the
book. Were he to get excited again he might tear
out more pages. When he had first come into my
room I had been discourteous, standing and staring
at him, and now I did not want to speak of the book,
to warn him. I wanted to pick it up casually when
he wasn't looking. "I'll walk across the room with
it and put it out of his reach," I thought but just as
I was about to put out my hand he put out his hand
and took it again.

And now as he fingered the book nervously his mind
jumped off in a new direction. He told me that during the Summer before he had got hold of a book
of verses by an American poet, Carl Sandburg.

"There's a fellow," he cried, waving my Balzac
about. "He feels common things as I would like to
be able to feel them and sometimes as I work in my
garden I think of him. As I walk about in my town
or go swimming or fishing in the Summer afternoons
I think of him." He quoted:

*"Such a beautiful pail of fish, such a beautiful peck of ap-
ples, I cannot bring you now. It is too early and I am not
footloose yet."*

It was pretty evident the man's mind was jerking
about, flying from place to place. Now he had forgotten the man who on Summer days came to lean
over his fence and was speaking of other people of his
New England town.

On Summer mornings he sometimes went to loiter

about on the main street of the town of his adoption, and there were things always going on that caught his fancy, as flies are caught in molasses.

Life bestirred itself in the bright sunlight in the streets. First there was a surface life and then another and more subtle life going on below the surface and the football-story writer felt both very keenly —he was one made to feel all life keenly—but all the time he kept trying to think only of the outside of things. That would be better for him, he thought. A story writer who had written football stories for ten or fifteen years might very well get himself into a bad way by letting his fancy play too much over the life immediately about him. It was just possible— well you see it might turn out that he would come in the end to hate a football game more than anything else in the world—he might come to hate a football game as that furtive fellow I had seen in the restaurant that afternoon no doubt hated a prison. There were his wife and child and his automobile to be thought about. He did not drive the automobile much himself—in fact driving it made him nervous—but his wife and the daughter from Vassar loved driving it.

And so there he was in the town—on the main street of the town. It was, let us say, a bright early Fall morning and the sun was shining and the air filled with the tang of the sea. Why did he find it so difficult to speak with anyone regarding the half-formed thoughts and feelings inside himself? He had always found it difficult to speak of such things, he explained, and that was the reason he had come to see me. I was a fellow writer and no doubt I also was often caught in the same trap. "I thought I would speak to you about it. I thought maybe you and I could talk it over," he said.

He went, on such a morning as I have described, into the town's main street and for a time stood about before the postoffice. Then he went to stand before the door of a cigar store.

A favorite trick of his was to get his shoes shined.

"You see," he exclaimed, eagerly leaning forward on the bed and fingering my Balzac, "you see there is a small fish stand right near the shoe-shining stand and across the street there is a grocery where they set baskets of fruit out on the sidewalk. There are baskets of apples, baskets of peaches, baskets of pears, a bunch of yellow bananas hanging up. The fellow who runs the grocery is a Greek and the man who shines my shoes is an Italian. Lord, he's a Wop like myself.

"As for the man who sells fish, he's a Yank.

"How nice the fish look in the morning sun!"

The story-teller's hand caressed the back of my book and there was something sensual in the touch of his fingers as he tried to describe something to me, a sense he had got of an inner life growing up between the men of such oddly assorted nationalities selling their merchandise on the streets of a New England town.

Before coming to that he spoke at length of the fish lying amid cracked ice in a little box-like stand the fish merchant had built. One might have fancied my visitor also dreamed of some day becoming a fish merchant. The fish, he explained, were brought in from the sea in the evening by fishermen and the fish merchant came at daybreak to arrange his stock and all morning whenever he sold a fish he re-arranged the stock, bringing more fish from a deep box at the back of his little coop. Sometimes he stood back of his sales counter but when there were no customers about he came out and walked up and down the sidewalk and looked with pride at the fish lying amid the pieces of cracked ice.

The Italian shoe-shiner and the Greek grocer stood on the sidewalk laughing at their neighbor. He was never satisfied with the display made by his wares but was always at work changing it, trying to improve it.

On the shoe-shining stand sat the writer of football stories and when another customer did not come to take his place at once he lingered a moment. There was a soft smile on his lips.

Sometimes when the story writer was there, sitting quietly on the shoe-shining stand, something happened at the fish-stand of which he tried to tell me. The fat old Yankee fish merchant did something—he allowed himself to be humiliated in a way that made the Greek and the Italian furious—although they never said anything about the matter.

"It is like this," the story writer began, smiling shyly at me. "You see now—well, you see the fish merchant has a daughter. She is his daughter but the American, the Yank, does not have a daughter in the same way as a Greek or an Italian. I am an American myself but I have enough memory of life in my father's house to know that.

"In the house of an Italian or a Greek the father is king. He says—'do this or that,' and this or that is done. There may be grumbling behind the door. All right, let it pass! There is no grumbling in his presence. I'm talking now of the lower classes, the peasants. That's the kind of blood I have in my veins. Oh, I admit there is a kind of brutality in it all but there is kindness and good sense in it, too. Well, the father goes out of his house to his work in the morning and for the woman in the house there is work too. She has her kids to look after. And the father—he works hard all day, he makes the living for all, he buys the food and clothes.

"Does he want to come home and hear talk of the rights of women and children, all that sort of bosh? Does he want to find an American or an English feminist perhaps, enshrined in his house?

"Ha!" The story writer jumped off the bed and began again walking restlessly back and forth.

"The devil!" he cried. "I am neither the one thing nor the other. And I also am bullied by my wife—not openly but in secret. It is all done in the name of keeping up appearances. Oh, it is all done very quietly and gently. I should have been an artist but I have become, you see, a man of business. It is my business to write football stories, eh! Among my people, the Italians, there have been artists. If they have money—very well and if they have no money—very well. Let us suppose one of them living poorly, eating his crust of bread. Aha! With his hands he does what he pleases. With his hands he works in stone—he works in colors, eh! Within himself he feels certain things and then with his hands he makes what he feels. He goes about laughing, puts his hat on the side of his head. Does he worry about running an automobile? 'Go to the devil,' he says. Does he lie awake nights thinking of how to maintain a

large house and a daughter in college? The devil!
Is there talk of keeping up appearances for the sake
of the woman? For an artist, you see,—well, what
he has to say to his fellows is in his work. If he is
an Italian his woman is a woman or out she goes.
My Italians know how to be men."

*"Such a beautiful pail of fish, such a beautiful peck of ap-
ples, I cannot bring you now. It is too early and I am not
footloose yet."*

VII

The story writer again sat down on the edge of the
bed. There was something feverish in his eyes.
Again he smiled softly but his fingers continued to
play nervously with the pages of my book and now he
tore several of the pages. Again he spoke of the
three men of his New England town.

The fish-seller, it seemed, was not like the Yank
of the comic papers. He was fat and in the comic
papers a Yank is long and thin.

"He is short and fat," my visitor said, "and he
smokes a corncob pipe. What hands he has! His
hands are like fish. They are covered with fish scales
and the backs are white like the bellies of fish.

"And the Italian shoe-shiner is a fat man too. He
has a mustache. When he is shining my shoes sometimes—well, sometimes he looks up from his job and
laughs and then he calls the fat Yankee fish-seller—
what do you think—a mermaid."

In the life of the Yankee there was something that
exasperated my visitor as it did the Greek grocer and

434

the Italian who shined shoes and as he told the story
my treasured book, still held in his hand, suffered more
and more. I kept going toward him, intending to take
the book from his hand (he was quite unconscious of
the damage he was doing) but each time as I reached
out I lost courage. The name Balzac was stamped in
gold on the back and the name seemed to be grinning
at me.

My visitor grinned at me too, in an excited nervous
way. The seller of fish, the old fat man with the
fish scales on his hands, had a daughter who was
ashamed of her father and of his occupation in life.
The daughter, an only child lived during most of the
year in Boston where she was a student at the Boston
Conservatory of Music. She was ambitious to become
a pianist and had begun to take on the airs of a lady
—had a little mincing step and a little mincing voice
and wore mincing clothes too, my visitor said.

And in the Summer, like the writer's daughter, she
came home to live in her father's house and, like the
writer himself, sometimes went to walk about.

To the New England town during the Summer
months there came a great many city people—from
Boston and New York—and the pianist did not want
them to know she was the daugther of the seller of
fish. Sometimes she came to her father's booth to
get money from him or to speak with him concerning
some affair of the family and it was understood between them that—when there were city visitors about
—the father would not recognize his daughter as being in any way connected with himself. When they
stood talking together and when one of the city visitors
came along the street the daughter became a customer

435

intent upon buying fish. "Are your fish fresh?" she asked, assuming a casual lady-like air.

The Greek, standing at the door of his store across the street and the Italian shoe-shiner were both furious and took the humilation of their fellow merchant as in some way a reflection on themselves, an assault upon their own dignity, and the story writer having his shoes shined felt the same way. All three men scowled and avoided looking at each other. The shoe-shiner rubbed furiously at the writer's shoes and the Greek merchant began swearing at a boy employed in his store.

As for the fish merchant, he played his part to perfection. Picking up one of the fish he held it before his daughter's eyes. "It's perfectly fresh and a beauty, Madam," he said. He avoided looking at his fellow merchants and did not speak to them for a long time after his daughter had gone.

But when she had gone and the life that went on between the three men was resumed the fish merchant courted his neighbors. "Don't blame me. It's got to be done," he seemed to be saying. He came out of his little booth and walked up and down arranging and re-arranging his stock and when he glanced at the others there was a pleading look in his eyes. "Well, you don't understand. You haven't been in America long enough to understand. You see, it's like this—" his eyes seemed to say, "—we Americans can't live for ourselves. We must live and work for our wives, our sons and our daughters. We can't all of us get up in the world so we must give them their chance." It was something of the sort he always seemed to be wanting to say.

It was a story. When one wrote football stories one thought out a plot, as a football coach thought out a new formation that would advance the ball.

But life in the streets of the New England village wasn't like that. No short stories with clever endings—as in the magazines—happened in the streets of the town at all. Life went on and on and little illuminating human things happened. There was drama in the street and in the lives of the people in the street but it sprang directly out of the stuff of life itself. Could one understand that?

The young Italian tried but something got in his way. The fact that he was a successful writer of magazine short stories got in his way. The large white house near the sea, the automobile and the daughter at Vassar—all these things had got in his way.

One had to keep to the point and after a time it had happened that the man could not write his stories in the town. In the Fall he went to many football games, took notes, thought out plots, and then went off to the city, where he rented a room in a small hotel in a side street.

In the room he sat all day writing football stories. He wrote furiously hour after hour and then went to walk in the city streets. One had to keep giving things a new twist—to get new ideas constantly. The deuce, it was like having to write advertisements. One continually advertised a kind of life that did not exist.

In the city streets, as one walked restlessly about, the actuality of life became as a ghost that haunted the house of one's fancy. A child was crying in a stairway, a fat old woman with great breasts was leaning

437

out at a window, a man came running along a street, dodged into an alleyway, crawled over a high board fence, crept through a passageway between two apartment buildings and then continued running and running in another street.

Such things happened and the man walking and trying to think only of football games stood listening. In the distance he could hear the sounds of the running feet. They sounded quite sharply for a long moment and then were lost in the din of the street cars and motor trucks. Where was the running man going and what had he done? The old Harry! Now the sound of the running feet would go on and on forever in the imaginative life of the writer and at night in the room in the hotel in the city, the room to which he had come to write football stories, he would awaken out of sleep to hear the sound of running feet. There was terror and drama in the sound. The running man had a white face. There was a look of terror on his face and for a moment a kind of terror would creep over the body of the writer lying in his bed.

That feeling would come and with it would come vague floating dreams, thoughts, impulses—that had nothing to do with the formation of plots for football stories. The fat Yankee fish-seller in the New England town had surrendered his manhood in the presence of other men for the sake of a daughter who wished to pass herself off as a lady and the New England town where he lived was full of people doing strange unaccountable things. The writer was himself always doing strange unaccountable things.

"What's the matter with me?" he asked sharply, walking up and down before me in the room in the

New York hotel and tearing the pages of my book. "Well, you see," he explained, "when I wrote my first football story it was fun. I was a boy wanting to be a football hero and as I could not become one in fact I became one in fancy. It was a boy's fancy but now I'm a man and want to grow up. Something inside me wants to grow up.

"They won't let me," he cried, holding his hands out before him. He had dropped my book on the floor. "Look," he said earnestly, "my hands are the hands of a middle-aged man and the skin on the back of my neck is wrinkled like an old man's. Must my hands go on forever, painting the fancies of children?"

VIII

The writer of football stories had gone out of my room. He is an American artist. No doubt he is at this moment sitting somewhere in a hotel room, writing football stories. As I now sit writing of him my own mind is filled with fragmentary glimpses of life caught and held from our talk. The little fragments caught in the field of my fancy are like flies caught in molasses—they cannot escape. They will not go out of the house of my fancy and I am wondering, as no doubt you, the reader, will be wondering, what became of the daughter of the seller of fish who wanted to be a lady. Did she become a famous pianist or did she in the end run away with a man from New York City who was spending his vacation in the New England town only to find, after she got to the city with him, that he already had a wife? I am wondering about her—about the man whose wife ran away with his friend and about the running man in

the city streets.   He stays in my fancy the most sharply
of all.   What happened to him?   He had evidently
committed a crime.   Did he escape or did he, after
he had got out into the adjoining street, run into the
arms of a waiting policeman?

Like the writer of football stories, my own
fancy is haunted.   To-day is just such a day as the one
on which he came to see me.   It is evening now and
he came in the evening.   In fancy again I see him,
going about on Spring Summer and early Fall days,
on the streets of his New England town.   Being
an author he is somewhat timid and hesitates about
speaking with people he meets.   Well, he is lonely.
By this time his daughter has no doubt graduated from
Vassar.   Perhaps she is married to a writer of stories.
It may be that she has married a writer of cowboy
stories who lives in the New England town and works
in a garden.

Perhaps at this very moment the man who has
written so many stories of football games is writing
another.   In fancy I can hear the click of his type-
writing machine.   He is fighting, it seems, to maintain a certain position in life, a house by the sea, an
automobile and he blames that fact on his wife, and
on his daughter who wanted to go to Vassar.

He is fighting to maintain his position in life and
at the same time there is another fight going on.   On
that day in the hotel in the city of New York he told
me, with tears in his eyes, that he wanted to grow up,
to let his fanciful life keep pace with his physical life
but that the magazine editors would not let him.   He
blamed the editors of magazines—he blamed his wife

and daughter—as I remember our conversation, he did not blame himself.

Perhaps he did not dare let his fanciful life mature to keep pace with his physical life. He lives in America, where as yet to mature in one's fanciful life is thought of as something like a crime.

In any event there he is, haunting my fancy. As the man running in the streets will always stay in his fancy, disturbing him when he wants to be thinking out new plots for football stories, so he will always stay in my fancy—unless, well unless I can unload him into the fanciful lives of you readers.

As the matter stands I see him now as I saw him on that Winter evening long ago. He is standing at the door of my room with the strained look in his eyes and is bewailing the fact that after our talk he will have to go back to his own room and begin writing another football story.

He speaks of that as one might speak of going to prison and then the door of my room closes and he is gone. I hear his footsteps in the hallway.

My own hands are trembling a little. "Perhaps his fate is also my own," I am telling myself. I hear his human footsteps in the hallway of the hotel and then through my mind go the words of the poet Sandburg he has quoted to me:

"Such a beautiful pail of fish, such a beautiful peck of apples, I cannot bring you now. It is too early and I am not footloose yet."

The words of the American poet rattle in my head and then I turn my eyes to the floor where my destroyed Balzac is lying. The soft brown leather back is uninjured and now again, in fancy, the name of the author is staring at me. The name is stamped on the back of the book in letters of gold.

From the floor of my room the name Balzac is grinning ironically up into my own American face.